Philosophy of Education in Action

Philosophy of Education in Action is an innovative, inquiry-based introductory text that invites readers to study philosophy of education through the lens of their own observations and experiences. Structured according to a "Wonder Model of Inquiry," each chapter begins by posing a fundamental *What if* question about curriculum, pedagogy, and the role of the school before investigating the various philosophical perspectives that guide and influence educational practices. Classroom vignettes and examples of actual schools and educational programs help to ground philosophical perspectives in real-world scenarios, while the book's unique inquiry-based approach leads students to both think critically about philosophical questions and apply the concepts to their own teaching.

Features of the text include:

- *What if* questions that structure each chapter to pique students' curiosity, stimulate creativity, and promote critical thinking.
- Authentic classroom vignettes that encourage students to analyze *what it means to "do" philosophy* and to reflect upon their own practices, examine their role in the educational process, and articulate their own philosophical beliefs.
- A concluding section asking readers to imagine and design their own hypothetical school or classroom as a project-based means of analyzing, synthesizing, and evaluating the different philosophies discussed.

Accessible and thought-provoking, *Philosophy of Education in Action* provides a dynamic learning experience for readers to understand and apply philosophy in educational practice.

David W. Nicholson is Professor of Education at Stevenson University, USA.

Philosophy of Education in Action

An Inquiry-Based Approach

David W. Nicholson

Routledge
Taylor & Francis Group

NEW YORK AND LONDON

First published 2016
by Routledge
711 Third Avenue, New York, NY 10017

and by Routledge
2 Park Square, Milton Park, Abingdon, Oxon, OX14 4RN

Routledge is an imprint of the Taylor & Francis Group, an informa business

Library of Congress Cataloging-in-Publication Data
Names: Nicholson, D. W., author.
Title: Philosophy of education in action : an inquiry-based approach / by
    David W. Nicholson.
Description: New York : Routledge is an imprint of the Taylor & Francis
    Group, an Informa Business, [2016] | Includes bibliographical
    references and index.
Identifiers: LCCN 2015030211| ISBN 9781138843042 (hardback) |
    ISBN 9781138843059 (pbk.) | ISBN 9781315731179 (e-book)
Subjects: LCSH: Education—Philosophy. | Inquiry-based learning.
Classification: LCC LB14.7 .N497 2016 | DDC 370.1—dc23
LC record available at http://lccn.loc.gov/2015030211

ISBN: 978-1-138-84304-2 (hbk)
ISBN: 978-1-138-84305-9 (pbk)
ISBN: 978-1-138-73117-9 (ebk)

Typeset in Times New Roman
by Swales & Willis Ltd, Exeter, Devon, UK

Dedicated to the memory of my father, Rev. Ed Nicholson, Jr., and to my mother, Okie Lee Nicholson.

Contents

Preface

An Inquiry-Based Approach to Studying Philosophy of Education

The goal of this introductory textbook is to engage readers in inquiry into the influence of philosophical perspectives and concepts on educational practices that may be observed in actual schools and classrooms. The primary audience is teacher candidates in teacher preparation programs studying the social, historical, and philosophical foundations of education at the undergraduate and graduate levels. The textbook is also written to engage all educators – beginning teachers, experienced teachers, support staff, and administrators – in exploring the influence of philosophy on educational practices and decision-making. Parents, community members, policymakers, and others interested in educational matters can also benefit from examining the different perspectives presented in this book. Students of philosophy and other areas of humanities and social sciences can extend their scholarship by exploring the relationship of philosophy to the field of education.

One can take different approaches to studying educational philosophy. An encyclopedia approach arranges philosophies, philosophers, and philosophical concepts by name, defines key terms, and provides concise summaries. A biographical approach presents background information on various philosophers, explains their positions, and furnishes representative excerpts from their work. A historical approach surveys the chronological development of education and describes the philosophical arguments advanced to support or challenge educational systems at different periods in time. A "schools of philosophy" approach groups philosophers and their arguments according to similarity. A thematic approach examines issues related to education from a philosophical perspective.

In every approach, philosophical inquiry in education asks foundational questions about teaching and learning within the broader context of the nature of reality and existence. However, each approach has its limitations. Philosophy is a vast field of study consisting of myriad points of view. Both the encyclopedia and biographical approaches may serve as useful references to supplement the study of educational philosophy, but to the reader just beginning to study the field can appear as disjointed blurbs of arbitrary information lacking any particular focus. The thematic approach organizes information in a coherent fashion, but can create a distancing effect if the issues appear remote, esoteric, or unrelated to the experiences of the reader. Critics of historical or chronological approaches are skeptical of a "grand narrative" explaining how things came to be or how events should be interpreted and the meanings ascribed to them. A "schools of philosophy" approach categorizes philosophies into a convenient format. Deeper examination, however, reveals a great deal of overlap between schools of philosophy. Moreover, inconsistent, conflicting, or incompatible beliefs may be found not only among but within so-called schools of philosophy. Philosophers may even contradict themselves as their positions change and evolve over time. Many philosophers elude simple interpretation, fostering debate as to whether a given philosopher belongs in one school or another.

This textbook serves neither as a comprehensive survey of the entire scope of educational philosophy nor attempts to address (much less resolve) complex scholarly disputes within the field. Moreover, the author recognizes that the practice of education does not operate in a vacuum, dissociated from historical, social, economic, political, ideological, and other contextual factors. Findings from the natural and social sciences, psychology, and brain-based research inform practice as well. Our inquiry, however, focuses on the philosophical dimension of education. Furthermore, a distinction is drawn between educational philosophy and learning theory to delineate the scope of the inquiry. The domains, methods, and findings of educational research and other fields constitute areas for further inquiry by the reader seeking additional support for concepts encountered in different chapters.

This textbook takes a *What if* approach, a format suggested by the dialogue in Plato's *Republic* on the origin of a city. In Book II, Socrates proposes creating a city from its beginnings. Starting with the premise that a city is designed based on needs, he constructs a hypothetical city-state to serve those needs. As the construction of the city progresses, Socrates critiques the purpose and value of each citizen's role. Likewise, each chapter opens by posing a *What if* question about the purpose of education, followed by a classroom vignette. Each vignette has emerged from direct observations in classrooms. Although a few are composites of lessons observed at different times and in more than one classroom, each represents instruction conducted in a school setting.

Probing questions investigate philosophical perspectives and concepts related to practices depicted in the vignette. Taking an inquiry-based approach, the investigations rely on examining primary sources to reveal the perspective of philosophers and educational thinkers. Direct quotations connect concepts to practices described in classroom vignettes and examples. The influence of certain philosophers will recur in the textbook depending on the purpose of education of the chapter.

Readers will examine and evaluate the design of schools that fulfill the purpose of education presented in each chapter. Actual schools and educational programs are described, offering relevant, practical, and authentic examples. While analyzing the vignettes and examples, readers may recognize preferences for certain practices. In doing so, readers can begin to reflect upon their own practices, examine their role in the educational process, and articulate their own philosophical beliefs.

We will conduct our inquiry into philosophy of education within a framework called the *Wonder Model of Inquiry*. The model poses questions about the purpose of education (Wonder), collects data through "virtual observation" of a vignette (Observe), analyzes sources of information and connects practices to philosophical concepts and perspectives (Investigate), describes the design of schools organized according to that purpose of education (Design), applies criteria to interpret and evaluate the design (Evaluate), and reflects on the process and implications of the findings (Reflect). A graphic organizer, the *Continuum of Educational Philosophy*, will be used as a tool to organize and guide learning throughout the inquiry process. As readers examine each perspective, they will locate its purpose of education on the continuum and how that purpose is enacted in practice.

Part I examines why the study of philosophy in education is important and relevant, introduces basic philosophical concepts and terms, presents the *Wonder Model of Inquiry*, and formulates the inquiry questions that will guide the study of educational philosophy throughout the textbook.

Part II explores education from the perspective that the purpose of education is to learn objective, universal knowledge. Part III examines education from the contrasting point of view: that the purpose of education is to learn to construct subjective, changing knowledge.

Part IV synthesizes the learning by guiding readers through the process of imagining and designing a hypothetical school or classroom of their own. Readers will analyze, synthesize, and evaluate the different philosophies to create a product that expresses understanding of the philosophical viewpoints. In this way, the inquiry has a tangible goal for the reader. The design activity may take the form of an exercise to apply the inquiry process or serve as a long-term project developed in stages throughout the course of reading the textbook.

The inquiry-based approach offers an accessible introduction to philosophy of education grounded in the experiences of the reader. The theme of "wonder" runs throughout the book, posing *What if* questions to pique curiosity, stimulate creativity, and promote critical thinking. The interplay between hypothetical questions and authentic observations creates an accessible and dynamic learning experience for the reader, based on active, relevant, and engaging inquiry into philosophy of education *in action*.

Acknowledgments

I am indebted to all former students who participated in my Philosophy of Education courses and engaged in learning activities that led to the development of the inquiry-based approach of this textbook. Observations conducted by students in classrooms helped inform the vignettes described in several chapters.

In particular, I wish to express my appreciation to:

Former students Kelsye Piper, Zac Stavish, Alix Weyforth, and Allie Withrow for providing feedback on the format of the book; Rebecca Knolleisen for providing detailed feedback on drafts of chapters; and Molly Malloy, Megan Polis, and Milvelis Vargas for helping locate sources and verify references.

The following teachers for providing input and feedback on classroom vignettes: Donald Bufano, David Jaeger, Emma Oberlechner, Emily Stanley, and Tina Uddeme.

The staff of the Stevenson University library for going above and beyond in helping me secure resources crucial to the research for this project.

Stevenson University for supporting my scholarship and granting me sabbatical leave to research this textbook.

My colleague, Beth Kobett, for providing crucial guidance, invaluable advice, and constant support throughout the writing and revision process.

All my past teachers and professors who have served as inspiring role models and mentors.

I am also grateful to the administration, faculty, and staff of the following schools for graciously allowing me and my students to observe in your classrooms: Arts & Ideas Sudbury School, Baltimore Montessori Public Charter School, Greenspring Montessori School, Jemicy School, Monarch Academy Charter School (of Glen Burnie, Maryland), the Waldorf School of Baltimore, and St. John's College.

Finally, I am grateful for the faith and encouragement of my family.

Part I

How Does Philosophy Influence Education?

Part I examines why the study of philosophy in education is important and relevant, introduces basic philosophical concepts and terms, describes a model for conducting inquiry, and poses the inquiry questions that will guide the study of educational philosophy throughout the book.

Chapter 1 asks, "Why Study Philosophy of Education?" Following a brief overview of the field of philosophy, the chapter explores questions about the relationship of philosophy to teaching and learning, including how philosophy relates to learning theory, pedagogy, and instructional methods, strategies, and techniques. The "3Cs" criteria (consistency, compatibility, and coherence) are introduced as a means to evaluate educational practices and design.

In Chapter 2, we wonder, "How Do I Conduct Inquiry into Philosophies of Education?" Different types of inquiry are described and the kinds of questions philosophy asks are explained. The *Wonder Model of Inquiry* is introduced as a process for conducting inquiry into philosophy of education. The *Continuum of Educational Philosophy* serves as a tool for comparing educational practices to philosophical perspectives. The major inquiry questions are posed that will guide the study of philosophy in action.

1   Why Study Philosophy of Education?

What Is Your Philosophy of Education?

Teachers typically encounter this question at the beginning of their careers, when they may arguably be in the least qualified position to answer it. A foundation course in a teacher education program may require an essay on the topic, a job application may request a written response, or the subject may arise during an interview. How would you answer this question? In particular, how would you answer this question without resorting to vague generalities and empty platitudes?

One may not give the matter of philosophy much thought, or even be aware one has a philosophy of education, until encountering practices or decisions with which one agrees or disagrees. An occasion to assess one's personal philosophy of education surfaces when confronted with outlooks different from one's own. What you believe becomes more apparent when you begin to implement practices compatible with your thinking. A feeling of uneasiness or even discontent can result if asked or required to teach in a manner that conflicts with your preferences. If you are certain about what you agree with or support, you can discover what it is you believe. You may also find you modify your beliefs when exposed to the ideas of others or adjust your outlook after spending time acclimating to a new or altered environment.

Studying the viewpoints of others offers a way to develop your own philosophy of education. How have other educators expressed their thoughts about education? In discussing beliefs, we may ask how philosophers have explored the subject. More importantly, we may wish to know how philosophy influences education and directly relates to the process of teaching and learning.

To begin, imagine you have successfully completed a job interview and have been offered a teaching position. After celebrating your accomplishment, your mind will turn to preparing for the school year. The following questions immediately arise:

- How will I arrange my classroom space? How will the use of space relate to instruction?
- What will I teach? In what sequence will I present the curriculum?
- How will I teach? What kinds of instructional activities will I plan?
- What resources, supplies, and materials will I need?
- What kinds of assessments will I choose and develop?
- What will be my classroom management plan?
- How will I manage instructional time?

These practical, concrete concerns all relate to philosophy. How you organize learning spaces, enact the curriculum, implement instruction, use resources, assess learning, conduct yourself in the classroom, and expect students to conduct themselves reflect a way of thinking about education. Your classroom may represent your own beliefs, be created in collaboration with others, or be prescribed by the school or school district. Some values and habits of behavior may conform to institutional, social, and cultural traditions spanning generations that are rarely called into question. However your belief system is constructed, the practices observed in your classroom will convey to students, colleagues, administrators, parents, and others a particular mindset about the profession and the purpose of education. This textbook explores the influence of philosophy on the practice of education as it occurs in schools.

The Study of Philosophy

> "Philosophy begins in wonder."
>   (Socrates)

Philosophy asks fundamental questions about the nature of reality and existence. The word philosophy comes from the Greek word *philosophia*. *Philo* means "loving" or "love of" and *sophia* means "wisdom." Therefore, philosophy means "love of wisdom." Philosophy is concerned with the search for meaning. What is the meaning of life? What is the meaning of the things we think about? What is the meaning of the things we do? What does it all mean? "Philosophy begins in wonder," the Greek philosopher Socrates declares (Plato, *Theaetetus*, 155d).[1]

A common saying asserts, "Perception is reality." Philosophy reflects as well as examines one's view of the world. In turn, one's view of the world affects how one acts. If, for example, you believe an eternal and perfect reality exists beyond the physical and temporal world we inhabit, this affects how you view the world you inhabit and how you act in it. If, on the other hand, you believe the only true reality is the physical and temporal one that we experience in the here and now, and no other form of reality exists, that will affect how you view the world and how you act in it. One's belief system determines what knowledge is worth knowing and what values are deemed applicable to how one lives.

Philosophy as a field of study has a rich history. The original meaning of the word implies seeking truth and wisdom, which therefore can lead to pursing knowledge in any subject. For example, before the development of the field of natural sciences as we know it, the study of nature was known as *natural philosophy*. Universities retain the connection to the traditional connotation by awarding Doctor of Philosophy (PhD) degrees. Individuals with a PhD, however, have rarely attained an advanced education in philosophy. Professors and other professionals hold PhD degrees in the humanities, sciences, and many specialized areas. Someone who has earned a PhD in Education, for example, has conducted formal research that contributes to the knowledge base of the profession. In this sense, a Doctor of Philosophy is someone who has devoted extensive scholarship to an area of study. Philosophy as we will use the term connotes systematic inquiry into the nature and meaning of reality, existence, truth, knowledge, reasoning, and values.

A philosopher's outlook is general and reflective, examining major issues while attempting to account for a wide range of stances competing for attention at any given time. Many who are known as philosophers of education have been philosophers in the broadest sense, whose work has touched upon education within arguments dealing with matters on a grand scale. Others may have never referred to themselves as philosophers, but the contemplative nature of their work has impacted views on how to think about education. Some philosophers of education have been practitioners while others may have never worked directly in a school setting. Therefore, the field has sometimes been accused of lacking clear criteria for what constitutes philosophy of education, and who should be counted among its ranks.[2]

Notwithstanding such debates, schools offer educational programs and confer upon graduates a recognized status in the form of certificates, licenses, diplomas, and degrees. We acknowledge the existence of systems designed for the express purpose of providing education, and these systems make decisions affecting those they educate and society-at-large. Therefore, we will proceed by conducting an inquiry into beliefs about the purposes and practices of education.

What Is the Relationship of Philosophy to Teaching and Learning?

"Philosophy is not a theory but an activity."

(Ludwig Wittgenstein)

The influence of philosophy on teaching and learning may not be readily apparent, especially within the demands of planning and implementing instruction daily. We need to see the connection between philosophical perspectives and educational practices to understand the influence one has on the other. Picture philosophy as the most comprehensive way of thinking about education, with learning theory and other aspects of teaching arranged in order from the most general to the more specific (Figure 1.1).

In preparing to enter a career in education, and in pursuing ongoing professional growth, teachers focus primarily on developing a repertoire of effective teaching skills. Learning theories and educational research that support instructional approaches receive a great deal of emphasis, while underlying philosophical arguments may be downplayed, ignored, or deliberately avoided. The application of skills in isolation from a larger context, however, can lead to haphazard or even incoherent practice. As one acquires each new teaching skill, two questions should be asked: 1) "Why am I incorporating this skill into my practice?" and 2) "How will this skill help me achieve my overall goals?" Educational philosophy can help answer both of these questions by providing an underlying foundation.

Philosophy of education answers *why* you might choose to include certain techniques, strategies, methods, and learning theories in your pedagogy. As Figure 1.1 shows, every teaching decision (moving from the most specific element upward to the more general) answers the "Why?" question: Why am I using this technique? (Techniques can fulfill a strategy). Why am I using this strategy? (Strategies can combine to create a method). Why am I using this method? (Methods can develop pedagogy). Why am I using this pedagogy? (Pedagogy can represent one's philosophy of education in the classroom). Pedagogy can be developed and refined as you gain knowledge and experience.

Pedagogy, learning theories, methods, strategies, and techniques answer *how* to put one's philosophy of education into action. To answer the "How?" question, move from the most general element (at the top of Figure 1.1) downward: How can I put my philosophy of education into action? (Through pedagogy, methods, strategies, and techniques, informed by learning theory.)

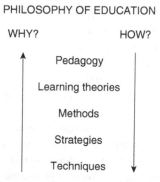

PHILOSOPHY OF EDUCATION

WHY?   HOW?

Pedagogy

Learning theories

Methods

Strategies

Techniques

Philosophy of education answers WHY to include certain techniques, strategies, methods, and learning theories in one's pedagogy.

Pedagogy, learning theories, methods, strategies, and techniques answer HOW to put one's philosophy of education into action.

Figure 1.1 Relationship of Philosophy to Teaching

How do I implement my pedagogy? (By selecting the appropriate methods, strategies, and techniques). Learning theory can support "Why" to select certain instructional techniques, strategies, and methods to include in one's pedagogy and help to justify each "How" decision.

The integration of these elements helps develop or reveal a philosophy of education. This is accomplished by consistently incorporating teaching techniques, strategies, and methods into pedagogy that are compatible with one another and with one's philosophical perspective. The role of philosophy is to question our assumptions, challenge our existing practices, and clarify our perspective. Wittgenstein (1922) asserts, "Philosophy is not a theory but an activity" (4.112).

To examine the relationship of philosophy to other aspects of instruction, we begin by discussing learning theory.

What Is the Relationship of Philosophy to Learning Theory?

Philosophy and theory are often used as interchangeable terms, but they can differ in significant ways. Philosophy contemplates complex and abstract issues about the nature of reality and the meaning of existence. Philosophy often asks questions that evade definitive answers, such as what constitutes happiness, virtue, beauty, and goodness. At times, philosophy seeks to explain a phenomenon or solve a problem, but not always. Philosophy sometimes analyzes and critiques the reasoning, use of language, and point of view of a given proposition. "Philosophy simply puts everything before us," Wittgenstein (1958) argues, "and neither explains nor deduces anything" (p. 126).

Learning theory seeks to identify, describe, and explain a problem or phenomenon occurring in education and offer solutions or suggest recommendations for practice, relying on empirical evidence to support its conclusions. In other words, learning theory depends on exacting scientific procedures, whereas philosophy can be an open-ended intellectual pursuit that asks fundamental, probing questions and challenges assumptions.[3] Learning theory describes a conceptual framework derived from systematic observation and empirical research to explain how students learn. Learning theory can support practice by justifying methods. The formulation of a learning theory follows the scientific method, posing and testing hypotheses. Theorists state conclusions they believe apply to learning in a variety of situations. Based on the findings, recommendations for practice may be implemented and evaluated.

Numerous learning theories have been proposed, such as behaviorism (B. F. Skinner), cognitive development (Jean Piaget, Jerome Bruner, David Ausubel), constructivism (Lev Vygotsky), multiple intelligences (Howard Gardner), and many others. Because competing theories exist, one may be skeptical that a theory can reliably predict what results will occur in every situation. For example, a law of nature (such as the Law of Gravity or the Law of the Conservation of Energy) provides verifiable results for every known instance. Although a learning theory may not be able to state with certainty its claims constitute unassailable proven fact, a large body of evidence can be cited indicating the degree to which a learning theory explains and predicts a particular phenomenon. Theory carries much more weight than opinion, anecdotal evidence, or speculation.

Theory may emerge from experience but is continuously tested to determine its validity. A hypothesis about how students learn can also arise from philosophical inquiry, but that hypothesis would need to be tested by collecting and analyzing evidence to move from the realm of philosophy to the sphere of learning theory. Some questions that philosophy poses may be beyond the reach of science to settle definitively, such as deliberations on moral, ethical, and spiritual matters.

Philosophy of education and theories about learning sometimes intermingle and reinforce one another. The questions raised by both areas of study can be examined to ascertain their impact on education. Philosophy, however, tends to dwell on a more abstract level, while learning theory attempts to produce tangible evidence to support its assertions. Figure 1.1 depicts this gradation from the most concrete and specific (techniques) to the most general and abstract (philosophy).

Learning theory is shown as engaging at all levels of instructional decision-making and practice. John Dewey, considered both a philosopher and theorist, offers this analysis: "Philosophy may even be defined as the general theory of education . . . it is the theory of education in its most general phases" (MW 9:338, 341).

What Is the Relationship of Philosophy to Pedagogy?

Pedagogy comes from the Greek *pais* or *paidos* (child) and *ago* (to lead) and means "to lead a child." Pedagogy involves more than planning lessons, selecting learning activities, or applying instructional strategies and techniques. Pedagogy entails accompanying the student throughout the learning process and providing direction or guidance. Viewed in this context, pedagogy encompasses the entire scope of a teacher's relationship with the student.[4]

Content pedagogy refers to teaching within a specific discipline or subject area, such as language, mathematics, the natural sciences, social sciences and humanities, and the arts.[5] Content pedagogy involves the interaction of knowledge about content matter, teaching practices, and learners. Delivering material to students with the objective of transmitting knowledge may not result in understanding. Even within the boundaries of a discipline, content pedagogy requires facilitating learning within a complex and diverse environment. How the teacher and students think about and express interest in the subject-matter, identify issues and define problems, apply learning, monitor progress, and evaluate performance transforms classroom activities into meaningful educational experiences.

If the definition of pedagogy extends beyond a technical set of teaching procedures to include all interactions with students, one's belief system comes into play. Teaching takes on moral, ethical, social, and personal dimensions. Separating the responsibilities of the teacher from principles and dispositions regarding equity, fairness, compassion, integrity, and credibility becomes problematic if not impossible. Reflecting on how one's actions in the classroom affect the emotional, physical, and academic well-being of a student has philosophical implications (Carr, 2006; Elliot, 1987; Elliot, 2000).

What Is the Relationship of Pedagogy to Instructional Methods, Strategies, and Techniques?

In planning a lesson, a teacher may search for an interesting activity to engage students in learning. Innumerable resources offer a vast array of activities from which to choose. How does a teacher decide which activity to select? A body of educational literature recommends selecting learning activities based on an intended outcome. Having an instructional goal in mind is preferable to choosing an activity that looks interesting or fun for several reasons. Students may enjoy participating in the activity but the teacher could find it difficult to indicate with confidence what the students learned and how the outcome relates to the curriculum standards. Meaningful instruction is purposeful.

Instruction is composed of techniques and strategies that combine to produce methods. Referring to Figure 1.1, begin at the bottom of the diagram and work upward. A technique is a specific applied skill. However, to achieve intended results or a particular outcome, proficient technique is not sufficient. Techniques must be applied strategically. A teacher must know not only how to apply techniques, but also when and why. Techniques are vital for success, provided techniques are not employed arbitrarily or erratically. Drawing on a repertoire of techniques, a teacher can carefully plan instruction to achieve consistent results. Over time, strategies reinforce and complement each other, helping the teacher develop a method.

Take, for example, the use of small groups. Dividing students into small groups is one technique for implementing instruction. One may have no more motivation for using small groups than to try something new, to see if the students respond positively. The technique may be successful in improving classroom management for a brief time, yet fail to help the students learn the content or develop the skill being taught. However, if small groups consistently produce the desired results, the teacher will arrange students in small groups more frequently. Used as a strategy, the teacher intends for the use of small groups to achieve certain outcomes. Ultimately, the teacher becomes convinced that having students work together in small groups achieves a variety of outcomes. In other words, this technique, used strategically over time in a variety of situations to achieve intended outcomes, has developed into a recognizable, coherent method. The use of small groups has evolved from completing one task at a time to a strategic plan of action to eventually characterizing the teacher's overall approach to the teaching and learning process.

Instructional techniques, strategies, and methods constitute pedagogy, which we have defined as the relationship of the teacher with the student throughout the learning process. Taken together, these considerations form an overall perspective on educational practice. Returning to our example, the use of small groups during instruction may achieve short-term outcomes but may also support broader convictions about the benefits of individuals engaging in social interaction and collaboration to construct knowledge within a learning community. Learning theory can be consulted to provide a rationale to justify the practice. Reflecting on how this practice relates to one's beliefs can reveal one's philosophy of education.

Thinking about these aspects of teaching can occur at any stage. A bottom-up approach begins at techniques and reasons upward to consider how techniques build to strategies, methods, pedagogy, and finally form a philosophy of education. A top-down approach begins with philosophy, which influences pedagogy, methods, strategies, and techniques, and can arguably influence the selection of learning theory to support decisions. Starting at the mid-point, methods can be examined to determine if techniques and strategies align, and how choices are impacted by learning theory to create pedagogy compatible with an educational philosophy.

The "3Cs" Criteria: Consistency, Compatibility, Coherence

Three key words express the relationship of philosophy to education: *Consistency*, *Compatibility*, and *Coherence*. To philosophize, evidence from observations must be evaluated according to some criteria (Rescher, 2014). A coherent system of thought implies consistency and compatibility, demonstrating congruence and alignment.

To evaluate a philosophy of education *in action*, we can ask three questions. Does the teacher demonstrate:

- Consistent use of educational practices?
- Compatible educational practices?
- Coherent overall educational design?

Consistency

Consistency implies that practices are regularly and systematically applied rather than implemented occasionally or sporadically. For example, a teacher may believe she has created a student-centered classroom that includes hands-on learning activities. However, she may inconsistently implement practices. A lesson may open with the teacher didactically presenting information, demonstrating a procedure, or modeling a skill. After several minutes of supervised guided practice, the students complete a worksheet that records single correct answers to basic recall questions. The practice portion of the lesson includes activities that incorporate hands-on materials (such as using manipulatives, objects, or technology) but the students follow a rigid step-by-step procedure. The teacher demonstrates or models and the students follow directions or imitate, with little or no opportunity for exploration or discovery. In this example, handling objects may appear to be student-centered practice, but instruction as a whole is teacher-directed and centered on the teacher's decisions, prescribed procedures, and pre-determined outcomes.

A teacher may exhibit consistent practices within lessons in a given subject area, but switch to different practices for lessons in another subject. For example, in reading or literature lessons, the teacher asks open-ended questions, encourages students to ask questions, probes student thinking with follow-up questions, and facilitates discussion. However, in social studies, this same teacher delivers information to students, who record notes or complete worksheets. Assessments consistent of quizzes requiring memorization and recall of material.

In another example, the source of content may be inconsistent across subject areas. The teacher may rely exclusively on a textbook during math instruction, yet supply primary sources for analysis during social studies or prepare labs for science lessons that investigate physical objects collected from natural settings. In certain subjects, the content comes from secondary sources while in other subjects the teacher values primary sources or items from the surrounding environment.

Therefore, depending on when one observes, a teacher may use different kinds of curricular materials and implement different instructional methods, offering the students widely disparate educational experiences during the school day. Choosing a variety of materials or techniques may be highly recommended, but the absence of a decision-making process that justifies each selection, and the lack of a strategy for applying these techniques, fails to exhibit consistency. Teachers should be prepared to explain and defend practices, not simply implement them.

Compatibility

Practices may be consistent yet not compatible. For example, a teacher may consistently drill students to memorize and recall material. However, the objectives focus on developing critical thinking, creativity, and collaboration. The instructional method and the outcomes are incompatible.

In another example, a teacher consistently leads discussions to foster an exchange of ideas, but the reading material consists of information sheets that only furnish bulleted facts. As students respond, the teacher confirms accurate answers and corrects those in error. Only one child responds to each question, directing their remarks to the teacher. Students do not interact with each other but focus on supplying correct answers to teacher questions, limiting participation and closing open-ended discussion. No interpretation of multiple points of view or evaluation of complex issues occurs. The discussion focuses on teacher questions while restricting the number or kinds of student questions. The results of the discussion are assessed using an objective-style test that does not allow for any divergent thinking. The instructional method, curricular materials, and assessment may be consistently implemented, but they are not compatible.

Incompatible practices can arise in all subject areas. A teacher may wish students to understand and practice civic responsibilities within the democratic process. However, students do not participate in decision-making during instruction but passively accept and follow rules determined by the teacher in advance. The teacher may state she expects students to take greater responsibility for their own learning, but this ends up simply requiring students to adhere to a checklist of behaviors, such as promptly submitting completed worksheets in the proper folder.

Incompatibility is often ironic, though not deliberately. Those enrolled in a teacher education program are familiar with lectures and PowerPoint presentations admonishing prospective teachers to avoid lecturing students in the classroom and engage students in active learning. The lecturer, however, may be reliably predictable in his methods, therefore remaining consistent. Consistency alone does not assure compatibility.

Coherence

Consistent choices and educational practices compatible with one another develop a coherent pedagogy. On a larger scale, the overall design of the school or educational program would reflect a philosophy of education. An observer in one classroom at a certain grade level in a particular subject area would perceive practices consistent and compatible with those in another classroom at the same grade level in the same subject area. This leads to a coherent grade-level approach to the teaching of that subject area. Furthermore, one could observe consistent and compatible practices in that subject area across grade levels. Not necessarily identical instructional methods, but methods consistent and compatible with the purpose of education for that discipline.

Expanding our scope, a philosophically coherent school or educational program would enact practices in all subjects across all grade levels that are inherently consistent and compatible with one another. For example, all science teachers conduct labs, all language arts teachers facilitate class discussions, all math teachers implement problem-based learning, and all social studies teachers assign projects. Beyond that, classes in all subjects also engage in discussions focused on higher-level thinking, students collaborate to problem-solve, and conclusions rely on evidence to support conclusions. Teachers in the different subject areas, even at different grade levels, exhibit a pedagogy that aligns with a broader purpose of education that represents the school as a whole. This creates a coherent framework that connects techniques, strategies, and methods into an integrated approach. One could observe school-wide decisions emerging from the same philosophical perspective. Moreover, all teachers and administrators in the school could articulate a rationale for their choices that corresponds to a stated purpose of education and shared philosophy of education.

If, however, individual teachers randomly select learning activities with no criteria (other than they might be fun to try), daily instruction in the classroom may appear arbitrary, disjointed, and even contradictory. The teacher becomes frustrated that students are not producing expected results, and students become aware each teacher is merely throwing different techniques against the wall to see which ones stick. Teachers try a variety of approaches—small groups, direct instruction, drills on facts, individual seatwork, discussion—but with no apparent strategy. Although each teacher may have a reason for each choice in isolation, no one is able to detect a rationale to explain the overall pattern of decisions at the classroom, grade, or school levels. The German philosopher Immanuel Kant (1797/1996) asserts that "the method of teaching . . . must be treated methodically; otherwise it would be set forth chaotically" (p. 221, 6:478).

Curriculum and pedagogy that lack the "3Cs" (consistency, compatibility, coherence) lack direction. According to the Chinese philosopher Lao Tzu, "If you do not change direction, you may end up where you are heading."[6] In other words, if you are frustrated or discouraged by choosing techniques without relying on a strategy, or implementing strategies that do not integrate with a broader method, by continuing in that manner you will remain frustrated and discouraged as you head down the same path. If a teacher continues to randomly grab learning activities from arbitrary sources, the teacher should come to expect random results and arbitrary outcomes. Having a destination in mind helps one make informed choices. In selecting activities, a teacher will begin to critique each one and decide how they help achieve the intended outcomes. Working collaboratively, teachers can examine and reflect on practice to determine a sense of purpose.

Lao Tzu calls a clear direction to knowledge and truth *Tao* or "The Way." Confucius beseeches his followers to act in accordance with "The Way" or Truth. The Buddha speaks of finding "The Path." Socrates urges his students to seek "The Good." By consistently selecting and implementing compatible choices, a coherent direction can emerge. Otherwise, in the words of the proverb, "If you don't know where you're going, any road will take you there."[7]

Notes

1 Also translated, "For this is an experience which is characteristic of a philosopher, this wondering: this is where philosophy begins and nowhere else." Aristotle also states, "For it is owing to their wonder that men both now begin and at first began to philosophize" (*Metaphysics*, 982b).
2 Recommended reading on issues in philosophy of education: Phillips, D. C., & Siegel, H. (2013). Philosophy of education. In E. N. Zalta (Ed.), *The Stanford encyclopedia of philosophy*. Retrieved from http://plato.stanford.edu/archives/win2013/entries/education-philosophy/
3 Recommended reading on distinctions between philosophy of education and learning theory: Carr, D. (2010). The philosophy of education and educational theory. In R. Bailey, R. Barrow, D. Carr, & C. McCarthy (Eds.), *The Sage handbook of philosophy of education* (pp. 37–53). Los Angeles: Sage.
4 Recommended reading on pedagogy: 1) Hansen, D. T., & Laverty, M. J. (2010). Teaching and pedagogy. In R. Bailey, R. Barrow, D. Carr, & C. McCarthy (Eds.), *The Sage handbook of philosophy of education* (pp. 223–235). Los Angeles: Sage, and 2) Smith, M. K. (2012). What is pedagogy? *The encyclopaedia of informal education*. Retrieved from http://infed.org/mobi/what-is-pedagogy
5 Recommended reading on content pedagogy: Shulman, L. (1986). Those who understand: Knowledge growth in teaching. *Educational Researcher, 15*(2), 4–14.
6 Widely attributed to Lao Tzu, although a precise citation remains elusive.
7 Variously attributed to several ancient sources, including Hindu texts and the Talmud. Lewis Carroll paraphrases the saying in *Alice in Wonderland*, and the line appears in the George Harrison song, "Any Road" (on the album *Brainwashed*, 2002).

References

Aristotle. (1984). *The complete works of Aristotle: The revised Oxford translation*. Jonathan Barnes (Ed.). Princeton, NJ: Princeton University Press.

Carr, W. (2006). Philosophy, methodology, and action research. *Journal of Philosophy of Education, 40*(4), 421–435.

Dewey, J. (1980). Democracy and education: An introduction to the philosophy of education. In J. Boydston (Ed.), *John Dewey: The middle works, 1916: Vol. 9* (pp. 192–361). Carbondale, IL: Southern Illinois University Press.

Elliot, J. (1987). Educational theory, practical philosophy and action research. *British Journal of Educational Studies, 35*(2), 149–169.

Elliott, J. (2000). Doing action research: Doing practical philosophy. *Prospero, 6*(3–4), 82–100.

Kant, I. (1996). *Metaphysics of morals*. (M. Gregor, Trans.). Cambridge, UK: Cambridge University Press. (Original work published 1797).

Plato. (1997). *Complete works*. J. M. Cooper (Ed.). Indianapolis, IN: Hackett.

Rescher, N. (2014). *Metaphilosophy: Philosophy in philosophical perspective*. Lanham, MD: Lexington.

Wittgenstein, L. (1958). *Philosophical investigations*. (G. E. M. Anscombe, Trans). (3rd ed.). Englewood Cliffs, NJ: Prentice Hall.

Wittgenstein, L. (1922). *Tractatus Logico-Philosophicus*. (C. K. Ogden, Trans.). New York, NY: Harcourt Brace.

2 How Do I Conduct Inquiry into Philosophies of Education?

How Does One Begin Inquiry?

> "The beginning is the most important part of the work."
>
> (Plato)[1]

One begins inquiry by asking questions. The simplest approach is based on the "Five Ws and one H" method: *Who, What, When, Where, Why,* and *How.* The order in which one asks these questions is not as important as investigating the different factors related to the phenomenon under examination. Three kinds of questions may be asked: 1) *factual* (*Who, What, Where, When* questions that identify concrete details and cite evidence), 2) *interpretation* (*How* and *Why* questions that infer meaning and probe understanding), and 3) *evaluation* (questions that elicit judgments, affirm conclusions, and justify beliefs) (Adler, 1955; Moeller & Moeller, 2002; Great Books Foundation, 2014).

Philosophy asks these same questions, focusing on: 1) *What* we observe occurring, 2) *How* these things connect or relate to one another, and 3) *Why* things are as they are (or *Why* things should be as they are and not otherwise). In doing so, philosophical questions address three issues: 1) *informative* ("determining what is the case"), 2) *practical* ("how to do things, how to achieve our aims"), and 3) *evaluative* ("what to aim at") (Rescher, 2001, p. 5). Our inquiry explores the influence of various philosophical perspectives on education. This entails asking informative questions (about what educational practices we observe in schools), practical questions (about how educational practices achieve their aims), and evaluative questions (about the consistency, compatibility, and coherence of practices in relation to their aims). Within these three basic categories, philosophical questions can probe the very purpose of education (Table 2.1).

In addition, philosophy asks *What if* questions. Speculative or hypothetical questions shift the direction of the inquiry and transform thinking. For example, beyond asking what curriculum students are currently learning, one might ask: "*What if* . . . students learned a different curriculum?" From this type of question, new questions emerge. If the curriculum changed, how would that affect instruction? How would changing instruction affect the role of the teacher? How would changing the role of the teacher affect the role of the student? Would changes in one major element of education lead to changes in the entire structure of a school, from the administration to a school's physical layout and resources? *What if* questions can: 1) *inform* (by describing what is, noticing what is not, and imagining what is possible), 2) influence *practical* actions (by supporting current practice or recommending changes in practice), and 3) *evaluate* (by examining and challenging the purposes of education).

What if questions begin in wonder. *What if* questions pique curiosity, stimulate creativity, and promote critical thinking. The following *What if* questions should guide your overall experience in reading this book:

Table 2.1 Examples of Philosophical Questions

Informative	Practical	Evaluative
• Who is educated in schools? Who decides?	• How are students educated in schools?	• Why should students learn in schools?
• Where and when does learning take place? Who decides?	• How is the curriculum developed? Who develops the curriculum?	• Why should learning occur on a schedule?
• What do schools teach? Who decides	• How do teachers teach? Who decides how teachers teach?	• Why should the curriculum include that content and those skills?
• What is the purpose of school? Who decides?	• How is the purpose of school determined?	• Why should learning require a teacher? What kind of teacher?
• What needs do schools fulfill? Whose needs do schools fulfill?	• How do schools fulfill this purpose? How do schools meet these needs?	• How do schools define an educated person?

- *What if* . . . schools taught in a different way than what I have observed or experienced?
- *What if* . . . I preferred schools taught in a different way than I have observed or experienced?
- *What if* . . . I could design my own school?

How meaningful and relevant this inquiry will be depends on your willingness to pose thought-provoking questions. The quality of our learning rests in our questions. A famous aphorism advises, "Judge a man by his questions rather than his answers."[2]

What Are the Different Types of Inquiry?

A familiar process for conducting inquiry follows the scientific method: 1) Pose a question, 2) Make a prediction or state a hypothesis, 3) Conduct an experiment and collect data, 4) Analyze and interpret the findings, 5) Report the findings and state a conclusion.

Not all modes of inquiry test hypotheses through experimentation. Different disciplines may employ modes of inquiry specific to those fields of study. Most general models, however, recognize the circular nature of inquiry, wherein each stage of the process informs the others, more questions are asked, and new investigation emerges. For example, the Stripling Model of Inquiry (2003) describes the following steps: 1) Connect (connect to self and previous knowledge, gain background knowledge to set context for new learning, observe and experience); 2) Wonder (develop questions, make predictions, and state hypotheses); 3) Investigate (find and evaluate information to answer questions and test hypotheses, think about information to illuminate new questions and hypotheses); 4) Construct (construct new understandings connected to previous knowledge, draw conclusions about questions and hypotheses); 5) Express (express new ideas to share learning with others, apply understandings to a new context or situation); 6) Reflect (reflect on own process of learning and on new understandings, ask new questions).

The inquiry process is closely related to general principles of critical thinking (Paul & Elder, 2008; The National Council for Excellence in Critical Thinking, 2013): 1) All reasoning has a purpose; 2) All reasoning is an attempt to figure something out, settle a question, or solve a problem; 3) All reasoning is based on assumptions (beliefs taken for granted); 4) All reasoning is done from some point of view; 5) All reasoning is based on data, information, and evidence; 6) All reasoning is expressed through, and shaped by, concepts and ideas; 7) All reasoning contains inferences or interpretations by which one draws conclusions and gives meaning to data; 8) All reasoning leads somewhere or has implications and consequences.

In addition to the steps or stages of the process, inquiry may also be based on the degree of structure afforded students during the process. For example, in *open* (or *full*) inquiry, students identify the problem, develop the questions, locate and select resources and materials, determine what evidence to collect, decide how to collect and analyze the data, and report and explain their findings. In *guided* inquiry, the teacher identifies the problem, poses the question, supplies resources and materials, provides the data, and suggests possible ways for students to analyze the data, explain the findings, and communicate the results. In *structured* inquiry, the teacher identifies the problem, poses the question, furnishes resources and materials, supplies the data for students to analyze, and provides the method for reporting or communicating the results (Colburn, 2000; Martin-Hansen, 2002). Models may be combined, such as in a *coupled* inquiry approach that begins with teacher selection of the problem and question while students assume greater responsibility as the inquiry progresses. In other variations, students may select from among questions or revise the questions, students may begin by using assigned resources then choose additional resources to continue the inquiry, and other options for shifting the balance between teacher direction and student initiative.

Wonder Model of Inquiry

We will conduct our inquiry into philosophy of education within a framework called the *Wonder Model of Inquiry* (Figure 2.1). Beginning with hypothetical *What if* questions, the model asks all three kinds of questions (factual, interpretation, and evaluation) that address all three philosophical issues (informative, practical, and evaluative) and incorporates all eight elements of critical thinking (purpose, questions, assumptions or beliefs, points of view, information and evidence, concepts and ideas, inferences or interpretations, conclusions and implications). The Wonder Model follows the structured inquiry process by posing questions, collecting data through

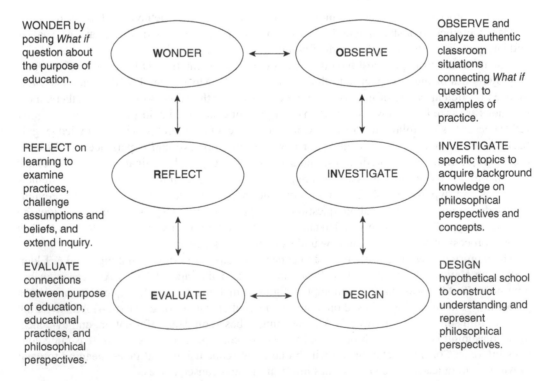

Figure 2.1 Wonder Model of Inquiry

observation, analyzing sources of information and connecting to philosophical concepts and perspectives, describing a method to communicate learning, applying criteria to interpret and evaluate the results, and reflecting on the process and the implications of the findings.

> WONDER: Pose a *What if* question about the purpose of education to serve as a hypothetical situation to examine.

> OBSERVE: Observe and analyze an authentic classroom situation (depicted as a vignette) connecting the *What if* question to examples of practice.

> INVESTIGATE: Investigate specific topics to acquire background knowledge on philosophical perspectives and concepts related to the observation.

> DESIGN: Design a hypothetical school (and/or examine example schools) to construct understanding and represent philosophical perspectives and concepts, based on the purpose of education and practices presented in the vignette.

> EVALUATE: Evaluate connections between the purpose of education, educational practices, and philosophical perspectives depicted in the vignette and represented by the school design.

> REFLECT: Reflect on learning to examine practices, challenge assumptions and beliefs, and extend inquiry.

As indicated in Figure 2.1, the steps of the model interact. The Wonder phase poses the purpose of education. The vignette described in the Observe phase illustrates the purpose of education. During the Investigate phase, we will be referring back to the vignette and projecting forward to design a hypothetical school. In the Design phase, we will compare our hypothetical school to examples of actual schools or educational programs. The Evaluate phase applies the "3Cs" criteria from Chapter 1 (consistency, compatibility, and coherence) to the examples.

Finally, the Reflect phase asks how prior observations and experiences in schools relate to the educational practices depicted in the vignette and examples. In doing so, readers can begin to reflect upon their own practices, examine their role in the educational process, question assumptions, and begin to articulate their own philosophical beliefs. As Albert Camus advises, "Philosophical thought only begins when we challenge the logic of clichés with rigor and honesty" (Todd, 1997, p. 92).

What Tools Will Help Guide and Organize My Inquiry into Philosophy of Education?

Philosophy is a vast field of study consisting of myriad points of view. A common way to determine similarities and differences among philosophies is to ask fundamental questions about the nature of reality, knowledge, values, and reasoning. These four areas of inquiry in philosophy are known as Metaphysics, Epistemology, Axiology, and Logic.

Metaphysics: Questions about the Nature of Reality

Metaphysics asks questions such as: What is reality? What is ultimately real? What truly exists? What is the purpose or meaning of existence? The Greek prefix *meta* means "after" or "beyond." Therefore, we can think of metaphysics as the area of philosophy that explores what may exist "after or beyond the study of nature or the physical." One can believe in a single possible reality or questions may arise asking how many different possible realities exist and what would be the nature of those realities. The philosopher William James (1890) explains, "Metaphysics means nothing but an unusually obstinate effort to think clearly" (p. 145).

Why is thinking about perceptions of reality important for teaching and learning? One's view of reality directly affects how one perceives the world and our place in it. If education concerns itself with learning knowledge and skills deemed reasonable and valuable, how reality is conceptualized ultimately determines the knowledge and skills we teach. Teachers are not in the habit of intentionally presenting to students information they believe not to be true. What is "real" can be argued to form the basis of education.

Epistemology: Questions about the Nature of Truth and Knowledge

Epistemology asks questions such as: What is true? How do we know it is true? What is "real" knowledge? Where does it come from? How do we know what we know? The word comes from the Greek *episteme*, which means "to know" and refers to knowledge, understanding, or belief.

Why is thinking about what constitutes true knowledge, and where it comes from, important for teaching and learning? As mentioned above, we can assume teachers believe they offer students "real" and "true" knowledge. A fundamental question to ask is, "How do we know the knowledge we teach is true?" The sources of the knowledge we teach, and our confidence in the credibility and reliability of these sources, directly influence decisions about teaching. The integrity of the knowledge we teach is a primary issue in education.

Axiology: Questions about Values

Axiology asks questions such as: What is good or bad, right or wrong, moral or immoral, ethical or unethical? Axiology also asks questions such as: What is desirable or undesirable, attractive or unattractive, appealing or unappealing, beautiful or ugly? The Greek word *axia* stands for value or worth. Axiology examines the nature of values such as morals, ethics, and virtues, as well as the nature of aesthetic matters such as beauty or taste in art, architecture, music, nature, etc.

Why is thinking about values, and where they come from, important for teaching and learning? Dispositions of students such as conduct and character attributes directly affect the learning environment of the classroom. Research cites classroom management issues and expectations for student behavior as a chief concern of beginning teachers. In what ways do we teach values in school? Every school and classroom establishes rules and posts reminders regarding traits such as responsibility, honesty, trustworthiness, and respect. Character education has become an explicitly identified part of the curriculum. From the beginning of educational philosophy, identifying and examining these values has been a central concern of inquiry.

Why is thinking about aesthetics important for teaching and learning? Changing priorities sometimes result in art and music education receiving less attention in schools. Nonetheless, aesthetics are present in classrooms. Instruction frequently involves presenting visual representations. Students create using art materials to express their learning. Music is employed to teach topics. Technology and other media convey visual and audio information. In more subtle ways, aesthetics permeate the classroom environment. Hallways and classrooms are decorated to express a theme, walls are painted different colors to indicate locations in the building as well as providing a comfortable, pleasing setting for learning. Students display their work on posters and other types of exhibits. The importance of aesthetics to the learning process cannot be overlooked.

Logic: Questions about Reasoning

Logic asks questions about reasoning. The Greek word *logos* means "word" as well as "reason." Schools emphasize reasoning skills in all subjects. Essay writing stresses offering coherent arguments. Mathematics and science apply logical processes to solve problems. Historical reasoning informs social studies. Two types of reasoning are most often modeled and practiced in classrooms. Deductive reasoning is top-down reasoning where one reasons from the general (abstract ideas or propositions) to the particular (concrete examples or evidence). Inductive reasoning is bottom-up reasoning from the particular (concrete examples or evidence) to the general (abstract ideas or conclusions).

Why is thinking about how students think and reason important for teaching? The logic or sequence of instruction changes depending on the content, desired outcomes, students, and learning situation. How we ask students to express their understanding involves logic.

These four areas of inquiry (Metaphysics, Epistemology, Axiology, and Logic) can help organize philosophical perspectives along a *Continuum of Educational Philosophy* (Figure 2.2).

The continuum displays educational practices above the arrow and corresponding philosophical perspectives below. Overall, philosophical perspectives and educational practices on the left side of the continuum place greater emphasis on ideas-based, rational approaches to thinking and learning. Perspectives and practices on the right side favor experience-based, empirical approaches. Rationalism argues that knowledge can be gained through systematic, logical reasoning and intuition. Empiricism claims that acquiring or constructing knowledge is dependent on sense experiences, providing the source for all our ideas and concepts. The continuum does not divide these two major positions into distinct, mutually exclusive sections. Certain philosophers insist that knowledge can only be attained through reason. Others propose that phenomena must be observed and verified through the senses for reasoning to have any meaning. However, overlap does exist between rational and empirical approaches, and both can be employed and justified to support one another. The continuum permits us to locate the different outlooks we will encounter along a range, rather than isolate the work of each educational philosopher to a single fixed location.

As one moves from left to right on the continuum, the philosophical perspectives range from belief in a single absolute reality that exists prior to our sense experience to multiple possible views of reality that exist after experiencing with our senses (Metaphysics). Philosophical perspectives on the left side of the continuum believe in universal knowledge that exists independent of subjective experience whereas perspectives on the right believe knowledge is gained from

EDUCATIONAL PRACTICES

RATIONAL   EMPIRICAL

Ideas-Focused	Experience-Focused
Content-Oriented	Process-Oriented
Fixed Curriculum	Flexible Curriculum
Teacher-Centered/Teacher-Directed	Student-Centered/Student-Directed
Pre-Determined Outcomes	Open-Ended Exploration
Whole-Class Activities	Differentiated/Individualized Activities

←————————————————————————————————→

Objective External Reality	Internal Subjective Reality
Absolute Universal Truth	Changing Relative Truth
Pre-Existing Knowledge	Constructed Knowledge
Knowledge Independent of Experience	Knowledge Dependent on Experience
Autonomous Knowledge	Interdependent Knowledge
Absolute Universal Values	Relative Local Values
Values Independent of Experience	Values Dependent on Experience

PHILOSOPHICAL PERSPECTIVES

Figure 2.2 Continuum of Educational Philosophy

one's direct personal experiences (Epistemology). Between the two extreme positions on the continuum, rational reasoning as a way to achieve and defend understanding merges with the requirement to verify truth based on experience and the demand to take variables into account while proposing tentative conclusions (Logic). Morals, ethics, and virtues also range from belief in absolute and inerrant universal values to the need to consider context (including social, cultural, economic, political, religious, and other factors) with respect to human conduct (Axiology).

Educational practices on the left side of the continuum support an ideas-focused, content-oriented curriculum that is teacher-centered. Practices on the right prefer a process-oriented, experience-focused curriculum supporting student-centered learning activities. The edges of the continuum represent polar positions. At the far left, the curriculum consists of a fixed body of content knowledge. Instruction emphasizes teacher-directed methods with students participating in whole-class activities. Assessment consists of meeting prescribed outcomes and achieving pre-set standards. At the far right, a flexible curriculum values student experiences to construct knowledge. Students engage in open-ended exploration with no pre-determined outcomes. Student interests and needs affect the kinds of instruction offered. Individual students initiate and direct their own learning and are responsible for monitoring their own growth.

The majority of the continuum falls between the two extremes, observing different educational practices that invoke interplay among philosophical perspectives. As one moves from left to right, the curriculum becomes less rigid and more flexible. Instruction comprises a variety of methods from teacher-directed to student-centered. The process of learning becomes as valued as the content. Students collaborate or study individually depending on adaptable goals based on the context. Decisions about learning are based on student differences to an increasing degree.

The continuum as a guide permits fluid movement. One is not restricted to an either/or choice between viewpoints. A school or classroom may at times demonstrate practices located in one direction on the arrow (i.e., more content-oriented and teacher-centered) and at times gravitate in the other direction (i.e., more process-oriented and student-centered). For example, some teachers may ask questions such as, "What do I want my students to learn and how do I want to teach it?" Other teachers may ask, "What do my students want to learn and how would they like to learn it?" Many teachers may navigate between these positions, negotiating the curriculum and selecting instructional methods based on the needs of the students, the demands of school administrators, the expectations of parents and other stakeholders, and their own sense of what is appropriate in the situation.

The continuum can accommodate a range of practices and philosophical perspectives. The continuum in no way implies that practices or beliefs on one side are better than or more highly recommended than those on the other. The continuum serves as a tool for conducting our inquiry. As we encounter different examples of educational practices, we will locate these examples along the continuum and investigate philosophical perspectives that relate to those practices.

One word of caution. Practices that appear at locations far apart from one another on the continuum begin to contradict one another. In those instances, instruction loses consistency, practices lack compatibility, and educational programs become less coherent. A school or classroom exhibiting drastically contrasting philosophies creates a tension that becomes difficult to justify. For example, a teacher may wish to act as a guide in the classroom to facilitate collaborative learning, promote critical thinking, and encourage creativity. Yet this same teacher may spend a disproportionate amount of time behaving in a mostly teacher-centered manner, such as delivering content and drilling on prescribed skills to prepare students for testing. We will apply the "3Cs" criteria (consistency, compatibility, and coherence) introduced in Chapter 1 to the observations examined in each chapter to reveal contradictions.

In our inquiry, we will challenge assumptions about existing practices by asking *What if* questions. In addition, we will ask fundamental questions about the nature of reality, knowledge, values, and reasoning in education, locating examples of these four areas along the *Continuum of Educational Philosophy*. In the process, we will envision designing schools based on different beliefs about the purpose of education.

What Are the Big Questions about Teaching and Learning?

"Philosophical thought only begins when we challenge the logic of clichés with rigor and honesty."

(Albert Camus)

To explore philosophical perspectives that have influenced educational practices, we will focus on the following inquiry questions:

- What is the purpose of education?
- What do teachers teach?
- How do teachers teach?
- How are schools organized?

What Is the Purpose of Education?

Schools or school systems commonly offer a purpose statement to the public, published on their websites and in other materials such as brochures and student handbooks. Sometimes the purpose will be called a mission statement or a statement of the school's philosophy. While these statements focus on the learning needs of students, many attempt to generally address all or most of the expectations of prominent stakeholders such as families, policymakers, business interests, and community leaders. However, some schools (especially independent or private schools, charter or model schools, alternative schools, and other schools that serve a specific population of students or are designed according to a particular theme or approach) will express in a purpose statement the qualities or features that make the school unique.

The key questions to ask about the purpose of a school are:

- How would one design a school to fulfill that purpose?
- How does the school define an educated student?

To answer these two broad questions, and to get past the generic language that typifies many purpose statements, specific questions must be asked about the curriculum, the teaching and learning process, and the organization of the school. They include informative, practical, evaluative, and hypothetical types of questions.

The purpose of education differs from its aims or objectives. Aiming implies attempting to hit a target (Peters, 1973). Objectives set specific outcomes to be accomplished under certain conditions within a given time limit. Aims and objectives can conceivably be achieved, with effort and concentration. The possibility of failing is always a potential consequence. "The term 'purpose' carries no such suggestions," Peters concludes (p. 13). The purpose of education is broader, formulating an explanation as to why we endeavor to educate in the first place.

The purpose of education, and the definition of an educated person, changes over time. Frequent calls to reform education represent deeply held opinions that reflect fundamental beliefs, not only about the teaching and learning process but also about how society functions and how the world is viewed. Nevertheless, public discourse regarding education can fall into the trap of spouting superficial slogans or proposing sweeping solutions with scant evidence to support them beyond impassioned conviction.

What Do Teachers Teach? Questions about the Curriculum

More than one kind of curriculum may be found in schools (Eisner, 1994; Marsh, 1992; Posner, 1992). The *official* curriculum is the formal version—written, documented, published, and disseminated to administrators, teachers, and the public. The official curriculum may be developed at a school, within a school system, and/or produced at the state level. The official curriculum generally guides instruction and forms the basis of the assessment of students and the evaluation of teachers. However, this curriculum varies when implemented. Time and resources may tend to emphasize certain subject areas and content matter, and standardized testing identifies and measures only some aspects of the curriculum for accountability purposes.

Many students also engage in *extracurricular* activities. These are offered as part of the function of a school, but fall outside of the official curriculum. For example, students may perform in the marching band, join the chess club, compete on debate teams, play athletics, act in school plays, and voluntarily participate in other pursuits the school supports and endorses but does not require.

The *hidden* curriculum lies beneath the surface. Students are expected to learn and conform to social and procedural expectations, such as adhering to a schedule, earning grades, maintaining acceptable conduct, respecting authority, assuming responsibility, demonstrating respect for peers, displaying integrity, and other norms and values considered essential to the operation of the school environment and the preservation of the school culture.

The *null* curriculum (Eisner, 1985) refers to what schools do not teach. The official curriculum includes recognizable, familiar subjects such as languages, mathematics, sciences, history and social studies, physical education and health, and the visual and performing arts. Some schools incorporate vocational and technical subjects into their curriculum while in other communities these kinds of courses are offered in a separate school setting. While many schools continue to offer a variety of classes in the visual and performing arts (including drama and dance), other schools have severely curtailed or discontinued these classes, whether due to budget cuts or other reasons.

The subjects that schools emphasize, and the areas reduced or eliminated, reflect decisions with philosophical implications. The knowledge and skills deemed of the highest value (to students or society) represent beliefs about what is worth knowing. The official curriculum codifies a set of values, the hidden curriculum enforces a set of values, and the null curriculum reinforces a set of values. Philosophical inquiry asks questions about *What* knowledge students are taught, *How* these decisions are made, and *Why* this knowledge is taught (or *Why* certain knowledge is taught and not other knowledge). Fundamental questions about the curriculum may include:

- What do schools ask teachers to teach? Why require that curriculum?
- Who decides what to include and what to omit? Does some knowledge receive greater emphasis and other knowledge less? Why emphasize that knowledge?
- Where does that knowledge come from? What are the sources of knowledge the school accepts and values? How do we know the selected content is accurate or valid? How do we know the content is relevant?
- Does some knowledge change while other knowledge remains constant? Is some knowledge universal and useful to all while other knowledge only applies to certain people in certain situations?
- What content and skills do teachers get to decide to teach or to emphasize in their own classrooms?
- *What if* . . . the purpose of the school changed; how would that affect the curriculum? What would teachers teach?

How Do Teachers Teach? Questions about Pedagogy

As we discussed in Chapter 1, pedagogy involves more than inserting activities into a lesson plan. Techniques, strategies, and activities can be combined into coherent and consistent methods of instruction. Questions to ask about pedagogy include:

- How do teachers teach? Why use those methods of instruction?
- How do teachers prefer to teach? Does the school encourage and support those methods or require a different set of teaching methods?
- How do students prefer to learn? Should how students prefer to learn determine how they are taught?
- How do teachers assess learning? Why assess learning using those methods?
- How do teachers prefer to assess learning? Does the school encourage and support those methods or require a different set of assessment methods?
- How do students prefer to demonstrate their learning? Should how students prefer to demonstrate learning determine how they are assessed?
- How do teachers manage instructional time? Who decides how teachers use instructional time?
- How do students prefer to use their time? Should how students prefer to use time determine how instructional time is allocated and managed?
- *What if . . .* the purpose of the school changed; how would that affect instruction? How would teachers teach?

Beyond issues regarding instructional and assessment methods, pedagogy involves asking questions about the role of the teacher and the role of the student in the learning process. The way teachers behave in classrooms is greatly influenced by their own experiences as students, how they were taught in the past, how fellow teachers behave, how students respond, and expectations of administrators, families, and others in a position to influence school policy and practice. Questions asked to challenge assumptions about the role of the teacher may include:

- How are teachers expected to act or behave in the classroom? How do teachers act or behave in the classroom? How do teachers want to act or behave in the classroom?
- How are teachers expected to interact with the students in the classroom? In what ways do teachers interact with the students in the classroom? How do teachers want to interact with the students in the classroom?
- *What if . . .* the purpose of the school changed; how would that affect the role of the teacher? What metaphors might we suggest for the role of the teacher?

The curriculum, instruction, and role of the teacher influence the role of the students and how they are expected to conduct themselves in the classroom setting. Questions may be asked to challenge assumptions about the role of the student, such as:

- How do students learn? In what different ways do students learn?
- How are students expected to act or behave in the classroom? How do students act or behave in the classroom? How do students want to act or behave in the classroom?
- How are students expected to interact with the teacher in the classroom? In what ways do students interact with the teacher in the classroom? How do students want to interact with the teacher in the classroom?
- How are students expected to interact with each other in the classroom? In what ways do students interact with each other in the classroom? How do students want to interact with each other in the classroom?

- *What if* . . . the purpose of the school changed; how would that affect the role of the student? What metaphors might we suggest for the role of the student?

How Are Schools Organized? Questions about the Role of the School

Teachers may overlook asking, "What role does the school play in the learning process?" Perhaps this question is not always consciously asked. How the school supports teachers may be taken for granted over time. However, a school is more than a building or location. A school represents the education a student receives. Myriad decisions made at various levels of the institutional structure determine the kinds of things students learn, how they are taught, the methods of assessment, the time allotted for subject areas and specific topics within subjects, and even the space used for instruction. These decisions communicate the kinds of learning valued by the school. Broad questions to consider include:

- How is the school organized to fulfill the purpose of education?
- How does the school manage instructional time? How does the school acquire and allocate resources?
- How does a school's decision-making processes affect teaching and learning?
- How is the school's physical environment and arrangement of space related to teaching and learning?
- *What if* . . . the purpose of the school changed; how would that affect the way a school is organized and its role in the teaching and learning process?

Philosophy of Education in Action

Asking questions about the purpose of education and the value of educational practices enters into the domain of philosophy. Examining one's teaching and offering a rationale based on reasoning and reflection reveals assumptions, beliefs, and values about education. The Greek philosopher Aristotle describes practical activity (*praxis*) as action toward the Good, concerned with matters of human conduct such as ethics and politics (*Nicomachean Ethics*). Inquiry into what actions are good or worthwhile may be called "practical philosophy" (Haldane, 2011, p. 5). One need not formulate a philosophical perspective in advance to engage in practical philosophy. For instance, the process does not require starting with a philosophical position and either looking for examples of it in practice or applying its principles to an area of practice. Practical philosophy may begin "with questions posed by some area of human practice," investigating the activity, and interpreting and evaluating its consequences (Haldane, 2011, p. 11). Questions about whether the purposes and outcomes of practice are reasonable, appropriate, and worthwhile (or good) have philosophical implications.

The American philosopher John Dewey argues that philosophy should venture beyond a specialized field contemplating arcane issues, restricted to studying itself or caught up in internal disputes. Problems that arise in social practice, and in education in particular, offer rich opportunities for philosophy to have a direct influence on situations that matter to the people involved and affected. He states, "Education offers a vantage ground from which to penetrate to the human, as distinct from the technical, significance of philosophical discussion" (MW 9:338). Philosophical inquiry should emerge from conditions and experiences encountered in daily living and offer practical guidance. "Philosophy of education," Dewey writes, "is not an external application of ready-made ideas to a system of practice" (MW 9:341). Philosophical inquiry can bring problems to light so they may be rigorously examined and honestly addressed.

According to British philosopher R. S. Peters, we assume education results in some condition of life or state of being we find desirable. He reasons, however, that "even though there may be value in being educated it must be associated with some specific types of value" (1973, p. 239). One view values breadth of understanding and the pleasure of attaining knowledge for its own sake. Another view looks to the utility of what we learn and how it can be applied in the interests of achieving some social or individual purpose. A third view seeks truth that can be regarded as "having a worth which is independent of its benefit" (p. 251). The merits of these views are perpetually discussed and debated, and each places demands on the process of education. Why these different approaches come into conflict, and how they might be reconciled, raise philosophical questions concerning the values that underlie practice. "Philosophy has an important contribution to make to practical wisdom," Peters concludes, although it is not in a position to prescribe specific solutions (p. 29). As an activity, philosophy has significance for the questions it asks.

Two quotations from Chapter 1 convey the theme of this textbook. In the classic Greek period, Socrates stated, "Philosophy begins in wonder" (*Theaeteus*, 155d). In the 20th century, Wittgenstein (1922) claimed, "Philosophy is not a theory but an activity" (4.112). By combining these two ideas, drawn from different eras of philosophical thought, we will describe philosophy as a *wonder activity*. This synthesis represents our view of the inquiry process as an activity that begins by asking questions. The goal is to engage in active and relevant inquiry, focused on philosophy of education *in action*.

Notes

1 *The Republic*, 377b.
2 Frequently misattributed to Voltaire. The original quotation, "It is easier to judge the mind of a man by his questions rather than his answers," has been sourced to Pierre-Marc-Gaston, duc de Lévis (1808) in *Maxims and Reflections on Various Topics of Morals and Politics, Vol. 1* (Maxim xvii).

References

Adler, M. J. (1955). *A guide for leaders of great books discussion groups*. Chicago, IL: Great Books Foundation.

Aristotle. (1984). *The complete works of Aristotle: The revised Oxford translation*. J. Barnes (Ed.). Princeton, NJ: Princeton University Press.

Colburn, A. (2000). An inquiry primer. *Science Scope, 23*(6), 42–4.

Dewey, J. (1980). Democracy and education: An introduction to the philosophy of education. *The middle works of John Dewey, 1916: Vol. 9* (pp. 192–361). Carbondale, IL: Southern Illinois University Press.

Dewey, J. (1986). How we think: A restatement of the relation of reflective thinking to the educative process. In J. Boydston (Series Ed.), *The later works of John Dewey, 1933: Vol. 8* (pp. 105–352). Carbondale, IL: Southern Illinois University Press.

Eisner, E. (1994). *The educational imagination: On the design and evaluation of school programs* (3rd ed.). New York, NY: Macmillan.

Great Books Foundation. (2014). *Shared inquiry: Handbook for discussion leaders and participants*. [PDF file]. Chicago, IL: Great Books Foundation. Retrieved from http://www.greatbooks.org/wp-content/uploads/2014/12/Shared-Inquiry-Handbook.pdf

Haldane, J. (2011). *Practical philosophy: Ethics, society and culture*. [Electronic]. Andrews UK Limited. Retrieved from www.andrewsuk.com

James, W. (1890). *Principles of psychology*. New York, NY: Henry Holt.

Marsh, C. J. (1992). *Key concepts for understanding curriculum*. London: Falmer Press.

Martin-Hansen, L. (2002). Defining inquiry. *The Science Teacher, 69*(2), 34.

Moeller, M., & Moeller, V. (2002). *Socratic seminars and literature circles*. New York, NY: Routledge.

The National Council for Excellence in Critical Thinking. (2013). A draft statement of principles. [Website]. Retrieved from http://www.criticalthinking.org/pages/the-national-council-for-excellence-in-critical-thinking/406#top

Paul, R., & Elder, L. (2008). *The miniature guide to critical thinking: Concepts and tools*. Dillon Beach, CA: Foundation for Critical Thinking.

Peters, R. S. (1973). Aims of education: A conceptual inquiry. In R. S. Peters (Ed.), *The philosophy of education* (pp. 11–57). London: Oxford University Press.

Peters, R. S. (1973). The justification of education. In R. S. Peters (Ed.), *The philosophy of education* (pp. 239–267). London: Oxford University Press.

Plato. (1997). The Republic. In J. M. Cooper & D. S. Hutchinson (Eds.), *Plato: Complete works* (pp. 971–1223). Indianapolis, IN: Hackett.

Posner, G. J. (1992). *Analyzing the curriculum*. New York, NY: McGraw-Hill.

Rescher, N. (2001). *Philosophical reasoning*. Malden, MA: Blackwell.

Stripling, B. K. (2003). Inquiry-based learning. In B. K. Stripling & S. Hughes-Hassell (Eds.), *Curriculum connections through the library*. Westport, CT: Libraries Unlimited.

Todd, O. (1997). *Albert Camus: A life*. (B. Ivry, Trans.). New York, NY: Alfred A. Knopf.

Wittgenstein, L. (1922). *Tractatus Logico-Philosophicus*. (C. K. Ogden, Trans.). New York, NY: Harcourt Brace.

Part II

What If . . . The Purpose of Education Were to Learn Objective, Universal Knowledge?

The *Wonder Model of Inquiry* begins by posing a hypothetical wonder question about the purpose of education. Part II asks the overarching question, *"What if . . . the purpose of education were to learn objective, universal knowledge?"*

Each chapter in Part II begins by posing a *What if* question focused on one aspect of the overarching question.

Chapter 3 wonders, *"What if . . . the purpose of education were to learn enduring ideas and eternal truths?"*

Chapter 4 asks, *"What if . . . the purpose of education were to learn structure and principles?"*

Chapter 5 poses the question, *"What if . . . the purpose of education were to learn essential knowledge?"*

Following the steps of the Wonder Model, in each chapter we will observe a classroom lesson based on the purpose of education and investigate philosophical concepts that support the practices observed. From the investigation, we will design a hypothetical school to represent this perspective and compare it to examples of actual schools organized according to this purpose. Using the "3Cs" criteria, we will evaluate the design for consistency, compatibility, and coherence. Finally, you will be asked to compare the educational practices described to your own observations and experiences in schools, and reflect on how they relate to your beliefs about the purpose of education.

The *Continuum of Educational Philosophy* will help guide and organize our inquiry. In Part II, we will examine philosophical perspectives on the left side of the continuum, which takes a rational approach to learning. According to this point of view, a single absolute reality ultimately exists prior to our personal sense experiences of the world. Through rational thinking, one may attain objective, universal knowledge that exists independent of individual, subjective interpretations. Morals, ethics, and virtues also represent absolute and inerrant universal values. Education focuses on learning ideas and concepts in a content-oriented curriculum. The teacher directs the learning of the students to discover a pre-determined body of knowledge.

3   What If . . . The Purpose of Education Were to Learn Enduring Ideas and Eternal Truths?

Wonder

We begin our inquiry into philosophies of education by asking the wonder question, *"What if . . . the purpose of education were to learn enduring ideas and eternal truths?"*

On the *Continuum of Educational Philosophy* (Figure 3.1), this purpose of education views knowledge as objective and unchanging, existing independently from an individual's subjective experiences. Ideas and subject matter are highly valued, and the teacher assumes a leadership role in directing the learning of students. Students follow the direction set by the teacher and express their learning through rational thinking and logical argument.

Observe

Classroom Vignette: A Socratic Discussion in a Fifth-Grade English/Language Arts Classroom

In Mrs. A's fifth-grade classroom, the desks are arranged in a circle in the center of the room. Each student is grasping a copy of a *Junior Great Books* anthology of stories, turned to the short story

EDUCATIONAL PRACTICES

RATIONAL	EMPIRICAL
Ideas-Focused	Experience-Focused
Content-Oriented	Process-Oriented
Fixed Curriculum	Flexible Curriculum
Teacher-Centered	Student-Centered
Teacher-Directed	Self-Directed
Pre-Determined Outcomes	Open-Ended Exploration
Whole-Class Activities	Differentiated/Individualized Activities

Objective External Reality	Internal Subjective Reality
Absolute Universal Truth	Changing Relative Truth
Pre-Existing Knowledge	Constructed Knowledge
Knowledge Independent of Experience	Knowledge Dependent on Experience
Autonomous Knowledge	Interdependent Knowledge
Absolute Universal Values	Relative Local Values
Values Independent of Experience	Values Dependent on Experience

PHILOSOPHICAL PERSPECTIVES

Figure 3.1 Continuum of Educational Philosophy (Ideas and Truth)

"Charles" by Shirley Jackson. Mrs. A, sitting in the circle with the students, begins the discussion by asking a question.

"Why did Laurie invent Charles?"

Five students eagerly raise their hands. Mrs. A waits a few more seconds. Some students exchange glances as others flip through the pages of the book. More hands rise. Mrs. A calls on a student.

"To not get in trouble," Justin says.

Mrs. A does not respond. She smiles and calls on another student.

"He wanted to see how his parents would act first," Kate explains.

"Act first?" Mrs. A inquires. "Act before what?"

"Before he tells them that Charles is really him."

After hearing more responses, Mrs. A asks, "How do we know Charles does not exist?"

"The teacher says so," Shirley answers. "It says so right here." The girl reads aloud the closing sentence of the story.

"Laurie invented an imaginary student, Charles," Nat states to the class, "to describe to his parents how he had been behaving in kindergarten."

Several students nod and voice their agreement. Mrs. A's eyes focus on the book. She places her finger on a sentence near the beginning of the story. She looks up from the page and asks, "How did Laurie start to dress when he began to go to kindergarten?"

"He began wearing blue jeans," Patty answers.

"What reasons might Laurie have to change how he dressed when he began school?"

Students share their opinions. Mrs. A asks for evidence from the story to support their answers. Mary attempts to respond, but stumbles over unfamiliar vocabulary words such as *swaggering*, *raucous*, *insolently*, and *fresh*. Mrs. A encourages the students to infer the meaning of the words based on their context in the text.

After the words have been defined, Mrs. A returns to her line of questioning. "Why did Laurie leave for the first day of kindergarten as a *swaggering* character?" she asks. "Why did he return acting *insolent*, *raucous*, and *fresh*?"

The students suggest reasons, and begin to wonder aloud why Laurie's parents didn't figure out sooner that Charles is actually Laurie.

"What clues or hints do they have that Charles might actually be Laurie?" she asks.

The students scramble to look for clues in the story. One girl murmurs that she had picked up right away on the fact Laurie had made up Charles. Another disputes this claim, leading to a minor quarrel before Mrs. A intervenes.

"Why," Gina wonders, "did Laurie tell his parents about Charles every day?"

Before Mrs. A can respond, Malcolm asks, "Why did he say Charles is bigger than him?"

"We will return to your question, Gina," Mrs. A replies. "Malcolm, where does it say in the story that Charles is bigger than Laurie?"

Malcolm tells the class what page he is on and reads the sentence aloud. "And he says Charles doesn't have to wear rubbers and a jacket."

Students jump into the discussion as Mrs. A silently observes.

"I think he wanted to get kicked out of kindergarten so he could stay home," Patrick conjectures.

Without confirming or refuting his assertion, Mrs. A asks the class, "What caused a sudden *reformation* in Charles's behavior in school?" She stops to make sure all the students understand the meaning of the word "reformation" before calling on students. She asks students to supply evidence directly from the story to support their responses.

Victoria indicates that after a week of good conduct, Charles returned to "normal." Mrs. A asks why she believes he resumed his disruptive behavior.

"Because he figured out he could get away with it," she replies. "He got a little girl in trouble and pretended like he was just passing out crayons."

"Michael does stuff like that," Gina remarks, and the class giggles.

Mrs. A switches the direction of the discussion. "Why is Laurie's mother so anxious to meet Charles' mother?" she asks.

Ted points out that the father wants to invite her to tea to "get a look at her." Skipping down the page, he reads the passage where Laurie's mother scans the classroom to try and spot Charles' mother.

"What did Laurie's mother conclude?" Mrs. A asks.

"That none of the mothers looked 'haggard enough,'" Martin replies.

Mrs. A helps the students determine the meaning of *haggard*. "Why would Laurie's mother expect Charles' mother to look haggard?" she asks.

The students explain how looking after a boy like Charles would be frustrating and exhausting. Finally, Gina exclaims in exasperation, "But she *is* Charles's mother!"

"Do you think Laurie's mother suspects that Charles is actually Laurie?" Mrs. A asks.

Some students express the belief she did, and others disagree. Mrs. A alters the question.

"Do you think Laurie's mother wants to know that Laurie is Charles?"

The students howl a chorus of "No!"

"Why not?"

Attitudes initially center on how the mother would be disappointed in her son. However, the possibility is raised that she might have been disappointed in herself and worried how Laurie's behavior would reflect on her as a mother. Victoria believes the mother simply cannot see herself as the kind of mother who would raise a Charles, that she doesn't see herself as that kind of mother.

"She probably doesn't think she's haggard," the girl suspects.

Mrs. A offers another tack. "Why would Laurie want his parents to know he is Charles?" she asks.

Some students are convinced Laurie does not want his parents to know. Others, however, wonder if he is trying to tell them about his own struggles to adjust to kindergarten by conveying them through this invented character. A few suggest Laurie is worried how his parent will react if they know he is actually Charles.

Mrs. A returns to the question why Laurie told his parents stories about Charles. "Do you agree or disagree with Laurie's decision to tell his parents made-up stories about Charles?"

Some students condemn Laurie, stating that a lie is always wrong. A few students suggest that a lie can be told under certain circumstances if hiding the truth causes no harm or protects someone. Patrick claims that a lie will always be found out and will only make things worse.

Mrs. A takes the opportunity to connect the two issues. "Do you think Laurie's mother wants to know that Laurie is Charles?"

Some students agree she does want to know; others are not so sure.

Mrs. A asks, "What is the author trying to tell us about Laurie, and what is she trying to tell us about Laurie's parents? Why don't we break into pairs and discuss these two ideas before we come to a conclusion as a class?"

As the students grapple with the questions, Mrs. A remains seated and scans the circle. Voices rise and fall as students express their thoughts. Mrs. A softly calls students by name when their conversations veer off topic.

"Alright," she says after a few minutes. "What have we decided?"

Mrs. A listens attentively to every idea. She continues to ask questions and begins to combine ideas, guiding the students to support their reasoning.

To conclude the lesson, Mrs. A gives directions for a writing assignment. "Here are two writing prompts for today's journal entries," she says.

"What can we learn from this story about how families might act when a young child begins attending school for the first time?" The students scribble her question into their notebooks.

"Here's a second question to think about," Mrs. A continues. The students look up from their notebooks.

"Why is the story called 'Charles'?" she inquires. "Why not call the story 'Laurie'? Or 'Laurie's Mom'? In your journal entry, suggest a title and explain why you believe that title best expresses the meaning of the story."

Investigate

To examine philosophies that have influenced this view of the purpose of education, we will investigate the following inquiry questions:

- What Do Teachers Teach? Questions about the Curriculum
- How Do Teachers Teach? Questions about Pedagogy
- How Are Schools Organized? Questions about the Role of the School

What Do Teachers Teach? Questions about the Curriculum

If we were to design a school based on learning enduring ideas and eternal truths, what curriculum would we teach? Where would this knowledge come from? What philosophical perspectives would support this curriculum?

What Is Lasting Knowledge?

"The truth is everywhere the same."
(Robert M. Hutchins)

In the classroom vignette above, the students are reading a story from the *Junior Great Books* series. This source represents the thinking of those who argue students should read works and study ideas of enduring value. *Great Books of the Western World*, first published in 1952, contains writings by an illustrious roster of poets, playwrights, historians, scientists, and politicians. The *Great Books* consider ideas from great minds of the past relevant to understanding problems in the present, and believe that these enduring works will continue to inform and inspire in the future. *Junior Great Books*, first published in 1962, includes a wide selection of readings selected for young readers.

The editor of *Great Books*, Robert M. Hutchins (1899–1977), served as President and Chancellor of the University of Chicago from 1929–51. Hutchins (1936) proposes a general curriculum consisting of "permanent studies," a body of knowledge that remains valid for all time (p. 70). Hutchins believes knowledge and truth to be universal. He reasons:

> Education implies teaching. Teaching implies knowledge. Knowledge is truth. The truth is everywhere the same. Hence, education should be everywhere the same.
>
> (p. 66)

Hutchins (1952) praises what he calls the "Great Conversation" that typifies the spirit of inquiry associated with Western civilization (Vol. 1, p. 1). The *Great Books* are intended to engage readers in that ongoing dialogue, to better understand society and themselves while preserving and transmitting the cultural heritage those ideas represent. Hutchins supports a general education in the liberal arts. A liberal education is one that is *liberating*, promoting freethinking across a wide and rich spectrum of knowledge to reach one's fullest potential. A general or liberal education cultivates the intellect. This approach does not support offering a vocational or specialized curriculum that trains students in practical skills or prepares them for specific careers.

The educational philosophy associated with this point of view is known as Perennialism. Perennialism attests that certain knowledge continues to have value for every learner. The root word of Perennialism (*perennial*) means perpetual or recurring. Perennialism believes in teaching important truths and knowledge that persist with each succeeding generation.

Mortimer J. Adler (1902–2001), a student of Hutchins, also believed all students should follow a general or liberal education. He co-edited the *Great Books* and *Junior Great Books* with Hutchins and published *The Paideia Proposal*. *Paideia* comes from the Greek *pais* or *paidos* (child) and means "the upbringing of a child" (the word *pedagogy* comes from the same Greek root). Paideia principles follow the tenet, "The best education for the best is the best education for all" (Adler, 1982, p. 6). This echoes the Greek philosopher Aristotle's declaration that "education should be one and the same for all" (*Politics*, Book VIII, 21).

The prominent place of philosophy in the *Great Books*, and the use of *Paideia* in the title of Adler's program, is not coincidental. Classical Greek philosophers express a belief in lasting knowledge and universal truth that continues to influence thinking about education today.

What Is Ultimately Real and True?

The Greek philosopher Socrates (469/70–399 BCE) is one of the most celebrated names in Western philosophy. Although Socrates never wrote down any of his thoughts for posterity, writers and historians of his day depict him as a tireless seeker of truth and virtue. Socrates frequented the public places of Athens, engaging in conversations and provoking people to deliberate the fundamental nature of such matters as beauty, virtue, justice, and goodness. "The unexamined life is not worth living," Socrates states (Plato, *Apology*, 38a).

Much of what we know about Socrates' thinking is derived from the writings of his well-known pupil, Plato (424/3–347 BCE). Plato wrote numerous *dialogues*, or conversations between Socrates and one or more of his students based on a series of probing questions. Many dialogues likely represent Plato's beliefs as much as they do those of Socrates. Socratic dialogues form the basis of Idealism (or Platonic Idealism). Idealism contains both the words *idea* and *ideal*, emphasizing the paramount significance of ideas in this philosophy's perspective about truth and knowledge.

In Book VII of *The Republic*, Plato recounts one of Socrates' most famous dialogues, often referred to as the "Allegory of the Cave." Socrates asks his pupil, Glaucon (Plato's older brother), to imagine people living in a cave since birth, chained by their legs and necks so they are unable to move or even turn their heads from side to side. All they are able to do is stare directly ahead at the cave wall in front of them. On the cave wall appear images of animals, trees, vessels, and other objects. We learn in the dialogue that these images are shadows being cast by a fire located behind the prisoners. The objects themselves are merely replicas or facsimiles of the things they display, made of wood, stone, and other materials. To the prisoners, however, these shadows are the actual things. The shadows represent the only reality they have ever experienced.

Socrates then asks Glaucon to imagine a twist to the story: What if a prisoner were to escape? Socrates describes how the journey up the path out of the cave would be difficult for the prisoner. The glare of the fire, which he is seeing for the first time, would be painful to endure in the dimness of the cave. Exiting the cave exposes him to a far more dazzling light, nearly blinding him. As his eyes adjust, he sees for the first time the actual objects that were displayed in the cave as shadows. He sees trees, rocks, and rivers, and the moon and stars in the sky. Finally, he gazes upon the Sun itself, in all its brilliance. He becomes aware that the Sun is the true source of light, of heat, and of the seasons.

Socrates explains that the cave is the physical world we all live in, that the fire in the cave is the Sun we see in the sky, and that the shadows on the wall are those things we perceive with our senses and believe to be real. Ultimate reality lies beyond the cave, where the actual objects exist and the radiance of true knowledge shines. The journey out of the cave represents our quest for true knowledge. Socrates calls the ultimate source of all knowledge, the creator of all things, the Good.

The "Allegory of the Cave" raises a provocative question: *What if* reality as we know it is not true? *What if* the reality we experience and believe to be true is only an illusion, a shadow of true reality? Where does true, ultimate reality exist? The implications for education are significant. Socrates concludes, "There is only one good, knowledge."[1] But what knowledge? If the reality we experience in our daily lives is not necessarily true, what knowledge should we learn?

For Socrates, reality is not what we experience in the physical world. The physical world is unreliable and changing. The only reliable source of true knowledge is the perfect world of ideas. Ultimate reality is composed of Forms. Forms are the perfect ideal versions of everything in reality. Forms exist for all things, not only for physical objects but also for abstract concepts such as goodness, beauty, and justice as well as for character traits and moral virtues. All conceivable reality exists first and foremost as Forms.

True knowledge is universal, meaning it applies to everyone everywhere at all times. This reality is autonomous and independent of one's subjective experience. In Latin, this is known as *a priori* ("from the earlier") and contends that reality exists first, prior to our experience of it. This objective knowledge is discovered, neither constructed by individuals nor subject to change based on context.

Plato's pupil, Aristotle (384–322 BCE), disagrees with his teacher about the nature of reality regarding Forms. In Aristotelian Realism, Form does not exist independent from Matter. Aristotle perceived a duality to all things, with Form being the design or structure and matter the substance. For example, a human being possesses both an intellect (rational mind) and a physical body. Physical matter has particular characteristics or properties that may be perceived as variable (such as variations in physical appearance, shape, color, etc.) but ultimately each thing that exists has an essential characteristic that defines it. Aristotle calls that defining characteristic "essence" (*Topics*, 101b37). For example, all oak trees have within them the *essence* of an oak tree, that which distinguishes one object from all other objects (such as an oak tree from other things, even from other kinds of trees). By studying an oak tree, one can determine its essence, or that distinguishing characteristic or property that makes it what it is. Therefore, each thing contains within it the essence of its Form. Instead of disregarding the physical world as an unreliable source of knowledge, Aristotle believes that Forms can be discovered by studying the characteristics of things to reveal their Essence.

According to this philosophy, people possess an essence as well. The essence of a human being, the enduring characteristic that makes a human being a unique entity, is rational intelligence. "All men by nature desire to know," Aristotle states (*Metaphysics*, 980a 21). The goal of education is to develop rational thinking, which leads to universal knowledge. (The influence of Aristotle on education is explored further in Chapter 4.)

Various religions believe humans possess an essence (or soul) that connects us to a divine creator. The physical world we inhabit is temporal, transitory, and ephemeral. True reality resides on an eternal plane that transcends the physical world. We are admonished not to trust in knowledge gained only through our senses. Rather, we are counseled to seek true and perfect knowledge that can only be attained in a higher realm of abstract and perfect goodness. Socrates cautions that, although we may regard what we perceive with our physical senses as true knowledge, our eyesight "does not see wisdom" (Plato, *Phaedrus*, 250d).

One Western religious figure greatly influenced by classic Greek philosophy is St. Augustine of Hippo, a Bishop in the Roman Catholic Church. Augustine (ca. 413–426/1950) believes that the material world (the earthly city or City of Man) derives its essence from the spiritual world (the City of God). True knowledge cannot be revealed through our senses, only through insight (or by divine revelation, which Augustine calls *illumination*). In the theology of Augustine, however, the role of rational thinking holds as high a value as in the philosophy of Plato. Augustine (1953) argues, "We could not believe at all if we did not have rational souls" (p. 302). The essence of a human being, for Augustine, is a rational soul.

What Is the Relationship between Reality and the Mind?

Philosophers continue to ponder the relationship between reality and the mind. René Descartes (France, 1596–1650), considered by many the father of modern philosophy, famously declares, "I think, therefore I am" (1998, p. 33).[2] As an exercise, Descartes purposely doubted all reality and, from that starting point, began to construct an argument for what is real. Through his doubting, he affirmed his own existence by acknowledging the act of thinking came first. His method became known as Skeptical Idealism. "If you would be a real seeker after truth," Descartes (1644/1984) explains, "it is necessary that at least once in your life you doubt, as far as possible, all things" (Part I, 1). Our perceptions of the physical world can be in error. Everything we claim to know as truths are ideas. "We exist," Descartes concludes, "insofar as our nature is that of a thinking thing" (Part I, 75).

Other philosophers have contemplated the role of the mind in determining reality. George Berkeley (1685–1753), a Bishop in the Episcopal Church of Ireland, believes all existence depends upon the mind to know it. Berkley (1710/1988) sums up his argument with the phrase, "*esse* is *percipi*" ("to be is to be perceived") (p. 54). For a material object to exist, the mind must perceive it. When we perceive objects, we perceive them with the mind. All that we perceive in the physical world are ultimately ideas.

The German philosopher Georg Hegel (1770–1831) argued that all reality is unified into one system with an inherent rational order. The "Absolute Idea" that Hegel describes (1816/1989) has "an existence of its own," "exists wholly as form," comprises "all truth," and is "the sole subject matter and content of philosophy" (p. 824–5). His philosophy maintains the centrality of the mind in understanding a reality composed of ideas.

Immanuel Kant (1724–1804), another German philosopher, believed that our sense perception of physical reality does not constitute ultimate knowledge. "But though all our knowledge begins with experience," Kant reasons (1781/2007), "it does not follow that it all arises out of experience" (p. 41). He proposes that humans perceive only the appearances of things, not the actual things themselves. "All our intuition is nothing but the representation of appearance," he explains. "As appearances, they cannot exist in themselves, but only in us" (p. 82). Breaking from Platonic Idealism, Kant does not equate appearance with illusion. He believes material objects have their own existence. However, our rational minds relate knowledge of appearances to universal categories that exist beyond the physical world of the senses. "Thus all human knowledge begins with intuitions, proceeds from thence to concepts, and ends with ideas" (p. 569). Ideas envision perfection that we can aspire to, whether or not this reality has yet to be experienced.

How Would One Design a Curriculum Based on Learning Enduring Ideas and Eternal Truths?

In the *Republic*, Socrates describes the kind of education citizens should receive. He begins with stories, poetry, speech, and music. He also recommends instruction in physical training, balancing the education of the soul with the education of the body. However, he stresses that a fit body does not make for a good soul. On the contrary, a good soul will make for a good body. The emphasis remains on one's soul, on the mental and spiritual. Socrates later introduces mathematics, which he argues produces not only practical knowledge but leads the soul upward by seeking understanding of true and lasting knowledge. Ultimately, Socrates arrives at philosophy, which strives to discover Form and ultimately grasp the Good itself. According to Socrates, the ideal education integrates all learning into a complete whole that seeks true, lasting knowledge.

To design a school based on learning enduring ideas and eternal truths, the curriculum would focus on classic works that have endured the test of time and convey universal truths and values all students should learn. A generalized curriculum based on the liberal arts develops the intellect, teaching one how to think. In the *Paideia Program*, Adler (1982) proposes using "books that are not textbooks and products of human artistry" in the curriculum (p. 28–9). In other words, the products of minds expressed in fiction, poetry, essays, philosophy, historical accounts, visual arts, music, dance, theater, and other first-hand, primary sources that exemplify intellectual curiosity, imagination, and understanding of the human condition. Socrates advises, "Employ your time in improving yourself by other men's writings, so that you shall gain easily what others have labored hard for."[3]

In this vision of education, one does not learn through compulsion or coercion, but comes to the truth on one's own. In the dialogues, as in so many other writings through the ages, light is used as a metaphor for truth or knowledge. When one discovers the truth, we often say one has "seen the light" or has become "enlightened" (what Augustine calls *illumination*). This leads to the next question in our inquiry: How should one teach? If we were to design a school to teach enduring ideas and eternal truths, what would be the method of instruction?

How Do Teachers Teach? Questions about Pedagogy

"The power to learn is present in everyone's soul."
                                                                    (Socrates)

Socrates observes, "Education isn't what some people declare it to be, namely, putting knowledge into souls that lack it, like putting sight into blind eyes" (*Republic*, 518b–c). Socrates believes each person possesses a capacity for learning that already exists in every soul. A familiar saying goes, "Education is not the filling of a pail, but the lighting of a fire."[4] The role of the teacher is to engage the learner in the discovery of truth and knowledge.

The Socratic Method

In the classroom vignette, Mrs. A does not lecture the students or present information while students take notes. She begins the lesson by posing a thought-provoking question, and continues to ask probing questions to encourage the students to participate in a discussion. Teaching in this style is widely known as the Socratic Method.

In *Meno*, Plato recounts a dialogue between Socrates and a young aristocratic whose slave has no formal education. Using a stick, Socrates draws the figure of a square on the ground and asks the slave how to double the area. After several attempts, the slave arrives at the correct solution. Socrates argues that through being asked questions the slave was guided to discover the existing knowledge for himself. Socrates believes "the power to learn is present in everyone's soul" (Plato, *Republic*, 518c). We already possess truths about reality, which education brings out of the learner.

Socrates calls this technique the "dialectic" (*Republic*, 532b). The dialectic has come to be expressed as a three-part logical progression.[5] The dialogue begins with a *thesis* (Greek for "something put forth"), a statement or assumption that establishes a position. Next, a new perspective or opposing viewpoint is introduced, the *antithesis* ("setting opposite" or "against position"). The third part, *synthesis* ("placing with" or "putting together"), combines ideas to reconcile the original position with the new perspective.

For example, in the "Allegory of the Cave," Socrates asks Glaucon to picture people living in a cave since birth, chained by their legs and necks. Once this premise has been established,

Socrates poses a new development, asking what would happen if a prisoner were to escape. Finally, Socrates connects the allegory to the search for knowledge, explaining that each of us lives in a cave of illusions and must ascend into the light of true reality. This dialogue follows the three-part sequence of stating a thesis, proposing an antithesis or new perspective, and synthesizing the ideas to arrive at a greater understanding.

In the classroom vignette, Mrs. A begins the lesson by asking, "Why did Laurie invent Charles?" The opening question establishes the situation and introduces a proposition. She expects the students to reveal the essence of the story through their own reasoning. By opening with an interpretation question, Mrs. A encourages her students to make connections across the story and initiate a dialogue.

What new perspective or different way of looking at the situation arises in the discussion? The viewpoint of Laurie's parents is introduced. The motivations of the parents to meet Charles's mother, and the insight that might reveal, become as important an issue in the discussion as Laurie's motivations for inventing Charles. To help achieve synthesis, a writing prompt asks the students to ponder both points of view as they reflect on the meaning of the story.

What Is the Role of the Teacher in the Socratic Method?

TEACHER AS QUESTIONER

In the classroom vignette, the role of the teacher is one of questioner. In the Socratic Method, this role is also referred to as discussion leader. Although the Socratic Method is often portrayed as collaborative, the leader's use of deliberate questioning can direct the discussion. Adler refers to the teacher's role as "the first among equals" to aid in guided discovery (Adler, 1982, p. 54; Adler, 1984, p. 19). The teacher moderates and directs the discussion. The discussion leader (who may be the teacher or a student) should only ask questions. The leader of a Socratic discussion can prepare questions in advance to frame the issue and determine the fundamental ideas, how they relate, and what insights students should gain (Paul, 1993; Paul & Elder, 2007).

A Socratic discussion is not entirely open-ended, in the sense that students freely express opinions without demonstrating rational thinking. According to Socrates, opinions are the lowest level of argument because they can be distorted or inaccurate. In the vignette, Mrs. A does not confirm if students' responses are correct. Instead, she requests that the students support their answers with evidence from the text and asks follow-up questions to probe and clarify responses. The role of the teacher also includes being a good listener. An effective discussion leader models the process for the participants, so they may develop listening and questioning skills.

The Socratic Method employs questioning techniques as part of a strategy to examine and challenge opinions, develop argument skills, and refine critical thinking. As the discussion leader, Mrs. A's choice of questions steers the direction of the inquiry. She avoids opening with clichéd questions such as, "How did you like the story?" or "How did the story make you feel?" Mrs. A asks probing questions that require the students to support their responses by referring to evidence from the story (such as, "Why did Laurie change how he dressed when he began to go to kindergarten?"). Mrs. A refrains from stating her opinions to the students or providing her interpretation of the story's meaning. Instead, she uses systematic and purposeful questioning to guide her students to discover the meaning for themselves.

TEACHER AS ROLE MODEL

Reading the dialogues, one can view Socrates in the role of master and his students as followers or disciples. A master is one who has achieved a high level of knowledge and wisdom. The metaphor of master embodies the role of the teacher in leading students in the search for truth.

As master, the teacher would expect students to pass on his teachings to others. Truth in this sense encompasses cultivating virtues as well. Absolute truth includes absolute moral and spiritual truth. Socrates unequivocally dismisses relative moral values as a false belief system. Morals and values are innate in each of us, part of our latent knowledge to be recollected.

Aristotle, on the other hand, believes morality to be a rational choice arrived at through deliberation and habit (*Nicomachean Ethics*, Book II). Things cannot act in a way contrary to their nature or essence. A rock, for example, will not continue to rise when tossed in the air, but will fall to the ground according to its nature. Therefore, Aristotle reasons, unethical or immoral conduct indicates we must not have virtues instilled in us from birth. We do, however, possess the potentiality to act with virtue. Aristotle contends ethical principles can be cultivated as part of a student's education.

Like Aristotle, Kant does not believe humans are born possessing innate morals but that the capacity to develop moral reasoning is part of our rational nature. Morality is developed through reason. A teacher can develop morals in children using catechisms (maxims committed to memory) or through dialogue, appealing to their reason through discussion and questioning.

Perennialism reflects this view of the teacher as role model. Hutchins (1952) calls for "an education that draws out our common humanity" (Vol. 1, p. 50). Adler (1982) advocates for an education that "most befits human nature" (p. 19). Teachers are to aid in the personal growth of students, which includes moral and spiritual development. Therefore, the teacher imparts education in morals, virtues, and character as well as academic content. Although Kant (1797/1996) does not believe a child can learn moral principles merely through imitation of others' behavior, he advises teachers to provide guidance and discipline, and set a "good example" for students by their "exemplary conduct" to assist them on the path to gaining moral autonomy (p. 223).

While entreating the teacher to serve as an exemplary model and leader, the Socratic Method avoids a pedantic or didactic approach to instruction. The teacher should not dominate the discussion or provide conclusions for the students to passively accept. The development of the intellect and moral reasoning requires active participation by the learner, with the teacher directing the process.

What Is the Role of the Student in the Socratic Method?

STUDENT AS DISCUSSANT

Students in the Socratic Method actively participate in the discussion. Students must support their answers with evidence from the text. For older students who can read independently, participation requires reading the text in advance. Many teachers require students to annotate the text – taking notes, generating questions, and making inferences as they read.

The role is also one of active listener and questioner. This includes respectfully considering different points of view. *Junior Great Books* calls the method Shared Inquiry. Students are expected to respond directly to each other, not express their remarks to the teacher. A true dialogue should emerge among learners.

STUDENT AS SEEKER

The role of the student is to be a seeker of truth and wisdom. The student should actively participate in discussion to discover knowledge. They should also seek moral truths. In the vignette, Mrs. A asks the students if they agree or disagree with Laurie's decision to invent "Charles," in essence to tell his parents a lie. This evaluation question requires the students to make a moral judgment about Laurie's ethical behavior. Mrs. A refrains from stating her own position on the subject, instead using questioning to draw the appraisal from the students.

STUDENT AS FOLLOWER

The student is also to strive for virtue and integrity, and regard the teacher as an exemplary role model. If the teacher is the leader or master, then the student is a follower or disciple. This role recalls the original Greek definition of *pedagogy*, "to lead a child." Following the teacher's example, the child will develop listening, questioning, and critical thinking skills to arrive at conclusions about the issue under discussion. With practice in the process, students can each become discussion leaders and conduct a Socratic dialogue for peers.

Design

Plato began teaching his students at the *Akademia*, a grove of trees located outside of Athens named for the Greek mythological hero, Akademos. In this setting, Plato and his students engaged in dialogues. From these origins, Plato's Academy was founded and the word *academy* has become associated with a school.

How Are Schools Organized? Questions about the Role of the School

In our school design (Table 3.1), the curriculum would emphasize *Great Books* and primary sources. The pedagogy features the Socratic Method, which determines the role of the teacher and the role of the student in instruction. To remain consistent with the purpose and offer a coherent educational program, the entire school would be organized to support this curriculum and pedagogy.

The school administrator (whether a principal, director, or headmaster) would function as a lead teacher, a fellow educator who supports the academic mission of the school. Decision-making on the selection of the curriculum, the choice of instructional materials, and instructional and assessment methods would reflect the purpose of the school and represent the philosophical perspective.

School decisions determine a great deal besides curriculum and instruction. Schools control time. Students report to school, and function within the school day, according to a schedule. The schedule determines the time allocated for instruction in different subjects. In doing so, the schedule designates what subjects are most valued. Moreover, time influences instructional methods. A school devoted to the search for truth using the Socratic Method would schedule time for class discussions in which all students could participate. The schedule would permit ample time to allow students to engage in intellectual inquiry that ponders foundational questions, examines reasoning, and probes deeply into issues.

Table 3.1 Design a School (Ideas and Truth)

Purpose of Education	Learn universal knowledge and eternal truths
Curriculum	Permanent body of knowledge (e.g., *Great Books*, *Junior Great Books*, Paideia Program), primary sources
Instruction	Socratic Method (questioning and rational inquiry)
Role of Teacher	Questioner, Listener, Leader, Role Model
Role of Student	Discussant, Seeker, Follower
Role of School	Head or lead teacher (Headmaster)
	Seminar classes organized around discussion of fundamental ideas and issues
Educated Person	Rational thinker, skillful in logical argument and abstract reasoning, lifelong learner

The arrangement and use of space would reflect and aid the school's purpose. Rather than filling a room with desks arranged in rows facing the front, seating would be arranged in circles or rooms would be furnished with tables and chairs to accommodate discussion in a seminar style. The physical layout of the classroom would encourage interaction among students. Smaller class sizes or working in small groups would also facilitate learning in this environment.

Paideia Partner Schools

Paideia Partner Schools are schools that have adopted the Paideia approach to education.

Each school completes an application process to formally assess the school's alignment with Paideia philosophy and teaching methods. Paideia Partner Schools receive support, professional development, and consulting from Paideia Center staff and faculty to create a learning community based on Paideia Principles. Partner schools offer Paideia Seminars, and instruction in advanced Paideia Schools take the form of Paideia Projects that incorporate the three columns of learning.

The *Paideia Program* (Adler, 1982, 1984) outlines a three-column approach to instruction: 1) acquisition of organized knowledge, 2) development of intellectual skills, and 3) understanding of ideas and values. These three kinds of learning should be integrated with one another into a single coordinated program. The National Paideia Center proposes that 15–20% of instruction should be composed of seminars that use Socratic dialogue to foster understanding of ideas and values. To develop critical thinking skills, 70% of instruction should be intellectual coaching (i.e., modeling and questioning). Only 10–15% of instruction should be didactic (or direct) teaching of factual knowledge.

Paideia Schools have been recognized across the United States and internationally. For example, the Barret Paideia Academy in Shreveport, Louisiana serves over 300 children from preschool through fifth grade. All students are provided with a challenging learning environment to become independent life learners. The Jones Paideia Magnet School in Nashville, Tennessee uses seminars and Socratic questioning to "embed the Paideia philosophy throughout all areas of student learning" (Jones Paideia Magnet School, n.d., About Our School section, para 3). Participation in coached projects engages students in problem solving and the application of knowledge through performance. The Sylvan Park Paideia Design Center, also in Nashville, serves elementary-grade students. The school follows the three columns of learning to engage students in civil dialogue, real-world projects, and critical thinking. The principal is considered a lead teacher working cooperatively with faculty, who are committed to lifelong learning.

St. John's College

Another model of a school designed in the Socratic tradition is St. John's College in Annapolis, Maryland. The curriculum focuses on philosophers (such as Plato, Aristotle, Augustine, and Descartes), authors (such as Homer, Chaucer, Shakespeare, Cervantes, and Tolstoy), scientists (such as Galileo, Newton, and Darwin), and musicians (such as Beethoven and Mozart). This roster represents the kind of curriculum St. John's has offered since its founding (originally as King William's School) in 1696. The purpose of the school is to provide a liberal arts education in the true sense of the word, "the liberation of the human intellect" (2013, p. 7). The college motto, *Facio liberos ex liberis libris libraque*, is Latin for, "I make free adults out of children by means of books and a balance" (St. John's School, 2015, History section, para 1).

St. John's requires the same course of studies for all students, who earn a Bachelor of Arts degree in Liberal Arts. The curriculum is based on reading and discussing great works from across the spectrum of Western thought. Beginning in freshman year, each class of students is assigned the same readings, organized into Literature, Philosophy and Theology, History and Social Science, Mathematics and Natural Science, and Music. Classes are arranged as seminars, conducted by tutors using a questioning approach modeled on Socratic dialogue. The goal is to cultivate habits of thought, methodical and careful study, and precise discussion and writing.

How Does a School Designed to Teach Enduring Ideas and Eternal Truths Define an Educated Person?

In the school we have designed (Table 3.1), an educated person would be defined as one skillful in rational thinking, exhibited in large part through discussion. In *Theaetetus*, Socrates examines several definitions of knowledge to distinguish between wisdom and judgment. One argument defines knowledge as "true judgment with an account" (*Theaetetus,* 202c).[6] That is, beliefs or conclusions having rational support.

Reading and discussing great ideas develop valuable skills applicable in all situations, helping justify decisions, actions, and practices. Hutchins argues that the purpose of education is to develop the habits of mind for lifelong learning. Adler (1982) states, "Education is a lifelong process of which schooling is only a small but necessary part" (p. 10). In the philosophical perspective explored in this chapter, learning through reasoning reflects the human nature shared in common by all people. The goal is for the thinker to apply rational reasoning to clarify issues, solve problems, cultivate moral development, and advance society.

Evaluate

Chapter 1 introduced the "3Cs" criteria: consistency, compatibility, and coherence. We will apply these criteria to a school designed to teach students enduring ideas and eternal truths.

Consistency

If the purpose of education were to teach enduring ideas and eternal truths, what would be the sources of the curriculum? We have used the *Great Books* as an example of a source that contains this kind of knowledge. "The great books of the western world cover every department of knowledge," Hutchins (1936) argues (p. 80). Adler (1984) states that reading primary sources can "inculcate a respect, even a piety, for the past and allow students to participate in the creative process of discovery" (p. 107). The primary goal of education is not to specialize in a particular field of study or to train in skills for future employment, but to gain a well-rounded liberal education that asks foundational questions about the nature of human existence and develop habits of mind that can guide lifelong learning. For the curriculum to remain consistent with this purpose, primary sources such as those contained in the *Great Books* would serve as the foundation of the curriculum in every subject.

The Socratic Method would permeate instruction in all subjects as well. For example, a seminar approach to teaching mathematics can bring out the relationship of concepts to one another and the nature of their application, including within other fields. The place of mathematics in the broader scope of the curriculum can be explored. "Mathematical reasoning," Adler (1984) argues, "is one of the most human things that human beings do" (p. 85). Socratic questioning can elicit reasoning from students on concepts in all subjects. Limiting the Socratic Method to only the study of literature or the humanities would be inconsistent with a school devoted to the purpose of teaching students to discover truths.

Compatibility

Is the Socratic Method always compatible with the purpose of teaching students enduring ideas and eternal truths? This depends on how the Socratic Method is used. Teachers may use three kinds of Socratic discussion: spontaneous questioning, exploratory questioning, and focused questioning (Paul & Elder, 2007). *Spontaneous questioning* asks a student to clarify a response, support a conclusion, or elaborate on an idea that emerges during instruction. *Exploratory questioning* probes student thinking on issues or concepts, assesses prior knowledge, reveals opinions, or discovers student interests. In *focused questioning*, the teacher prepares questions in advance and structures the discussion to explore a particular topic or issue. All three kinds of questioning can examine student thinking and seek meaning, representing teaching that is "imbued with the Socratic spirit, when you maintain your curiosity and sense of wonderment" (p. 48).

However, a lack of structure or direction may allow students to voice unsupported opinions or to freely interpret texts without grounding their conclusions in evidence. The rigor of a logical approach to instruction will be lost. Discussion leaders using the Socratic Method may pose an open-ended interpretation question having no single correct answer, but the question will be carefully crafted to elicit analysis and examination of the ideas and values in the text. Seminar leaders do not open discussion by asking, "So, what did you think of the story?" and accept responses such as "I liked it" or "It was boring." The method would not be compatible with the purpose without continued questioning to search for verifying or contradictory evidence. Brief bouts of unstructured discussion that interrupt planned instruction then quickly revert to didactic teaching would not be Socratic in nature. For instruction to remain compatible with the purpose, the teacher would seek "true judgment with an account" from students.

Coherence

How would a *Great Books* curriculum and the Socratic Method produce a coherent educational program? The curriculum and instruction of the entire school would need to align with the same purpose of education. The Socratic Method should not exist as isolated and detached portions of the school day by one or two teachers interested in encouraging student participation. If the majority of instructional time remains focused primarily on the acquisition of discrete factual knowledge, the purpose of understanding abstract concepts, discovering universal truths, and cultivating virtues and values will not be achieved. If the school has not adopted the same curriculum, agreed on consistent methods, and participated in professional development to practice and refine skills in implementing and integrating those methods throughout the educational program, an incoherent design will result. Paideia Partner Schools and St. John's College represent examples of designing schools to offer a coherent education. A visitor to a school designed for the purpose of teaching students enduring ideas and eternal truths should observe consistent, compatible practices throughout the school day, across grade levels and within all subject areas.

Reflect

To reflect on the philosophical concepts, compare your prior observations and experiences in schools and classrooms to the vignette, descriptions, and examples we have examined.

How Do Your Prior Observations and Experiences Relate to a Curriculum Designed to Teach Enduring Ideas and Eternal Truths?

You may not have necessarily observed the exact same sources of content (such as the *Great Books* series) in classrooms. Yet, what aspects of the curriculum have you observed that share qualities in common with a curriculum that relies on primary sources and works by established or recognized writers and thinkers? In what ways is the curriculum you are familiar with designed to help students discover enduring ideas and eternal truths? What subjects or content were emphasized or valued?

How Do Your Prior Observations and Experiences Relate to a Pedagogy Designed to Teach Enduring Ideas and Eternal Truths?

You may not have participated in or observed a Socratic discussion, but you may have observed, participated in, or conducted a class discussion of a text or issue. In what ways were your experiences similar to a Socratic discussion and how might they have differed? Was the purpose to reveal an existing truth or value, or was the aim to evoke a variety of interpretations based on personal experiences? Were diverse opinions equally valued, did the class reach consensus, or did the teacher present an overall conclusion?

In what ways is the role of the teacher you have observed or experienced in schools similar to and/or different from the examples? What kinds of teacher practices have you observed? Would you offer a similar metaphor for the role of the teacher, such as questioner, listener, leader, master, or role model?

In what ways is the role of the student you have observed or experienced in schools similar to and/or different from the examples? What metaphor would you offer for the role of the students you have observed, and how does the metaphor relate to the student as seeker or discoverer of truth, questioner and discussant, or follower and disciple?

How Do Your Prior Observations and Experiences Relate to a School Designed to Teach Enduring Ideas and Eternal Truths?

Have you observed schools organized to foster intellectual inquiry? Was time scheduled to permit the Socratic Method or other forms of participatory discussion? Was more time scheduled for subjects such as literature, humanities, and the arts than other subjects? Was probing deeply into issues emphasized more than acquisition of factual knowledge? Where would you place schools you have observed on the *Continuum of Educational Philosophy*?

How Do Your Own Practices and Beliefs Relate to the Purpose of Education as Learning Enduring Ideas and Eternal Truths?

At this stage in the inquiry process, where would you locate your beliefs about education on the *Continuum of Educational Philosophy*? From your current perceptive, is learning subject matter the most important purpose of education? Do you agree that all students should learn a certain body of knowledge? If so, what kind of knowledge and from what sources? Would you be comfortable teaching from the *Junior Great Books* series or some other approved reading list of classic or "great works?" If so, would that constitute most or all of the readings, or would you supplement the selections with other content? Would you make those decisions, or would you allow students to suggest their favorites?

Are you inclined to view learning from a teacher-directed point of view, or should students be permitted greater input based on their own interests? Should students be taught to adapt to the expectations of the school and the traditions of society, or is the role of the school to foster individuality and adjust to the student?

We instigated our inquiry at the far left side of the continuum, with the emphasis on seeking eternal truth and universal knowledge. We asked, *"What if the purpose of education were to learn enduring ideas and eternal truths?"* From this perspective, a story such as "Charles" from the *Junior Great Books* contains within it enduring, universal truths to be discovered through the Socratic Method of questioning and discussion.

How have other philosophies described the purpose of education? Alfred North Whitehead (1929/1967) remarks, "The safest general characterization of the European philosophical tradition is that it consists of a series of footnotes to Plato" (p. 63). Whitehead means that, in many ways, philosophy in the Western world has been a conversation responding to (and often arguing against) Plato's views about the nature of reality, knowledge, values, and reasoning. As we proceed along the continuum, philosophies of education will begin to gradually move from an ideas-based, rational approach to a more experience-based, empirical approach.

Notes

1 From Diogenes Laërtius, *Lives and Opinions of Eminent Philosophers: Book 2, Socrates, His Predecessors and Followers*. The full translation reads: "There is only one good, knowledge, and one evil, ignorance," or "The only good is knowledge and the only evil is ignorance."
2 Appears in French in the first edition of *Discourse on Method* (1637). The Latin phrase ("cogito, ergo sum") later appears in the 1644 edition of *Discourse* and in *Principles of Philosophy* (1644).
3 Attributed to Socrates, source uncertain. In *Memorabilia of Socrates*, Xenophon quotes Socrates as saying, "The thoughts of wise men enrich their possessors with virtue."
4 Variously attributed to Socrates, among others (including William Butler Yeats). Variations of the phrase include, "The mind is not a vessel to be filled, but a fire to be kindled."
5 In the dialogues, Plato does not describe the dialectic using the terms *Thesis-Antithesis-Synthesis*. Other philosophers and influential thinkers (such as Kant, Hegel, Engels, and Marx) have also reasoned using the dialectic, to which the triadic (or three-part) model has often been ascribed the terms *Thesis-Antithesis-Synthesis*. Kant calls the dialectic "the logic of illusion" because it is a method for reaching agreement, not a means to achieve certain or unequivocal understanding about the content of knowledge (B86).
6 Popularly referred to as "justified true belief."

References

Adler, M. J. (1982). *The Paideia proposal: An educational manifesto*. New York, NY: Macmillan.

Adler, M. J. (1984). *The Paideia program: An educational syllabus*. New York, NY: Macmillan.

Aristotle. (1984). *The complete works of Aristotle: The revised Oxford translation*. Jonathan Barnes (Ed.). Princeton, NJ: Princeton University Press.

Augustine. (1950). *The city of God*. (M. Dods, Trans.). New York, NY: Modern Library. (Original work published ca. 413–426.)

Augustine. (2008). *Letters* (Vol. 2). (W. Parsons, Trans.). Washington, D.C.: Catholic University of America Press.

Berkeley G. (1988). *Principles of human knowledge*. R. Woolhouse (Ed.). New York, NY: Penguin. (Original work published 1710, 2nd ed. published 1734.)

Descartes, R. (1998). *Discourse on method and meditations on first philosophy*. (4th ed.) (D. Cress, Trans.). Indianapolis, IN: Hackett. (*Discourse* originally published 1637, *Meditations* originally published 1641)

Descartes, R. (1984). *Principles of philosophy*. (V. R. Miller & R. P. Miller, Trans.). Dordrecht, Holland: D. Reidel. (Original work published 1644.)

Great Books Foundation. (2014). *Shared inquiry handbook for discussion leaders and participants*. Chicago, IL: Great Books Foundation.

Hegel, G. W. F. (1989). *Science of logic*. H. D. Lewis (Ed.) (A. V. Miller, Trans.). Atlantic Highlands, NJ: Humanities Press International. (Original work published 1644.)

Hutchins, R. M. (1936). *The higher learning in America*. New Haven, CT: Yale University Press.

Hutchins, R. M. (Ed.). (1952). *Great books of the western world*. Chicago, IL: Encyclopedia Britannica.

Jones Paideia Magnet School. (n.d.) About our school. [Website]. Retrieved from http://jonespaideiaes. mnps.org/pages/Jones_Paideia_Magnet_School/About_Our_School/ABOUT_OUR_SCHOOL

Kant, I. (2007). *Critique of pure reason*. (N. K. Smith, Trans.) New York, NY: Palgrave Macmillan. (Original work published 1781.)

Kant, I. (1997). *Groundwork of the metaphysics of morals*. (M. Gregor, Ed. and Trans.). Cambridge, UK: Cambridge University Press. (Original work published 1785.)

Kant, I. (1996). *Metaphysics of morals*. (M. Gregor, Trans.). Cambridge, UK: Cambridge University Press. (Original work published 1797.)

Kant, I. (2009). *Lectures on metaphysics*. (K. Ameriks & S. Naragon, Ed. and Trans.). Cambridge, UK: Cambridge University Press. (Original lectures presented 1760–90.)

Moeller, M., & Moeller, V. (2002). *Socratic seminars and literature circles*. New York, NY: Routledge.

National Paideia Center. (2015). Paideia active learning. [Website]. Retrieved from http://www.paideia.org/about-paideia/paideia-schools/

Paul, R. (1993). *Critical thinking: What every person needs to survive in a rapidly changing world* (3rd ed.). J. Willsen & A. J. A. Binker (Eds.). Santa Rosa, CA: The Foundation for Critical Thinking. Retrieved from http://www.criticalthinking.org/pages/richard-paul-anthology/1139

Paul, R., & Elder, L. (2007). *The thinker's guide to the art of Socratic questioning*. Dillon Beach, CA: The Foundation for Critical Thinking.

Plato. (1997). *Complete works*. J. M. Cooper (Ed.). Indianapolis, IN: Hackett.

St. John's College. (2013). Statement of the St. John's program section, 2013–2014. Retrieved from http://www.sjc.edu/files/5814/0899/9449/SJC_ProgStatement.pdf

St. John's College. (2015). History. Retrieved from http://www.sjc.edu/about/history/

Whitehead, A. N. (1967). *Process and reality: An essay in cosmology*. New York, NY: Macmillan. (Original work published 1929.)

4 What If . . . The Purpose of Education Were to Learn Structure and Principles?

Wonder

We continue our inquiry into universal knowledge by asking the wonder question: *"What if . . . the purpose of education were to learn structure and principles?"*

On the *Continuum of Educational Philosophy* (Figure 4.1), objective, universal knowledge remains highly valued. However, instead of relying only on abstract reasoning, direct experience in the physical world as well as rational thinking becomes a source of learning. The teacher directs students as they seek to understand the basic structure of the universe and the fundamental laws and principles that govern and unify existence.

Observe

Classroom Vignette: A Sixth-Grade Science Lesson on Cells

Mr. B calls his sixth-grade science class to attention and holds up a baggie.

"Can anyone guess what I have in here?" he asks.

A student in the front row points to the baggie and calls out in excitement, "I see Twizzlers!"

EDUCATIONAL PRACTICES

RATIONAL	EMPIRICAL
Ideas-Focused	Experience-Focused
Content-Oriented	Process-Oriented
Fixed Curriculum	Flexible Curriculum
Teacher-Centered	Student-Centered
Teacher-Directed	Self-Directed
Pre-Determined Outcomes	Open-Ended Exploration
Whole-Class Activities	Differentiated/Individualized Activities

Objective External Reality	Internal Subjective Reality
Absolute Universal Truth	Changing Relative Truth
Pre-Existing Knowledge	Constructed Knowledge
Knowledge Independent of Experience	Knowledge Dependent on Experience
Autonomous Knowledge	Interdependent Knowledge
Absolute Universal Values	Relative Local Values
Values Independent of Experience	Values Dependent on Experience

PHILOSOPHICAL PERSPECTIVES

Figure 4.1 Continuum of Educational Philosophy (Structure and Principles)

"Exactly," Mr. B replies. "Twizzlers and M&Ms and Gummie Worms." Holding up a container, he adds, "And here we have . . . "

"Icing!" the students shout in unison.

Mr. B smiles broadly. "Today we are going to make something yummy and learn too."

Mr. B announces that the objective for the day's lesson will be to construct models of animal and plant cells using candy and treats. They will label the parts of the cells and identify the function of each part. To begin, Mr. B reviews vocabulary with the class, such as defining photosynthesis and mitosis. He then projects a diagram of a cell on the screen showing all the parts labeled.

"Your model must accurately label each organelle just like in the diagram, "he tells them, "using different kinds of food for each."

Mr. B writes a list of the organelles on the white board and what foods will represent each, such as frosting for the cytoplasm, 'Nilla wafers for the nucleus, and Gummie Worms for the Golgi Bodies.

"Can anyone tell me what two parts the plant cell has that are not in the animal cell?" he asks. After a few guesses, two students correctly respond the chloroplasts and the cell wall.

"Right," Mr. B confirms. "Your group may choose to construct an animal cell or a plant cell. If you make a plant cell model, use Twizzlers to form the cell wall and green M&Ms as the chloroplasts."

A student passes out worksheets that include an unlabeled diagram. "Label each organelle on the worksheet before you add that organelle to the model," he instructs, "and write one sentence on the line below it to describe its function."

The students are divided into small groups that receive a baggie depending on which kind of cell they choose to construct. "No eating any of the food!" he commands. "Not until all the models have been completed and I have checked your group's worksheet."

As they begin work, Mr. B circulates to make sure each organelle is located in the correct place on the model. The room buzzes with activity. As each group completes the task, hands are raised and Mr. B comes to the table and reviews the finished product. He notes any corrections necessary on the worksheet. When each group has successfully constructed a model, he directs the students to write their names on the worksheets and drop them in the basket on his desk. Every group walks around the room to view the model of every other group.

"Can we eat now?" a student asks.

"Clean up your table first," Mr. B insists. A few students groan but follow his instructions. After all tables have been cleaned and the students are seated quietly, Mr. B claps his hands and proclaims, "Now, we eat!"

Investigate

In Chapter 1, the perspectives we investigated argue that what we perceive in the world of matter exists first as ideas (or Forms) in the mind. *What if*, however, reality possesses a structure governed by principles existing independent of the mind? To examine philosophies with this view of the purpose of education, we will investigate the following inquiry questions:

- What Do Teachers Teach? Questions about the Curriculum
- How Do Teachers Teach? Questions about Pedagogy
- How Are Schools Organized? Questions about the Role of the School

What Do Teachers Teach? Questions about the Curriculum

In the classroom vignette above, the objective of the lesson is to study the structure of cells and learn how each part functions. This information is not subject to interpretation according to an individual's opinion or personal point of view, but is considered factual knowledge supported by evidence based on research. What philosophical perspectives support teaching objective, universal knowledge to understand the nature of the universe?

How Is Reality Structured?

> "Nature is a cause that operates for a purpose."
>
>   (Aristotle)

The Greek philosopher, Aristotle (384–322 BCE), a disciple of Plato, assumes humans by nature are rational beings. Unlike Plato, however, Aristotle believes in a reality that exists external to and independent of the mind (or the world of ideas). Aristotle disavows the concept of latent knowledge posited by Socrates. He states that the mind is like "a writing-tablet on which as yet nothing actually stands written" (*On the Soul*, 430a1). This has become known as the *tabula rasa* or "blank slate" concept of the mind. Aristotle believes we use both our rational minds and our senses to gain knowledge. By studying the characteristics of matter, we detect evidence of laws and principles that govern the universe.

Aristotelian Realism believes in an objective order to reality, an underlying structure to the universe. Rather than accept the appearance of what we perceive as reality, we should seek to understand the internal significance of each object. Through observation and analysis of the physical world, one can perceive a universal balance, harmony, and purpose to nature. Aristotle conceives of a unity to existence in which each thing has a place in relation to a greater whole. We can trace to Aristotle the saying, "The whole is greater than the sum of its parts."[1]

Moreover, all things exist in an orderly progression. Matter can be organized, classified, and categorized according to a scale, proceeding from the lowest level (i.e., inanimate objects such as rocks), to plants and vegetation, to animals, to the highest level (i.e., humans). As rational beings, humans rank at the top of the hierarchy. The universe we occupy is also rational. All things fall into an order or pattern. Human beings possess the rational ability to study and classify the physical universe. Studying physical matter can reveal the structure of the rational universe.

This view has direct and powerful implications for teaching and learning, and has influenced education for centuries. Arising from Aristotelian Realism, the purpose of education becomes a process of learning the fundamental laws and universal principles that govern the universe. Aristotle chooses to study the physical world to discern truth. This became known as *natural philosophy*. Aristotle adds the natural sciences to the liberal arts curriculum (discussed in Chapter 3). For this reason, Aristotle is often referred to as the Father of Science or the Father of Biology. The source of knowledge is the observable world and the method of learning is through scientific investigation.

Aristotle divides knowledge into three kinds of sciences: 1) theoretical sciences, 2) productive sciences, and 3) practical sciences. *Theoretical* sciences, such as the natural sciences, explore physical phenomena to produce knowledge of universal fundamental principles that never change. The *productive* sciences produce useful things, such as furniture, or create things of an aesthetic nature, such as art. The *practical* sciences are concerned with matters of human conduct, such as ethics and politics. The principles that support the productive and practical sciences are contingent on context and less certain than those of the theoretical sciences. Each field of knowledge has a structure that can be determined by studying their underlying principles.

The curriculum of schools continues to organize knowledge into distinct subject areas or disciplines. In 1894, the Harvard Committee of Ten compiled a list of subjects for the secondary school curriculum: languages (Latin, Greek, English, German, French, and Spanish), mathematics (algebra, geometry, and trigonometry), history, "natural history" (astronomy, meteorology, botany, zoology, physiology, geology, and ethnology), and physics and chemistry (NEA, p. 36–7). One notices the concentration of scientific subjects in this list, despite concerns that a classical education traditionally emphasizes Latin, Greek, and mathematics over science. The Committee report stresses the need to allocate time and resources equally among subjects, and provide the same kind of instruction in each subject to all students. Sciences should devote a great proportion of learning time to laboratory work and experiments.

One justification for studying knowledge grouped into discrete subjects is that each discipline possesses a structure or conceptual framework based on fundamental principles. Cognitive theorist Jerome Bruner (American, 1915–) explains that "basic and general ideas" serve as the foundation for a discipline (Bruner, 1977, p. 17). "The curriculum of a subject," he proposes, "should be determined by the most fundamental understanding that can be achieved of the underlying principles that give structure to the subject" (p. 31). Starting with the hypothesis that "any subject can be taught effectively to any child in some intellectually honest form," Bruner recommends a "spiral curriculum" that introduces children to ideas, structures, and principles in a simple form and continues to return to that content in greater complexity at later ages (p. 52). Bruner proposes that "a curriculum ought to be built around the great issues, principles, and values" worthy of continual study (p. 52).

In the classroom vignette, students construct a model of the structure of the cell to understand the function and purpose of each part and how all parts interconnect. A model or other conceptual framework helps place details in a structured pattern that provides a generalized model for understanding. The study of cell structure and the functions of organelles can be revisited by students in increased depth and specificity as they progress through higher levels of education. The fundamental process remains the same:

> Intellectual activity anywhere is the same, whether at the frontier of knowledge or in a third-grade classroom. What a scientist does at his desk or in his laboratory . . . are of the same order as what anybody else does when he is engaged in like activities—if he is to achieve understanding. The difference is in degree, not in kind. The schoolboy learning physics is a physicist, and it is easier for him to learn physics behaving like a physicist than doing something else.
>
> (Bruner, 1960/1977, p. 14)

An emphasis on structure and principles appears in many aspects of educational practices, including in teacher education programs. For example, The Interstate Teacher Assessment and Support Consortium (InTASC) recommends standards for teaching that "outline the common principles and foundations of teaching practice" (InTASC, 1992, p. 6). InTASC Standard 4, Content Knowledge, states: "The teacher understands the central concepts, tools of inquiry, and structures of the discipline(s) he or she teaches and creates learning experiences that make these aspects of the discipline accessible and meaningful for learners to assure mastery of the content." In the framework for teaching published by the Danielson Group, Standard 1a, "Demonstrating Knowledge of Content and Pedagogy," states that "every discipline has a dominant structure" (Danielson, 2013, p. 6). Describing the practice of teaching in terms of *standards*, *principles*, *foundations*, *concepts*, *tools of inquiry*, and *structure* reveals the influence of Realism. Even the phrase "mastery of the content" to define learning implies a pre-determined outcome to the learning process. The purpose of education is to investigate the world to reveal its structure. The more one investigates, the closer one comes to the discovery of principles that govern everything, leading to universal knowledge.

As an exercise, draw a triangle. If you measure the three angles of the triangle and add them together, what would be the sum total degrees? Continue to draw different types of triangles (e.g., acute, right, obtuse) and measure their degrees. Whatever type of triangle you draw, you will discover that the three angles always total 180 degrees. The study of the properties of different specific triangles will lead to the universal knowledge that all triangles equal 180 degrees. Scientists continue to search for a "theory of everything" that will unify all knowledge of the universe into a single coherent structure (e.g., Hawking, 2002; Weinberg, 1994).

In the vignette, students are studying the structure and parts of cells. Each organelle serves a specific function. For example, DNA (deoxyribonucleic acid), located in a human or animal cell, contains the genetic code that determines an organism's function and purpose. A sort of "blueprint," DNA possesses the design and structural information for a living thing. Through the study of specific characteristics of matter, one can discover patterns that lead to fundamental principles about the structure of reality.

Studying nature involves investigating cause and effect, inquiring into why phenomena occur and the reasons for the activity observed. Knowledge consists of knowing the causes of things and discovering their underlying principles. "Nature is a cause that operates for a purpose," Aristotle maintains (*Physics*, 199b30).

Aristotle believes that all matter contains *potentiality*, the potential to become something, to fulfill a purpose, to become actualized. Aristotle determines that things achieve *actuality* through a process named the Four Causes:

- *Material Cause*—the matter from which something comes (potentiality).
- *Formal Cause*—the form, design, or structure, and its features.
- *Efficient Cause*—factor or agent.
- *Final Cause*—purpose, ultimate reality (actuality).

To understand how things come into being, we will use the example of a bronze statue. The bronze is the *Material Cause*, the matter or raw material from which the statue will come into existence. The *Formal Cause* is the shape the bronze will take. The form originally exists as a design in the artisan's mind, and he fashions a mold to produce a representation of what the finished statue will look like. The *Efficient Cause* is the artisan and his tools, who melts the bronze, pours it into the mold, and gives the bronze its physical shape and features. The *Final Cause* is the finished statue, the product of the idea or mental image of the artisan. The Final Cause is the end result of the design conceived by the designer. In the form of a statue, the bronze has achieved *actuality*; it has achieved its purpose.

The famous artist Michelangelo purportedly said, "In every block of marble I see a statue as plain as though it stood before me, shaped and perfect in attitude and in action. I have only to hew away the rough walls that imprison the lovely apparition to reveal it to the other eyes as mine see it." A similar expression has been attributed to Stradivari: "To make a violin, take the wood and carve away all that is not the violin." The form exists in the mind of the artist who, as the Efficient Cause, produces a finished product from the raw material. The Final Cause always existed as *potentiality* in the raw material.

However, we cannot readily see how everything achieves its final form. We are not able to peer into the mind of the artist as he deliberates or perceive the form he imagines. Likewise, especially in Aristotle's time, one cannot always observe the four causes as they occur in nature. One could reasonably ask if the raw bronze was not itself the product of causes (of forces or a process) that brought it into being. To this kind of question Aristotle counters, "If the ship-building art were in the wood, it would produce the same results by nature" (*Physics*, 199b28). That is, wood does not fashion itself into a ship. The wood is the material cause, but a form is conceived in the mind of the shipbuilder, who through deliberate effort causes the wood to take the form of a ship. Shipbuilding is a purposeful process, and Aristotle supposed all things present in nature occur through a purposeful process, even one we are not able to yet observe.

The structure and function of the parts of a cell were unknown to those in Aristotle's time, but the system for discovering that knowledge follows principles he advocated. The students in the vignette rely on a diagram and pictures produced by the research of others to represent the interior of a cell. The curriculum depends on a hierarchy of knowledge the teacher can transmit to the students, relating what they learn about cells to an organized body of knowledge about living things in general. The students will be introduced to a taxonomy that classifies organisms according to species, genus, family, order, class, phylum (animals) or division (plants), and kingdom.

"Reason is to man what God is to the world."
(St. Thomas Aquinas)

A religious form of Realism has its origins in the writings of St. Thomas Aquinas (1225–74), a Benedictine monk. Aquinas (1265/1949) believes, like Aristotle, that "the light of reason is placed by nature in every man" (Book 1, 4). Theistic Realism, or Thomism, believes in a Creator (God) of all existence and reality. All reality has its origins in a divine Creator. Thomism combines the reason of Aristotle with the faith of Christianity, creating a synthesis of Aristotelian Realism and Christian theology. According to Aquinas, one can come to know God through studying physical objects in the material world, just as Aristotle believes one can come to know eternal truths and knowledge from studying physical matter.

In Thomism, the essence residing in a human being is the soul. The soul is a creation of God, and gives meaning and purpose to each person. Similar to Aristotle's assertions about potentiality and actuality, everyone in existence is moving toward enlightenment. Also similar to Aristotle, who conceived of a structured hierarchy to knowledge, Aquinas (1265–74/1947) describes a Great Chain of Being that represents all existence in the universe. God resides at the top of the scale, the only omniscient, omnipotent, and perfect being. Below God exist angels, humans, animals, plants, and inanimate objects. Below matter, nothing exists but emptiness and void. Just as Aristotle posits a perfect order and structure to the universe, Thomism believes in a perfect order and set of principles that guide reality and give everything in existence its purpose.

The parallels between Aristotle and Aquinas continue. Aristotle believes the study of matter could lead to knowledge of principles. For Aquinas, the first principle is God. Aquinas claims that proof of God's existence could be empirically observed in nature. He famously offers five ways to prove the existence of God (*Summa Theologica*). The origins of each of the five proofs can be traced back to God:

Motion—Everything in motion had to be put into motion. Things may have the potential to be in motion but a thing cannot put itself into motion. All causes for motion lead back to God, the first mover.

Causation—Nothing can be the efficient cause of itself; some cause will always exist prior. Only God is the first cause.

Possibility/Necessity—There may be many things that are possible to exist, but only certain things that are necessary to exist. Nothing is necessary except that a necessary being created it. That being can only receive it necessity from itself, which is God.

Gradation—There are degrees of all things (e.g., more or less, hotter or colder, etc.). Only by comparing to other things can we determine these degrees (e.g., something is hotter than something else). Only God is fully actualized to the maximum or ultimate degree that nothing else can exceed.

Governance—All things in existence are governed by underlying laws and principles to achieve their purpose. Some intelligence must be the designer of all creation who directs all things to achieve their purpose, and that ultimate divine intelligence is God.

God's presence can be observed through the rational order manifested in the world, which sees its apogee in humankind. "Reason is to man what God is to the world," Aquinas professes (1265/1949, Book 2, 94).

How Can We Know Structure and Principles?

Francis Bacon (British, 1561–1626) combines the reasoning of Plato and Aristotle with the scientific revolution to build a bridge between the classical and modern eras of philosophy. Like Aristotle, he believes that true knowledge is to be found in causes. Bacon criticizes generalizations based on scanty evidence and advocates for investigation to gather evidence and test hypotheses. In *Novum Organum* (1620/1902), he describes four Idols, or sources of accepted knowledge, that can interfere with one's reasoning. The Idols of the Tribe refers to generalizations or assumptions that arise as preconceived notions due to human nature, whether these beliefs have been empirically verified or not (such as believing the planets and stars revolve around the Earth). The Idols of the Den refers to individual beliefs based on limited personal experience, in which one's perceptions of reality may be incomplete or inaccurate (similar to living in Socrates' cave). The Idols of the Marketplace are the meanings imbued in things by language and labels, which may be fallacies (think of the distortions promulgated by advertising and various media outlets). The Idols of the Theatre challenge ideologies presented as truths by authorities or institutions (such as religious, political, educational, and philosophical systems). Bacon promotes the use of the scientific method to rid one of misconceptions and discover the basic structure and general principles of reality.

John Locke (British, 1632–1704) denies the mind contains innate ideas. A proponent of the *tabula rasa* (blank slate or blank sheet) concept of the mind, he believes knowledge is based on experience. "Let us then suppose the mind to be, as we say, white paper," Locke (1964) proposes, "void of all characters, without any ideas" (p. 89). He insists that knowledge is gained through investigations of matter. However, unlike the senses, the mind does not experience nature firsthand. Instead, we indirectly experience the world through representations that our perceptions form in the mind. "The mind makes the particular ideas received from particular objects become general," Locke writes. "Ideas taken from particular beings become general representatives of all the same kind" (p. 129). This view is known as Representative Realism. Abstract ideas are artificial representations of the mind, which collects particular characteristics and unites them into a single conception referred to by the name of that thing.

In the vignette, students study a diagram and pictures to construct a model. They do not directly observe the interior of a cell or the functions of the organelles. Rather, they learn from the representations of that knowledge and the corresponding labels and definitions. An objective reality exists independent of our individual consciousness, and we apply our rational minds to understand the sensory data we perceive. The concepts we form in our minds are not in and of themselves reality; the external objects exist independent of our rational thinking about them.

As discussed in Chapter 3, Immanuel Kant (1724–1804, Germany) believes our rational minds relate knowledge perceived by the senses to universal categories. Kant (1900) explains:

> Understanding is the knowledge of the general. Judgment is the application of the general to the particular. Reason is the power of understanding the connection between the general and the particular.
>
> (p. 71)

Learning should develop general understanding. Mere memorization of facts has no use unless one can exercise judgment. He calls such a person a "walking dictionary" (p. 71). Memory must be exercised in the service of intelligent reasoning, so universal principles have meaning and purpose.

Alfred North Whitehead (1861–1947), a British mathematician and philosopher, proposes a curriculum that balances specific and general knowledge, with an emphasis on literature, art, philosophy and theology, science, and applied technical knowledge. Whitehead (1929/1949) disdains "inert ideas" and reasons that only knowledge applied to life has value (p. 13). Whitehead considers reality to be a process composed of events. These events can be observed to reoccur, producing sustained or lasting knowledge. "Organized thought is the basis of organized action," he writes (p. 106). Nature operates according to a logical system, as should education. The goal should be to study general principles that can be applied to concrete cases in practical living.

Bertrand Russell (1872–1970), a British mathematician and philosopher, agrees with Locke that much of our knowledge is not directly observed. Russell (1926/1961) distinguishes between two types of data: "hard data" and "soft data" (p. 77). Hard data are indisputable facts that can be verified by direct observation using the senses and supported by evidence. Hard data cannot be refuted by logical argument or critical analysis. The effects of gravity would fall under this category. Soft data are beliefs that have been inferred and are therefore open to doubt. For example, quantities are hard data (quantities of matter exist whether a human mind perceives them or not). However, numbers belong to a symbol system that the human mind has devised to represent quantities. Therefore, numbers (as symbols) are soft data, and the physical quantities they represent are hard data.

Russell grapples with the question of whether we can know of the existence of any reality that is independent of our own senses. We rely on the observations of others to verify what we are unable to observe first-hand. A taxonomy, for example, would represent soft data as it displays knowledge but is in itself not composed of direct, first-hand objects that constitute reality.

From this viewpoint, one might argue that the parts of a cell the students are studying in the vignette may at first be considered soft data because students infer knowledge of their characteristics from representations produced by others and trust the data without direct verification. However, the students are relying on observations that, over time, have been repeatedly verified by empirical evidence and have not been refuted. The materials the students inspect are representations of things they wish to examine, but the methods of observation and the findings that result have been verified. The knowledge enters into the world of hard data based on the exactness of the reproductions.

Similar to Locke, John Searle (American, 1932–) argues that any statement we make about reality is a representation of reality. Representations are necessary for us to be understood by others. However, some facts do not require representation to exist. Searle (1995) refers to "brute physical facts" that can exist independent of representation (p. 191). Phenomena such as falling rain can exist without needing to be represented in a social context. Social facts, however, exist within social institutions and social relationships, and are imbued with meaning only through language and symbols. The raw materials of a dollar bill (e.g., cotton fiber, linen, ink, etc.) are brute facts. That a dollar bill is considered currency is a social fact; the value attributed to it as legal tender is based on social agreement. A brute reality exists that is independent of representation, but language and interactions among people imbue these facts with socially constructed meaning. "You cannot have institutional facts without brute facts," Searle concludes (p. 191). We assume the existence of an external realism when we communicate our understanding of reality.

Schools often teach information to students without distinguishing between what is a physical fact according to the laws of nature (existing independent of observation and identification by the human mind) and a fact that derives meaning solely through the human mind in agreement with others. In other words, social facts would not exist if the human mind did not exist to label it a fact. The color red, for example, would exist as a wavelength in the electromagnetic spectrum whether humans perceived it or not. However, "red" as a color is a label humans have placed upon this physical phenomenon. This can be convincingly argued by observing that not all creatures perceive this wavelength, not to mention different human languages have invented a different word to refer to this color (and assign it social attributes such as claiming red symbolizes passion).

The perspectives we have investigated would present the curriculum as organized bodies of knowledge. The curriculum would be divided into disciplines or subject areas, each with a structure or conceptual framework connecting ideas into a hierarchy. Students would learn about objective knowledge that exists independent of the learner. Facts can be verified as true through a systematic process of observation and analysis.

How Do Teachers Teach? Questions about Pedagogy

"From many notions gained by experience one universal judgment about similar objects is produced."

(Aristotle)

The Scientific Method

Aristotle began what could be considered initial investigations into laws of nature or natural law. Knowledge can be classified, categorized, and organized according to levels from the concrete to the abstract. The hierarchy of knowledge this produces places an emphasis on knowledge derived from the scientific method. In Chapter 2, we generally defined the steps of the scientific method: 1) Pose a question, 2) Make a prediction or state a hypothesis, 3) Conduct an experiment and collect data, 4) Analyze and interpret the findings, 5) Report the findings and state a conclusion.

Comparable to the three kinds of sciences, Aristotle describes three kinds of human activity. *Theoria* (or theory) is contemplative activity, such as observation and study in the theoretical sciences to derive general principles that can be applied universally. Productive activity (*poieses*), related to the productive sciences, has an end purpose in mind and requires technical skill (or *techne*), such as an artisan casting a bronze statue or a sculptor chiseling marble. *Praxis* is action toward the Good (also action for its own sake), which can be practical sciences concerned with matters of human conduct, such as ethics and politics.

Aristotle maintains that theory (*theoria*) must agree with empirically observed facts. "The truth in practical matters is discerned from the facts of life" (*Nicomachean Ethics*, 1179a18). Seeking truth through an ordered system of thought, Aristotle combines existing ideas or propositions to arrive at inferences or conclusions. Empirical evidence from the study of the physical world connects to verify this universal knowledge. This reasoning can proceed deductively, stating a general proposition and presenting particular examples, or inductively, observing particular instances and arriving at general conclusions. Both kinds of reasoning can be used together to discover and verify universal knowledge.[2]

Reasoning through Syllogism

Aristotle applies a version of the dialectic, called a syllogism, to deductively arrive at truth. In a syllogism, a major premise or general assumption is stated. A minor premise, a more specific statement, is offered as evidence. If the evidence presented by the minor premise agrees with the major premise, a conclusion may be reached. A famous example proposes:

Major premise: All humans are mortal.
Minor premise: Socrates is human.
Conclusion: Therefore, Socrates is mortal.

Using this model, we can suggest:

Major premise: All children can learn.
Minor premise: John is a child.
Conclusion: Therefore, John can learn.

Many variations of the syllogism are possible. The basic structure applies deductive reasoning to support a conclusion. In a syllogism, the major premise is assumed true. If one can question the validity of the major premise, the integrity of the syllogism falls apart. Syllogism errors (or fallacies) can lead to questionable conclusions. For example:

> *Major premise*: All men are created equal.
> *Minor premise*: Thomas is a man.
> *Conclusion*: Therefore, Thomas is created equal.

However, if Thomas is owned as a slave, the major premise is false. One can detect an error in the logic that claims all men are created equal while at the same time allowing for glaring exceptions. However, one could argue Thomas is created equal but not everyone is recognizing this fact. In that case, the major premise is not in error; the error lies with the conduct of those who deny the major premise. The form of the syllogism allows contradictory evidence to refute conclusions or revise premises.

Inductive reasoning involves studying particular qualities of specific objects, which exist independently of the perceiver, to discover generalizations or principles. Aristotle states, "From many notions gained by experience one universal judgment about similar objects is produced" (*Metaphysics*, 981a5). Through observation, a hypothesis can be verified. As each observation supports the hypothesis, one becomes more confident of its veracity. In a variation on our first example above, if every human we meet is mortal, we can eventually conclude with confidence all human are mortal until new evidence contracts this conclusion. We can even begin to use the conclusion as the major premise of a syllogism and begin to reason deductively. However, when one observes an exception, the inference must be considered false, or at least altered or modified. For example, if every swan you have seen is white, you might conclude all swans are white. However, when you see a black swan, you can no longer assert, "All swans are white."

The goal of the scientific method is to arrive at valid conclusions. Aristotle seeks to discover the essential qualities of each thing, allowing him to classify and categorize the object into the scheme or structure of the universe. In the example above, by observing swans we determine that white feathers must not be the swan's defining characteristic; it must be something else. Aristotle would argue that there must remain an essence that makes every swan a swan (its "swan-ness"), despite differences in physical characteristics that individual swans may be observed to possess. He would continue the investigation to determine the defining feature so he could accurately locate it within a structure (such as in a taxonomy).

Bacon disavows the use of syllogisms to logically argue conclusions. In *Novum Organum*, he maintains, "The subtlety of Nature is greater many times over the subtlety of argument" (Book 1, Aphorism 24). Bacon prefers that scientific investigations proceed incrementally, always closely associated with empirical observations. However, a conclusion arrived at inductively may serve as a hypothesis for further investigation. Picture a range or gradation of conclusions of different levels of specificity. Some conclusions may be situated between more specific and more general ones. Investigation may proceed in either direction to validate empirical findings or produce new directions for inquiry.

In addition to the natural sciences, the scientific or inquiry method can be used in other subjects. In mathematics, the teacher or students can identify a problem or pose a question and experiment with different techniques, operations, or formulas to determine a solution. In history and social studies, students can examine primary sources, combining different pieces of information to form hypotheses or suggest conclusions about past events, their relationship to other events, and their relevance in the present day. Field trips, guest speakers, and interviews with local community members can simulate fieldwork to learn about topics in civics and government, economics, geography, and culture. Lessons in language arts and literature can be approached as a detective approaches a case, searching for clues to arrive at conclusions. Writing assignments may begin with questions requiring investigation using reference materials and other sources of data to examine evidence and report information or argue a position. In the arts, while a drawing, painting, or other form may or may not seek to accurately reproduce the physical characteristics of a subject, the artist can venture to reveal the essence of a subject. Apart from being a purely emotional expression, art can represent a rational thought process, a syllogism presented in terms of visuals, audio, music, and/or movement.

What Is the Role of the Teacher in the Scientific Method?

TEACHER AS DIRECTOR

For the Scientific Method, the metaphor offered is Teacher as Director. The teacher directs student investigations into the topic of study. The teacher in the role of chief investigator (such as in structured inquiry) selects the topic, poses the questions, determines the process, defines the steps, monitors the procedures, and verifies the conclusions. The method involves active participation by the students, but (as in the Socratic Method) the teacher retains the authority by maintaining control of the process and validating that students have learned accurate knowledge.

TEACHER AS PRESENTER

The role of the teacher is also to present accurate representations of the world. Aristotle explains, "Teachers are those who tell the causes of each thing" (*Metaphysics*, 982a30). Describing principles, explaining models, and demonstrating procedures help students learn the underlying structure of each discipline.

What Is the Role of the Student in the Scientific Method?

STUDENT AS INVESTIGATOR

In the Scientific Method, the student acts in the role of Investigator. The student follows directions and carries out procedures defined and explained by the teacher. The goal is to discover the basic structure and fundamental principles of reality. Personal opinion or one's subjective point of view do not influence the outcome. Conclusions must be verified by evidence. External standards of measurement can be used to assess the degree to which a student achieves the objectives determined in advance by the teacher.

STUDENT AS ACHIEVER

Another role of the student is to achieve. Aristotle believes that human beings, like everything in nature, have a purpose and the potential to achieve that purpose. Included in this role is to exhibit high qualities of character. Aristotle believes we are engaged in the search for excellence and to live the "good life." Likewise, just as all things seek the ultimate end or result closest to actualization, we too endeavor to find not only what is good for the moment but the highest good. These are questions about Axiology (morals, ethics, virtues, character). Aristotle believes one's conduct should embody the Doctrine of the Mean, meaning to strive for the mean between extremes, to exhibit self-control and not indulge in excess (*Nicomachean Ethics*, Book II). Virtuous behavior falls between the two extremes of excess and deficiency. This reinforces the viewpoint that the underlying structure of reality consists of unity, harmony, balance, and rational control.

Design

How Are Schools Organized? Questions about the Role of the School

A school designed to teach structure and fundamental principles (Table 4.1) would resemble a laboratory, where experiments would be performed. Rather than circles of students engaging each other in discussion, small groups would concentrate on delving into the particulars of an object to ascertain its structure, identify its parts, determine their functions, and reveal the principles that govern its operation.

Different types of inquiry follow steps that align with the scientific method. In Chapter 2, we examined structured inquiry (where the teacher directs the process), guided inquiry (where the teacher proposes alternative ways to engage in the process), open inquiry (where students direct the process), and alternatives that vary the degree of teacher and student control. By employing the scientific or inquiry method in classrooms, a cycle can be established wherein the results of one inquiry raise questions that produce an ongoing inquiry or instigate a new investigation.

The key factor in each of these models is the process of investigation. Learning activities begin with a question or hypothesis to be tested and verified. Even when a teacher provides students with generalizations they are to accept as facts (such as definitions, categories of information, principles, axioms, etc.), these serve as major premises. Students still investigate (directed, guided, or coached by the teacher) to discover and analyze evidence and/or locate additional examples that support conclusions. In all instances, the ability for others to reproduce the process in an attempt to replicate the results can evaluate and validate the method.

Although science has been part of the curriculum since the natural philosophy of Aristotle, the emergence of science, technology, engineering, and mathematics (STEM) education as an integrated field of study has increased emphasis on connecting science concepts and methods across disciplines (Honey, Pearson, & Schweingruber, 2015). STEM instruction reinforces a unified approach to learning about underlying structures and principles. "For example, an understanding of the general idea of systems may be aided by examining electrical systems, mechanical systems, ecosystems, and even mathematical systems to identify their common characteristics" (pp. 36–7).

In 1988, fifteen schools founded the National Consortium for Specialized Secondary Schools of Mathematics, Science, and Technology. In 2014, the Consortium shortened its name to the National Consortium of Secondary STEM Schools (NCSSS, About section). NCSSS has grown to nearly 100 institutional members in thirty states. Affiliate members include summer programs, colleges and universities, government agencies, private businesses and corporations, foundations, associations, and other nonprofit organizations that support STEM education.

Four schools initially collaborated to start the STEM consortium: North Carolina School of Science and Mathematics, Thomas Jefferson High School for Science and Technology in Virginia, Louisiana School for Mathematics, Science, and the Arts, and Illinois Mathematics Science Academy (NCSSS, History section). These public schools offer a comprehensive

Table 4.1 Design a School (Structure and Principles)

Purpose of Education	*Learn structure and fundamental principles*
Curriculum	Liberal arts and sciences
Instruction	Scientific method, syllogism (logic)
Role of Teacher	Director, presenter
Role of Student	Investigator, achiever
Role of School	Seminars and laboratories

curriculum specializing in science, mathematics, engineering, and technology. North Carolina School of Science and Mathematics, Louisiana School for Mathematics, Science, and the Arts, and Illinois Mathematics and Science Academy are residential institutions offering advanced-level and accelerated classes. Thomas Jefferson High School for Science and Technology serves students in four counties and two cities. Students at Illinois Mathematics and Science Academy conduct research in scholars at more than 100 institutions and present their findings at state, national, and international conferences. All seniors at Thomas Jefferson complete a culminating technology laboratory project in one of the school's laboratories or through a mentorship under the supervision of experienced scientists, engineers, and other professionals. North Carolina School of Science and Mathematics also offers online classes and a summer program. Students at Louisiana School for Mathematics, Science, and the Arts conduct research during the academic year and in the summer, and may participate in the Future Scientist Program.

Thomas Aquinas College

An example of a school offering a curriculum that adheres closely to the principles of both Realism and Thomism is Thomas Aquinas College in California. Thomas Aquinas College offers a "single, integrated curriculum employing the liberal arts and sciences in the pursuit of truth and wisdom" (Thomas Aquinas College, 2015, About section, para 2). The curriculum reveals its roots in both theistic and classical Greek conceptions of knowledge. For example, the college uses the term "science" more broadly than in reference to the natural sciences. The college defines science as "any systematically arranged branch of knowledge," explaining:

> The Thomas Aquinas College curriculum therefore rightly regards philosophy and theology as sciences—indeed, the greatest of the sciences, with theology as the queen—because they systematically arrange the highest sorts of knowledge, those of wisdom and of God Himself.
> (Thomas Aquinas College, 2015, The Liberal
> Arts & Sciences section, para 5)

This hierarchy of knowledge has its antecedents in Aristotelian Realism and Thomism. The college's description of its curriculum acknowledges its debt to Aristotle and Aquinas when explaining that philosophy and theology are "the greatest of sciences" taught in all four years of the program (Thomas Aquinas College, 2015, The Liberal Arts & Sciences section, para 5). The curriculum is viewed as a comprehensive whole, with a unity and an order. All students earn a Bachelor of Arts in Liberal Arts degree.

Classes are taught as seminars, tutorials, and laboratories. Thomas Aquinas College uses the *Great Books* in their curriculum, not merely as examples of great writings or to familiarize students with Western culture, but to reveal truths about reality. Thomas Aquinas College represents a school designed to teach a rational approach to divining the order, structure, and unity of existence. The college asserts, "To learn is to discover and grow in the truth about reality," with the objective that students are to "grasp something of the order of the universe" (Thomas Aquinas College, 2015, A Liberating Education section, para 1).

How Does a School Designed to Teach Structure and Principles Define an Educated Person?

The goal of learning, and of becoming an educated person, is to reveal the structure and purpose of all things. Purpose and meaning can be discovered by the rational and empirical study of the material world. Synthesis and unity are the goals of learning. Both deductive and inductive reasoning have the same goal: to determine the ultimate truth.

Evaluate

Consistency

A school with the purpose of teaching about structure and principles would investigate the fundamental cause and function of all things. To remain consistent, the scientific method or inquiry approach would permeate teaching and learning in all subjects and disciplines. Opinions would not be accepted as knowledge, but would be posed as hypotheses to be tested using systematic procedures. Contradictory evidence could disaffirm a tentative conclusion and require revising the hypothesis and engaging in further investigation. Individual interests or preferences would be integrated into the overall program, not offered as unrelated personal pursuits.

Compatibility

Discussion alone (such as in the Socratic Method) would not be compatible with this purpose of education. Even the use of syllogism, the logical process advanced by Aristotle, would not suffice without premises and conclusions being subject to rigorous empirical verification. Discussion must lead to revealing underlying truths about the nature of reality.

The teacher imparting information to students through lectures would also be incompatible with this purpose of education unless presented as prerequisite background information in preparation for students conducting a laboratory experiment or other form of inquiry. The scientist, for example, is not interested in memorizing isolated facts but in representing the facts within a larger system. Note-taking and exams need to support a research agenda. Public presentations and other means to report findings would serve as assessments and demonstrations of learning. Student work would be open to scrutiny and feedback from professionals.

Use of the scientific method can appear on both sides of the *Continuum of Educational Philosophy*, depending on the purpose. The purpose we have been investigating seeks objective, universal truth. Learning the skills of inquiry and problem-solving processes alone is not sufficient. The process must yield results that can be measured and evaluated. As a cognitive theorist, Bruner believes children learn not only by grasping general principles and mastering fundamental concepts, but also by constructing understanding through discovery. Knowledge is a process, not a product. As a child encounters new information in the environment, he begins to detect patterns and make associations. Through inference, the learner organizes facts in terms of principles and perceives structure in a body of knowledge. Although Bruner disagrees with a teacher providing all the information about principles to passive students, he acknowledges that the teacher should guide the discovery process in a systematic, structured way.

In the Realism view of reality, one does not construct new knowledge in the sense of creating new principles that have not previously existed in the universe. One can only speculate about what is yet to be discovered to find heretofore unidentified knowledge. New inventions – such as the telephone, powered flight, or semiconductors – function according to principles that have always existed. Inventing a new substance consists of combining existing chemicals in a new way or using a new procedure. The detection of a new planet, or observing a new element under laboratory conditions, tests a hypothesis and follows pre-existing principles and the discovery is classified within an existing system. Upon discovering a new species, the scientist refers to existing characteristics of other species to place it within a taxonomy.

The curriculum, therefore, should be designed with the belief that an underlying structure and basic principles are discoverable in a stable universe. Instruction, however, can range from teacher-guided discovery with pre-determined outcomes to more open exploration methods with no set criteria established at the outset. Active problem solving conducted with less structured guidance or supervision from the teacher is discussed in Chapter 8.

Coherence

A coherent design would embrace combining knowledge learned through rational inquiry and scientific investigation into a unified structure with inherent meaning and fundamental purpose. The comprehensive curriculum would integrate learning into a unified whole. Electives and other offerings must directly contribute to the single mission of reflecting order and reason.

Reflect

Refer to the *Continuum of Educational Philosophy*. Where do the curriculum, pedagogy, and purpose of education fall? Have you observed or experienced a curriculum that values objective, universal knowledge? Do direct experiences combined with rational thinking provide the sources and methods of learning? What are the roles of the teacher and student in this kind of education? How do schools endorse and support this kind of education?

How Do Your Prior Observations and Experiences Relate to a Curriculum Designed to Teach Structure and Principles?

How has the curriculum in schools you have observed or attended represented a coherent, comprehensive structure? Does the curriculum appear to have an underlying and consistent organization, or are subjects and topics arbitrarily included or omitted in response to shifts in the preferences of students, parents, or the community? In what ways does the curriculum emphasize unity or order?

What subjects do schools emphasize? Is science a priority, or do other subjects appear to have a greater standing? Even if science is not the field with the highest status, are the other subjects offered because they represent the nature of reality as ordered, rational, and purposeful? How is content represented by underlying principles or generalized ways of thinking unique to each subject area? Is knowledge open to individual interpretation or do conclusions need to be verified by evidence in all subjects? For example, are art, music, and dance taught purely as forms of self-expression, or to reveal truths about reality and the essence of human nature?

How Do Your Prior Observations and Experiences Relate to a Pedagogy Designed to Teach Structure and Principles?

How has teaching you have observed or experienced reinforced learning structures and principles?

In addition to labs required in science courses, how else have you observed or experienced the scientific or inquiry method used in schools? Are experiments restricted to the science lab? Do students engage in inquiry in other subjects?

How Do Your Prior Observations and Experiences Relate to a School Designed to Teach Structure and Principles?

Have you observed or experienced schools that explicitly state a mission or purpose to integrate all learning into a unified whole? Do schools offer a coherent program or may students personalize the curriculum by choosing from a menu of options? Does the school as an institution appear to reinforce the belief that reality is an orderly, rational, structured existence?

How Do Your Own Practices and Beliefs Relate to the Purpose of Education as Learning Structure and Principles?

After reading this chapter, and comparing it to Chapter 3, where would you locate your beliefs about education on the *Continuum of Educational Philosophy*? Has your perspective shifted or remained constant?

How have you taught or learned in a way compatible with the scientific method? Would this be your preferred way to teach? Can you envision teaching using inquiry in subjects other than science? Would you direct investigations or permit students to propose their own investigations, including choosing and devising their own methods?

Can direct observations of the world around us reveal an underlying structure to existence? Or do you believe that reality may be more arbitrary than that? Do you believe organized bodies of knowledge are created by people to impose order on a random universe, or is that structure inherent to the nature of all things?

Both Chapter 3 and the present chapter relate to the overarching wonder question posed at the beginning of Part II, "*What if . . . the purpose of education were to learn objective and universal knowledge?*" However, we have moved farther to the right on the *Continuum of Educational Philosophy*. Rational thinking continues to dominate the perspective of educators. However, the sources of knowledge include direct observation of the natural world in addition to abstract argument. Unsubstantiated opinions have no value in the absence of credible supporting evidence. Both views of education believe the ultimate truth about reality can be discovered. In the words of Francis Bacon (1605/1902), "If a man will begin with certainties, he shall end in doubts; but if he will be content to begin with doubts, he shall end in certainties" (Book I, V, 8).

Notes

1 As translated in *The Complete Works* (Jonathan Barnes, Ed.), "The totality is something besides the parts, there is a cause of unity" (*Metaphysics*, 1045a10).
2 A third kind of reasoning, abductive, refers to inferring an explanation based on the best available evidence. For example, Bertrand Russell (in this chapter) and Charles Sanders Peirce (Chapter 8) use the term, but conflicting definitions have been proposed. An overview of the concept may be read here: Douven, I. (2011). Abduction. In E. N. Zalta (Ed.), *The Stanford encyclopedia of philosophy*. http://plato. stanford.edu/archives/spr2011/entries/abduction/

References

Aquinas, T. (1949). *De regno ad regem Cypri*. (G. B. Phelan, Trans.). Toronto, Canada: The Pontifical Institute of Mediaeval Studies. (Original work published 1265.)

Aquinas, T. (1947). *Summa theological*. (Fathers of the English Dominican Province, Trans.). New York, NY: Benziger Brothers. (Original work published 1265–74.)

Aristotle. (1984). *The complete works of Aristotle: The revised Oxford translation*. J. Barnes (Ed.). Princeton, NJ: Princeton University Press.

Bacon, F. (1902). *Novum organum*. J. Devey (Ed.). New York, NY: P. F. Collier & Son. (Original work published 1620.)

Bacon, F. (1902). *The advancement of learning*. (Original work published 1605.) [Electronic version]. Retrieved from http://pages.uoregon.edu/rbear/adv1.htm

Bruner, J. S. (1977). *The process of education*. Cambridge, MA: Harvard University Press. (Original work published 1960.)

Danielson, C. (2013). *The framework for teaching evaluation instrument*. Princeton, NJ: The Danielson Group.

Hawking, S. W. (2002). *The theory of everything: The origin and fate of the universe*. Beverly Hills, CA: New Millennium Press.

Honey, M., Pearson, G., & Schweingruber, H. (Eds.) (2015). *STEM integration in K-12 education: Status, prospects, and an agenda for research*. Washington, DC: National Academies Press.

Interstate New Teacher Assessment and Support Consortium. (1992). *Model standards for beginning teacher licensing, assessment, and development: A resource for state dialogue*. [Electronic version]. Retrieved from http://programs.ccsso.org/content/pdfs/corestrd.pdf

Kant, I. (1900). *Kant on education*. (A. Churton, Trans.). Boston: D. C. Heath. (Original work published 1803.)

Locke, J. (1964). An essay concerning human understanding, A. D. Woozley (Ed.), Cleveland, OH: Meridian. (Original work published 1689.)

NCSSS (National Consortium of Secondary STEM Schools). (2015). About. [Website]. Retrieved from http://www.ncsss.org/about

NCSSS (National Consortium of Secondary STEM Schools). (2015). History and founders. [Website]. Retrieved from http://www.ncsss.org/about/history-and-founders

NEA (National Education Association). (1894). *Report of the Committee of Ten on secondary school studies: With the reports of the conferences arranged by the committee.* New York, NY: American Book Company.

Russell, B. (1961). *On our knowledge of the external world as a field for scientific method in philosophy.* London: George Allen & Unwin. (Original work published 1926.)

Searle, J. (1995). *The construction of social reality.* New York, NY: Free Press.

Thomas Aquinas College. (2015). About. [Website]. Retrieved from http://www.thomasaquinas.edu/about

Thomas Aquinas College. (2015). A liberating education. [Website]. Retrieved from http://www.thomasaquinas.edu/a-liberating-education

Thomas Aquinas College. (2015). The liberal arts & sciences. [Website]. Retrieved from http://www.thomasaquinas.edu/a-liberating-education/liberal-arts-sciences.

Weinberg, S. (1994). *Dreams of a final theory: The scientist's search for the ultimate laws of nature.* New York, NY: Knopf Doubleday.

Whitehead, A. N. (1949). *The aims of education and other essays.* New York, NY: New American Library. (Original work published 1929.)

5   What If . . . The Purpose of Education Were to Learn Essential Knowledge?

Wonder

This final chapter of Part II completes our inquiry into education based on learning objective, universal knowledge. We ask the wonder question: *"What if . . . the purpose of education were to learn essential knowledge?"*

We remain on the left side of the *Continuum of Educational Philosophy* (Figure 5.1) where ideas and content knowledge are more valued than subjective experiences or personal interests. However, the curriculum incorporates new knowledge from current sources. The teacher continues to make key decisions regarding the learning of students. The role of the student is to receive, accept, and retain essential facts and information to become a literate member of society and function as a productive citizen.

EDUCATIONAL PRACTICES

RATIONAL   EMPIRICAL

Ideas-Focused	Experience-Focused
Content-Oriented	Process-Oriented
Fixed Curriculum	Flexible Curriculum
Teacher-Centered	Student-Centered
Teacher-Directed	Self-Directed
Pre-Determined Outcomes	Open-Ended Exploration
Whole-Class Activities	Differentiated/Individualized Activities

Objective External Reality	Internal Subjective Reality
Absolute Universal Truth	Changing Relative Truth
Pre-Existing Knowledge	Constructed Knowledge
Knowledge Independent of Experience	Knowledge Dependent on Experience
Autonomous Knowledge	Interdependent Knowledge
Absolute Universal Values	Relative Local Values
Values Independent of Experience	Values Dependent on Experience

PHILOSOPHICAL PERSPECTIVES

Figure 5.1 Continuum of Educational Philosophy (Essential Knowledge)

Observe

Classroom Vignette: An Eighth-Grade History Lesson on Lincoln's Gettysburg Address

Ms. E's eighth-grade history class has been studying the Civil War. The unit has concentrated on identifying and examining the causes of the war, political figures, military leaders, major events, and key battles. Topics are being presented chronologically. In the most recent class, the students completed a quiz on the Battle of Gettysburg.

Today's lesson focuses on Abraham Lincoln's Gettysburg Address. The students take turns reading passages of the speech aloud. Next, Ms. E displays a photograph of Lincoln taken at Gettysburg while playing an audio recording of an actor reciting the speech, to allow students to imagine the scene while hearing the enunciation and intonation of the words for greater effect.

When the speech has ended, she asks the class. "What are the first words Lincoln speaks?"

"Four score and seven years ago," a student responds, reading from the text.

"Have any of you heard that phrase before?" Ms. E asks.

Several students raise their hands.

"What do you think it means?"

"My parents told me," Sally answers. "A score means twenty years."

"So that makes it . . . ?"

A student offers, "Eighty-seven years."

"That's a funny way of saying eighty-seven," Matthew interjects. "Why not just say eighty-seven?"

"That's an excellent question," Ms. E replies. "Before we discuss that, we need to know what Lincoln is talking about. What does he say happened eighty-seven years ago?"

The class determines the date to be 1776, the year of the signing of the Declaration of Independence. Ms. E asks questions to check what students recall about the Declaration of Independence. The sentence is dissected to indicate how it refers to the Founders and the beginning of a new nation. Most students have heard the phrase "all men are created equal" but not all know its origins or the context.

"That is one of the most famous quotes in history," Ms. E tells the class. "To get back to Matthew's comment, do you think the speech would be as memorable if Lincoln had begun by saying, 'Eighty-seven years ago . . . '?"

The class laughs.

"The eloquence of the speech helps make it memorable, although it may be the shortest speech in history," Ms. E continues. "We have spent more time discussing it in class today than it took Lincoln to deliver it. Why do you think the speech became so important?"

"Because Gettysburg was an important battle?" Alice suggests.

"Yes, but why would Lincoln's speech still be important to us today?" Ms. E responds. "Many speeches about important battles have been given throughout history but very few are remembered today or taught in schools. This speech is important for many reasons."

Ms. E hands out a two-column graphic organizer to the class. She breaks the speech into three sections and presents each section line by line. Students write down each line in the left column and its meaning in the right column. Ms. E instructs students to record key vocabulary words below the table and write a definition beside each one.

The final sentence entered in the table ends with the phrase, "that government of the people, by the people, for the people, shall not perish from the earth."

"The speech helped people remember our core national values at a time when the very existence of the nation was threatened," Mrs. E explains. "Lincoln says the Civil War was testing whether a nation conceived in liberty could endure. So liberty is one of the core values he said they were fighting to preserve. What are some other values the speech indicates we hold in common as a nation?"

Alicia raises her hand. "Equality," she answers.

"Freedom," another student suggests.

"Thank you, those are both values mentioned in the speech," Mrs. E responds. "What about responsibility?" she asks, "Is that in the speech?"

The students study the text of the speech. No student is able to find the word "responsibility." Mrs. E directs their attention to the final section.

"Right before the famous words about 'government of the people, by the people, for the people,'" she indicates, "Lincoln says the living must dedicate themselves to completing the unfinished work of those soldiers who fought and died in the battle. This means they also need to accept the responsibility to keep the nation united."

Mrs. E explains the speech is not just about dedicating the graveyard of the battlefield. Lincoln is urging the listeners to commit themselves to the values the nation stands for and to fight for freedom.

Mrs. E projects a photograph of the Lincoln Memorial in Washington, D.C. "The Gettysburg Address is so important in American history that it is inscribed on the wall of the Lincoln Memorial," she informs the class. She also points out that, from 1959 to 2008, the Lincoln Memorial appeared on the back of the penny and still appears on the back of the five-dollar bill. She passes around a 2008 penny, joking, "Now I want that penny back!" A student asks her to show them a five-dollar bill, but she tells the students she will need to wait until pay day to have that much money in her wallet.

Next, Mrs. E projects a photograph of Rev Martin Luther King, Jr. delivering his "I Have a Dream" speech on the steps of the Lincoln Memorial. She explains the significance of organizing the 1963 march on Washington to culminate at the Memorial, marking the hundredth anniversary of the signing of the Emancipation Proclamation. "Five score years ago," Mrs. E reads aloud from the speech, "a great American, in whose symbolic shadow we stand today, signed the Emancipation Proclamation." Mrs. E points out the parallels King draws to Lincoln by using "score" to denote the length of time, which is also one hundred years since the Gettysburg Address. The values expressed in King's speech, she says, form a continuity that extends from the revolutionary founding of the nation, to the tumult of Lincoln's time, to the present day. These same values have endured through periods of turmoil throughout the nation's history.

Ms. E returns to the table analyzing the Gettysburg Address and summarizes the key information. She notifies the class they will have a quiz on the material at the beginning of class tomorrow. She will expect them to know the meaning of important lines of the speech and to be able to define the vocabulary words.

At the end of the unit, the students prepare for a test on the Civil War. As part of the review, the class plays a Jeopardy-style game. The categories include names of famous generals, names of battles, important dates, famous quotations, and other vital information.

Investigate

What Do Teachers Teach? Questions about the Curriculum

If we were to design a school based on learning essential knowledge, what curriculum would we teach? Where would this knowledge come from? What philosophical perspectives would support this curriculum?

To examine philosophies with this view of the purpose of education, we will investigate the following inquiry questions:

- What Do Teachers Teach? Questions about the Curriculum
- How Do Teachers Teach? Questions about Pedagogy
- How Are Schools Organized? Questions about the Role of the School

What Knowledge Is Essential?

"To be culturally literate is to possess the basic information needed to thrive in the modern world."

(E. D. Hirsch)

In the classroom vignette, the students study the Gettysburg Address to learn about significant historical events as well as to understand the core values the speech represents.

In 1938, William C. Bagley (1874–1946), professor of education at Teacher's College (of Columbia University), founded the Essentialistic Education Society and published *The Essentialist's Platform*. For Bagley, cultural knowledge and democratic ideals comprise an essential education. He defines literacy as more than the ability to decode words as one reads but as developing understanding of the democratic ideals held in common by the national culture. Responsibility as well as freedom should be taught to create and sustain society.

Democratic society demands a "community of culture" that possesses "a common core of ideas, meanings, understandings, and ideals" (Bagley, 1938, p. 252). Bagley explains that "a knowledge of the world that lies beyond one's immediate experience has been among the recognized essentials of universal education" (p. 253). A universal education should consist of a specific common core of knowledge, in particular about American culture. Teachers would direct a systematic program of learning with rigorous standards that sequences subject-matter content according to grade level.

In the intervening years, experiments and innovations in education based on findings in psychology and educational research began to focus on student-centered learning. The curriculum took into account the developmental stage of the child, the learning needs of the child, differences in children's learning styles, each child's personal experiences and background, and the child's interests. The process of learning became emphasized, in the view of some, over the importance of teaching content. In 1983, the National Commission on Excellence in Education produced a report, *A Nation at Risk*, warning, "Our once unchallenged preeminence in commerce, industry, science, and technological innovation is being overtaken by competitors throughout the world" (p. 9). The report blames mediocre educational standards and decreased student performance for the dilemma. Mastery of a common subject-matter has been replaced by student choice. Students have gravitated to a fragmented curriculum offering electives and courses devoid of rigor.

Recalling similar sentiments expressed by Bagley during the crisis of the Great Depression, the Commission states, "A high level of shared education is essential to a free, democratic society and to the fostering of a common culture" (p. 10). The basic purpose of education is to form common understanding among citizens. The report recommends that schools return to a content-rich curriculum that establishes high expectations for all learners.

Following the report, a movement arose to reestablish a core curriculum consisting of essential knowledge. In 1986, E. D. Hirsch (Professor Emeritus of English, University of Virginia) founded the Core Knowledge Foundation. In his 1987 book, *Cultural Literacy: What Every American Needs to Know*, Hirsch argues that each member of American society needs to be literate in the shared knowledge of the national culture. He explains, "To be culturally literate is to possess the basic information needed to thrive in the modern world" (p. xiii). In the tradition of Bagley, Hirsch defines literacy as more than acquiring skills to be able to read, write, and speak, but as the ability to effectively communicate by sharing a common body of "cultural content" (p. 27). Hirsch asserts that the purpose of school is to acculturate children; that is, to assimilate children into a common national culture.

Hirsch advocates for a knowledge-based curriculum, complaining that reading skills and critical thinking skills have no meaning devoid of specific content. Hutchins (see Chapter 3) makes a similar argument against a content-free education. Instruction should emphasize understanding subject-matter knowledge. He believes universal knowledge exists that society takes for granted all educated people should have learned in school. This knowledge needs to be identified and articulated so that schools can uniformly and consistently teach relevant content. In addition, transmitting traditional civic values, such as equality and unity, is necessary to preserve democracy. Sharing common knowledge and values are essential to participating in society as well as succeeding economically.

Cultural Literacy: What Every American Needs to Know includes a preliminary list of the range of knowledge literate Americans should share. The Appendix alphabetically lists names (such as Abraham Lincoln), events (such as the Battle of Gettysburg), events (such as the Gettysburg Address), and dates (such as 1776), as well as terms from a variety of disciplines. Hirsch and his colleagues subsequently published *The Dictionary of Cultural Literacy* (1988), which organizes the information into sections (such as American History to 1865) and expands on each entry (such as offering brief background information on the Gettysburg Address). *The New Dictionary of Cultural Literacy* (2002) revises original entries and adds new ones to update the body of essential knowledge.

The New First Dictionary of Cultural Literacy: What Your Child Needs to Know (2004) contains over 3,000 entries intended for children through grade six. In addition to the dictionaries, a series of books arrange content knowledge by grade level. In titles that range from *What Your Preschooler Grader Needs to Know* to *What Your Sixth Grader Needs to Know*, these volumes recommend a curriculum for prekindergarten through grade eight. The *Core Knowledge Sequence* (2013) offers a cumulate grade-specific sequence of topics and skills in language arts, history and geography, visual arts, music, mathematics, and science for grades K-8. The topic of the classroom vignette, the Gettysburg Address, appears in *What Your Fifth Grader Needs to Know* (1993) and in the fifth grade of the *Core Knowledge Sequence*.

One purpose of the essential knowledge approach is to offer equal access to the common knowledge all citizens should share. Adherents to this philosophical perspective contend that adopting a national core curriculum would eliminate gaps in knowledge, reducing disparity among children's educational achievement. Another benefit of a common curriculum would be to provide teachers with clear guidance on what to teach and a coherent structure from which to plan instruction for all learners.

How Do Teachers Teach? Questions about Pedagogy

"Teaching can be defined as the process of making and implementing decisions."

(Madeline Hunter)

How do teachers teach essential knowledge? In the vignette, the class is studying a landmark speech from American history, the Gettysburg Address. The teacher leads the students through a line-by-line reading of the address to identify the historical and cultural references contained in each passage. The lesson emphasizes the meaning of the speech and the values it embodies. The unit on the Civil War builds on prior learning, stressing the accumulation of new knowledge. Students are frequently quizzed on their retention of the material, culminating in a summative end-of-unit test. To prepare for the test, the students review by playing a game of Jeopardy, which requires recall of specific names, dates, events, and other facts.

The vignette represents a systematic approach to learning. Instruction is teacher-directed and focused on conveying a well-defined body of knowledge that all students should know. The content is presented in an organized sequence, with routine monitoring to check for comprehension of key terms and vocabulary. Formal assessment is designed to provide evidence of achieving objective standards.

Bagley and Hirsch do not specify instructional methods for teachers to ensure students acquire the essential core content. Several models of instruction provide a teacher-directed approach that offers explicit teaching of content and skills with clear, unambiguous assessment that determines achievement of outcomes.

The Teacher Decision-Making model outlines seven elements for effective teaching: 1) learning objectives, 2) anticipatory set, 3) instructional input, 4) modeling, 5) checking for understanding, 6) guided practice, and 7) independent practice (Hunter, 1994). Productive teaching requires a systematic approach. Hunter explains, "Teaching can be defined as the process of making and implementing decisions before, during, and after instruction – decisions that, when implemented, increase the probability of learning" (p. 6). The model is designed to apply principles of learning, not prescribe a series of rigid steps. All seven elements should be incorporated into the teaching and learning process. However, merely including all seven elements in a lesson is not guaranteed to produce results. Teaching has been successful when "the output of [the] student is perceivable to the teacher and validates that learning has occurred" (p. 45).

Another common method for delivering content to students is the Direct Instruction model (Eggen & Kauchak, 2006; Joyce, Weil, & Calhoun, 2014). In the model, the teacher presents new content through lecture, presentation, demonstration, and/or modeling. Students engage in guided practice under the supervision of the teacher then apply their learning in independent practice. The lesson typically begins with a review of prior learning, stating the objective, overviewing the new content, providing explicit directions for learning activities, and supplying instructional materials. The teacher continually monitors student performance, frequently checks for understanding, and distributes practice over time to reinforce learning.

Related to direct instruction, the mastery learning approach expects students to master content; in other words, to bring students "to a certain predetermined standard of achievement" (Bloom, 1968, p. 7). The ideal situation for achieving mastery may be for each student to receive individual attention, as in a tutoring relationship. However, because classroom teaching does not lend itself to this kind of one-on-one instruction, mastery teaching divides learning into units and topics, each with a set of general objectives. Units are then broken into lessons, which state specific objectives (Bloom, 1968, 1971, 1974). The teacher frequently assesses student comprehension, providing data to the teacher and feedback to the student on progress toward achieving identified benchmarks. Content that the assessments indicate has been attained does not require further instruction. However, content that has not been acquired is re-taught, more practice is provided, and additional assessment is administered until student performance indicates mastery. "This implies some notion of absolute standards," Bloom (1968) explains, "and the use of grades or marks which will reflect these standards" (p. 8). Students should not be evaluated in comparison with each other, but according to a set of external, objective criteria.

The teacher may employ different strategies to ensure mastery, and need not focus only on basic skills but also on higher-level thinking, problem solving, and reasoning skills. Whatever the instructional techniques, the mastery of content remains the goal. In all types of instruction, teachers specify objectives and develop a sequence of tasks to incrementally accomplish each objective. Teachers should provide continuous, corrective feedback to address and correct errors.

Teach-Practice-Apply (TPA) presents a model for direct instruction (Reinhartz & Van Cleaf, 1986) that begins each lesson with explicit teaching of content and skills. In the Teach stage, the teacher directs instruction (by delivering, presenting, leading, showing, and telling). In the Practice phase, activity shifts from the teacher to the students. The teacher remains responsible for planning and implementing this phase and continues to direct student learning, monitoring student practice, and providing feedback. In Apply, students use the skill with less teacher supervision in another context. Students relate their learning to activities under similar but not identical conditions. The Apply component is often used as an assessment, such as seatwork or homework. The three components overlap, with re-teaching and corrective feedback continuing during the

Practice step and additional practice and review informing and strengthening the Apply step. The Teach-Practice-Apply model is designed to be flexible enough to permit teachers to employ a variety of deductive (lecture) and inductive teaching strategies (discussion, inquiry) "while allowing them to retain control of their classrooms" and ensure that lessons contain "essential instructional elements" (Reinhartz & Van Cleaf, 1986, p. 25). However, the stages of the TPA model are intended to be implemented in sequence.

The Gradual Release model (or gradual release of responsibility) represents a progression from total teacher responsibility (explicit direct instruction) to greater student responsibility (Fisher & Frey, 2008; Pearson & Gallagher, 1983). Instruction begins with the teacher presenting content and demonstrating and/or modeling the task, activity, or strategy for students. In the guided practice stage, the teacher gradually releases responsibility to the students while continuing to provide explicit instruction, reinforcement, and assistance. Independent practice focuses on students applying the skill. Although similar to direct instruction in structure (modeling, guided practice, independent practice), the model focuses more attention on guidance that leads to student independence. Feedback is "less corrective" (the teacher supplying the correct answer when a student struggles) and "more suggestive" (encouraging alternatives) (Pearson & Gallagher, 1983, p. 339).

Gradual release is also referred to as *I Do, We Do, You Do* (Fisher & Frey, 2008). The teacher provides a focus lesson on specific content and skills. The purpose or objective is stated, and the content, skill, or task explicitly named, defined, and explained. The teacher demonstrates or models (I Do). Next, the students engage in guided practice (We Do) with varying degrees of teacher assistance (such as cues, prompts, and questions). Finally, students complete independent learning tasks (You Do). An iteration of the model can have students collaborate (We Do Together) prior to independent practice.

What Is the Role of the Teacher in Teaching Essential Knowledge?

TEACHER AS CONTENT KNOWLEDGE EXPERT

Core knowledge advocates, such as Bagley and Hirsch, insist that teachers exhibit mastery of specific content knowledge. Knowledge of general teaching skills is not sufficient to effectively prepare students and achieve measurable learning objectives.

In this view, the metaphor for the role of the teacher would be Teacher as Content Knowledge Expert. The teacher is responsible for ensuring students have learned the necessary material. The assumption is the teacher possesses knowledge that the student does not. Therefore, the teacher is also the Transmitter of Information.

TEACHER AS SOURCE OF VALUES

The teacher serves as a Source of Values. In this philosophical perspective, the purpose of school is to acculturate students into a national culture of shared knowledge and democratic values.

What Is the Role of the Student in Learning Essential Knowledge?

STUDENT AS RECEIVER OF INFORMATION

In the classroom vignette, the students acted in the role of Student as Receiver of Information. The teacher carefully presented the content, directing students to identify each specific piece of information. Students were asked to recall prior learning and connect new information to their existing knowledge. The role of the student is to master a sequential comprehensive body of required knowledge.

STUDENT AS ACHIEVER OF STANDARDS

Objective assessment methods are key to determining mastery. Therefore, the student also acts in the role of Achiever of Standards. Performance is evaluated according to objective standards and criteria that apply to all students. Standardized testing is the common method for assessing that students have achieved standards.

STUDENT AS PRODUCTIVE CITIZEN

Among the reasons given for cultural literacy is to prepare to enter the workforce and begin a career. A culturally literate person contributes productively to the economic system of society.

Design

For a school designed to teach essential knowledge (Table 5.1), the curriculum would consist of core subjects sequenced by grade level. The school would hire well-prepared teachers who demonstrate mastery of content area knowledge. A teacher-directed pedagogy would be responsible for imparting the same basic information to all students.

Students would demonstrate competency through standardized assessments that verify mastery of common content knowledge.

How Are Schools Organized? Questions about the Role of the School

The first step to teaching cultural literacy is to identify and compile the essential information. The publication of *Cultural Literacy* (1987) and the dictionaries of cultural literacy that followed represent an attempt to explicitly provide a descriptive list. Such a list is not intended to be definitive, but aims for a level of competence. Hirsch recognizes "the traditionalism inherent" in the list, for it "must necessarily emphasize traditional materials" (p. 137). He does not view this as promoting any particular political bias, as the list represents accepted cultural knowledge consistent with the goals of universal education.

The list suggests a starting point for formulating a national curriculum. Resistance to teaching a national curriculum is to be expected. Although mandating a comprehensive curriculum at the federal level may not be feasible, schools should agree on fundamental core content and a grade-by-grade sequence. The basis of a literate education is a "national vocabulary," Hirsch (1987) explains (p. 139). He argues, "To repudiate the idea of a shared extensive curriculum is necessarily to accept the idea of an unshared extensive curriculum" (p. 144). A fragmented approach to curriculum will not ensure competence.

Table 5.1 Design a School (Essential Knowledge)

Purpose of Education	Learn essential knowledge
Curriculum	Common curriculum, core knowledge, cultural literacy
Instruction	Systematic, sequential, mastery learning
Role of Teacher	Content area specialist, transmitter of information, source of values
Role of Student	Receiver of information, achiever of standards
Role of School	Acculturation

Core Knowledge Schools

The Core Knowledge Foundation has developed the *Core Knowledge Sequence* (2013) to provide schools with a curriculum that describes specific, grade-level content knowledge. The Foundation publishes other educational books and instructional materials, offers professional development for teachers and administrators, and supports the establishment of Core Knowledge schools. Many schools integrate the *Core Knowledge Sequence* into their curriculum. Those demonstrating particular fidelity to the Core Knowledge content may be designated as Core Knowledge Schools of Distinction.

For example, Grayhawk Elementary School in Scottsdale, Arizona has offered a Core Knowledge curriculum for grade K-6 since opening in 1988. Grayhawk provides a detailed school-wide curriculum plan as well as domain and topic maps. The school has a Core Knowledge coordinator on staff to provide ongoing professional development. The school prides itself on purposeful student engagement. Academic and domain-specific vocabulary are infused into lessons and learning activities, and multiple opportunities are offered to practice using content-based knowledge and skills and transfer understanding in new applications.

Liberty Common School, a public charter school in Fort Collins, Colorado, is another K-6 school where continuous teacher collaboration produces a shared curriculum. The school's motto, *Commvnis Scientia, Virtvtes, et Prudentia* ("Common Knowledge, Common Virtues, Common Sense") embodies Core Knowledge principles (Liberty Common School, n. d., Home Page section). For example, Latin is fully integrated within all grade levels. Teachers and administrators plan together and engage in professional development activities to enhance their pedagogical and content knowledge. The cumulative curriculum teaches prerequisite knowledge while avoiding unnecessarily repeating content.

A unique example of a public charter school, Thomas Jefferson Classical Academy in North Carolina offers a college-preparatory education to students in grades Kindergarten through 12. Core Knowledge forms the foundation of the sequenced K-8 program. Grade-level teams collaborate to align instruction and assessment to the context-specific curriculum. The school employs a full-time Core Knowledge coordinator, and encourages parents to support their children at home through resources such as Hirsch's *What Your ___ Grader Needs to Know* series.

Common characteristics of Core Knowledge schools include the commitment of the administration to the adoption and implementation of the *Core Knowledge Sequence*, the integration of core knowledge into a coherent, comprehensive, content-rich curriculum, the collaboration of teachers in planning, aligning, and implementing instruction and assessment, and the cumulative building upon shared knowledge across grade levels.

No Child Left Behind

In a public school setting, curriculum standards and requirements had been traditionally selected and approved by local school boards. Over time, state boards of education began to exercise greater control and provide consistency among school districts. Private or independent schools possess more autonomy over the development of their curriculum, although some may belong to an association of schools or otherwise affiliate with peer schools. The federal government has no constitutional authority over the governance of schools. However, through laws designed to ensure equitable access to publicly funded services (such as IDEA, the Individuals with Disabilities Education Act), and others to ensure the civil rights of citizens (such as Title IX, regarding discrimination on the basis of gender), the federal government has increased its influence over how schools operate.

The Elementary and Secondary Education Act (ESEA), first authorized in 1965, offers federal assistance to grant educational opportunities to students previously underserved in public schools. The Act was reauthorized in 2002 under the name *No Child Left Behind* (NCLB). To receive continued federal funding, NCLB compels states to establish high curriculum standards and to measure annual progress in reading and mathematics in grades 3 through 8 (and at least once during grades 10 through 12) using standardized assessments. Testing in science began in 2007–8. Schools are held accountable for demonstrating Adequate Yearly Progress (AYP) on the measures. Based on testing results, schools in need of improvement receive assistance. A consequence of not meeting AYP over an extended period may be the restructuring of a school. In 2012, several states were granted waivers (or conditional waivers) from some of the requirements of the act.

NCLB does not impose a national curriculum on states. Each state is permitted to establish its own standards, develop its own curriculum, and develop or select its own testing instruments. Reporting and dissemination of testing results is required, however, and funding is withheld from states deciding not to participate. Despite not mandating a uniform national curriculum, NCLB has had an effect on state content standards. NCLB states, "State assessments must be aligned with challenging academic content standards and challenging academic achievement standards" (NCLB, 2002). The language of the act also defines competence as the mastery of core subject-matter according to two levels of achievement (proficient and advanced). NCLB identifies core academic subjects as English, reading or language arts, mathematics, science, foreign languages, civics and government, economics, arts, history, and geography. The emphasis on testing reading and mathematics, however, implicitly identifies those two areas as most essential.

NCLB also requires standards for the hiring and retention of highly qualified teachers. Each state establishes specific criteria, but in general a highly qualified teacher is certified to teach the core academic subjects of the classroom placement. Teacher candidates must take and pass texts of minimum competency in general content knowledge (reading, writing, and mathematics) and specific content area knowledge and pedagogy.

Common Core State Standards

In 2009, the Council of Chief State School Officers and the National Governors Association formed the Common Core State Standards Initiative to develop shared national curriculum standards. This consortium resulted in the publication of Common Core State Standards in English/Language Arts and Literacy (including literacy in History/Social Studies, Science, and Technical subjects) and Mathematics (CCSSO & NGA, 2010). As of 2014, forty-three states and the District of Columbia (as well as four U.S. territories and the Department of Defense Education Activity) adopted the K-12 College- and Career-Readiness standards. The Partnership for Assessment of Readiness for College and Careers (PARCC) and the Smarter Balanced Assessment Consortium represent a collaboration of states to develop assessments to measure the standards.

As part of the American Recovery and Reinvestment Act of 2009, the Race to the Top program offers funds to states that, among other criteria, adopt common content standards and assessments developed jointly with other states. The standards must support college and career readiness (although states are not required to specifically adopt the Common Core State Standards).

The Common Core State Standards Initiative anticipates collaboration among educators to interpret and implement the standards. Sharing knowledge will increase opportunities for collegiality and raise the level of teacher professionalism. "One hallmark of a professional is mastery of a body of knowledge" writes John Kendall (2011), Senior Director in Research at Mid-continent Research for Education and Learning (p. 31). "In a sense," Kendall continues, "the Common Core 'universalizes' a body of knowledge that is expected of all teachers" (p. 32). For students, the Common Core communicates a clear set of standards to prepare for college and entering a career. The standards do not classify these as two distinct paths. "Owing to the nature of today's career opportunities, students must be college-ready to be career-ready" (p. 39).

In addition to the Common Core, content areas have prepared standards that identify a core body of content knowledge. A goal of the Next Generation Science Standards "was to identify the core conceptual knowledge that all students need to know" as well as preparing future scientists, engineers, technologists, and technicians of the future (NGSS, Appendix C, p. 3). In addition, the standards state that science and technical knowledge and skills are vital to the "national long-term economic security" in a global economy (NGSS, Appendix C, p. 1). The new standards integrate content knowledge with application of skills. Goals of integrated science, technology, engineering, and mathematics (STEM) education include the development of STEM literacy, 21st century competencies, and workforce readiness (Honey, Pearson, & Schweingruber, 2015).

The College, Career, and Civic Life (2015) Framework for Social Studies Standards states, "The goal of knowledgeable, thinking, and active citizens . . . is universal" (p. 5). The C3 framework guides, but does not prescribe, the selection of content knowledge in the social studies. However, the framework contains key concepts and disciplinary ideas to support states in organizing a set of standards that prepare students for college, careers, and civic life.

The Framework for 21st Century Learning defines interdisciplinary knowledge and skills students need to succeed in work, life, and citizenship. The outcomes represent the "skills, knowledge and expertise students should master to succeed in work and life in the 21st century" (P21, 2015, About Us section, para 1). The framework incorporates core academic content knowledge with essential life and career skills needed to thrive in a competitive global economy.

How Does a School Designed to Teach Essential Knowledge Define an Educated Person?

Core knowledge and initiatives such as those described above define the purpose of school as learning knowledge essential for attending college or preparing for a career, and urge consensus among states to offer a common curriculum. According to an essentialist perspective, an educated person is a civically competent and economically productive citizen participating in a democratic society, sharing common cultural knowledge and national values.

Evaluate

Consistency

In the lesson on the Gettysburg Address, instruction focuses on learning basic facts as well as understanding the meaning the content has in the context of the national culture. The topic represents essential knowledge students need to know as American citizens, connecting references in the speech to core values. A school that follows a core curriculum would explicitly describe and define the content knowledge all students are expected to learn. Student choice would be limited to a standardized curriculum.

How does essential knowledge differ from perennial knowledge? In Chapter 3, we learned that Perennialists believe universal knowledge and truths do not fundamentally change. Essentialism embraces much of the same basic curriculum for the purpose of developing cultural literacy and participating in a society of shared knowledge. In many ways, this view correlates to how Hutchins envisions educated citizens joining in the "Great Conversation." This view also reflects belief in a basic human nature that possesses common characteristics and shared values.

Essentialism differs from Perennialism by recognizing that as society changes over time, new ideas and facts become introduced into the culture, adding to the growing body of essential knowledge. Reliance on a canon of "great" works to the exclusion of other sources of knowledge does not ensure that all students learn the information and skills necessary to function in contemporary society. For example, *The Great Books* series includes documents integral to the study of the United States such as the Declaration of Independence, the Articles of Confederation, the Constitution, and the Federalist. However, the series does not include the Gettysburg Address. One could argue that the Gettysburg Address belongs in the canon of great texts produced in the western world – and the Address appears in *Cultural Literacy*, the several dictionaries of cultural literacy, and the *Core Knowledge Sequence*.

Equally important, the education required to enter the workforce and pursue a career requires current knowledge. Hirsch and the Core Knowledge Foundation acknowledge that, beyond a common core curriculum, schools can and should incorporate knowledge that the state, school district, and/or local community may deem appropriate. However, this position presumes acquiring a comprehensive, cumulative, and sequential body of common knowledge among all learners. Additional content integrated into the curriculum should supplement, not alter, the core knowledge sequence.

Essentialism does not claim direct transmission of information is the only method of instruction, but advocates of this perspective have faulted the use of skill-based learning activities for failing to rigorously focus on teaching concrete facts and principles. Bagley (1938) concedes that activity and project methods may have value but these experiences should not "substitute for systematic and sequential learning" (p. 246). Hirsch (1987) argues that skill-based instruction can mistakenly dismiss factual content as irrelevant and deprive students of vital background information. "Facts are essential components of the basic skills that a child entering the culture must have," Hirsch contends (p. 28).

Core Knowledge Foundation emphatically states, "The Core Knowledge Sequence is not a list of facts to be memorized. Rather, it is a guide to coherent content from grade to grade, designed to encourage cumulative academic progress" (Core Knowledge Foundation, 2013, p. vi). However, Hirsch repeatedly asserts that learning is dependent upon the accumulation of prior knowledge that resides in one's memory, and the Core Knowledge Foundations implies that all of the specific grade-level topics are indispensable. The *Core Knowledge Sequence* guide emphasizes, "Effective Core Knowledge teachers recognize that topics from the Sequence must not be eliminated or changed from one grade level to another" and strongly discourages "picking and choosing" from among the content (p. vi).

Given the amount of content contained in the *Core Knowledge Sequence* (not to mention the dictionaries of cultural literacy and the grade-level series of books), teachers may wonder how to impart this wealth of information to students in a systematic and sequential manner without devoting large portions of instructional time to direct instruction. Critics accuse the process of accumulating cultural facts as mistaking literacy for memorization. The view of an educated person is one who has mastered the list. The cultural literacy approach reinforces the view that knowledge "can be directly imparted to students" (Estes, Gutman, & Harrison, 1988, p. 16). Learning is demonstrated through recall of facts and measured using objective assessments, rather than understanding the information in context. These critics argue that "telling is not teaching, told is not taught" (p. 17). Information and knowledge are not synonymous. Possessing information is not the same as having knowledge (Paul, 2012). Critical literacy, as compared to cultural literacy, requires students to interpret and evaluate information, not merely accept given information as accurate and important. This involves applying critical thinking skills of inference and analysis. This tension between memorization and understanding reveals a possible inconsistency between the goals of the curriculum and methods of instruction.

Compatibility

According to Hunter (2004), the purpose of instruction is to acquire information. "Information constitutes the foundation for learning and thinking," she states. "Once we have adequate information, we can proceed to build concepts, develop generalizations, and engage in higher level thinking" (p. 46). Hunter insists her model is not a direct teaching model but a teacher decision-making model. Nevertheless, the teacher must possess content area expertise, present information clearly and effectively, and demonstrate or model for students before they attempt practice. In addition, the model emphasizes retention and recall of information. The goal is for students to be able to learn independently, after they have demonstrated mastery of the skills necessary to complete the task and achieve the objectives established by the teacher.

Although the teacher in the vignette occasionally asks her students questions, she does not conduct a Socratic discussion. The teacher delivers knowledge and values rather than eliciting individual interpretations. Neither does the lesson employ the scientific method or inquiry approach. Analysis of the Gettysburg Address centers more on the teacher imparting the meaning to the students. Students are not asked to elaborate on their responses, nor do they scrutinize the logic of the speech's argument, defend its claims, or justify its views. The content is assumed to possess inherent, indisputable truth that the students are expected to accept.

When examining the curriculum for objectivity or universality, one asks how the required information has been selected, what are the criteria, and who makes the decisions. In a subject area such as history, *truth* and *fact* can be argued from different points of view. Participants may ascribe multiple subjective meanings to a verifiable event. For a topic such as the Civil War, with categorically labeled opposing sides, instruction naturally lends itself to considering opposing viewpoints. Yet those positions may be reduced to simple dualities: Union and Confederate, slaveholder and slave, industrial and agrarian. The complexities and nuances of numerous perspectives that do not readily fall under one heading or the other may be overlooked. Moreover, from an Essentialist perspective, certain content should be taught that aids in the acculturation of students and results in shared knowledge. The presence of myriad competing and perhaps subjective standpoints leads to a fractured curriculum.

Hirsch argues the community or culture at large decides what knowledge to incorporate into a core curriculum. Traditions, values, and ideals remain relatively constant from one generation to the next, or at least as each succeeding generation decides this to be their preference. Some information does become outdated or even discredited, but a core set of basic knowledge persists. Hirsch (2009–10) contends, "The taken-for-granted knowledge in the American public sphere is finite and definable" (p. 13).

This position may lead to incompatibility between the curriculum and pedagogy. How well would Hirsch's arguments stand up to interrogation by a figure such as Socrates? Or the other philosophers we have studied so far? What is the role of inference in learning a core knowledge curriculum? How consistent are interpretations of cultural knowledge such as historic events, autobiographies and biographies, primary as well as secondary sources?

This dispute relates to how a school defines an educated person. One must ask if sharing specific information in common translates to possessing essential knowledge. Will the acquisition, retention, and recall of discrete bits of cultural information lead to becoming educated? How deeply does one need to comprehend the information to understand it? In the digital age, how accurate and reliable are online sources of information? In the absence of refined critical thinking skills, how does the learner discern and discriminate? Are learning a core knowledge curriculum and developing critical thinking skills inherently at odds?

Coherent

To be coherent, a core knowledge school would identify the content all students should possess. However, is core knowledge a set quantity or a moving target? Since the publication of *The Dictionary of Cultural Literacy* in 1988, revised editions have been produced. For each succeeding generation, more core knowledge is accumulated. When would a school know a student has achieved sufficient core knowledge to be culturally literate? What room does that leave for offering electives or options to students?

A coherent educational program would also exhibit consistent pedagogy. Mastery learning identifies checkpoints or milestones. This implies a fixed body of information that can be measured, scored, and quantified. Mastery also implies an endpoint, a final outcome to be achieved, based on external, objective standards. Some critics suggest inquiry learning and core knowledge are incompatible.

One may also ask if the primary purpose of providing a core curriculum is cultural or economic. Bagley (1938), writing during the Great Depression, identifies economic as well as cultural reasons for adopting his essentialist platform. He cites several major changes that have affected the nation, including the transition from a predominantly agricultural to an industrial society, the rise in immigration, the growth of cities, and the increasing mobility of the population. He argues that the states that have best handled these challenges are those that have achieved the greatest level of assimilation during these times of shifting demographics. These states have also been "least dependent upon the federal government for 'relief' during the depression years" (p. 243). New opportunities await those educated to meet the demand for different kinds of occupations in the rapidly changing and volatile economy. An essential education safeguards not only against threats to the democratic system but also the perils facing the economy. "Generally speaking, then," Bagley writes, "'social security,' like responsible freedom, has been a conquest not a gift" (p. 256).

"To meet the needs of the wider economy," Hirsch (1987) argues, "the modern industrial nation requires widespread literacy" (p. 73). Literacy, as Hirsch defines it, consists of a common set of cultural facts. He declares that "literate culture has become the common currency for social and economic exchange in our democracy" (p. 22). "Most modern nations impose [compulsory education] because neither a democracy nor a modern economy can function without citizens who have enough shared knowledge to be loyal, competent, and able to communicate with one another" (Hirsh, 2009–10, p. 11). "We all have a stake in promoting an effective public sphere and a vibrant economy through our schools" (p. 12).

In justifying mastery learning, Bloom (1971) states, "The complexity of skills required by the work force of any highly developed nation like the United States" requires that students "acquire the skills and knowledge necessary to sustain the society's growth" (p. 48). He defends this position by citing evidence that investment in human resources has a greater rate of return than investment in capitol. This defines, at least in part, the education of students in terms of its economic value. Like Hirsch, Bloom also expresses a concern for the intellectual consequences resulting from a lack of specific concrete knowledge. However, he returns to his argument regarding the detrimental effects a knowledge deficit would have on the quality of the workforce.

As we have investigated, initiatives such as Common Core standards, NGSS science standards, STEM education, the C3 social studies framework, and 21st century skills all emphasize career readiness and workforce preparedness. Does a core curriculum equate cultural literacy with economic necessity? Can a school offer a coherent program in core knowledge without stressing the economic interests of society and the learner?

Reflect

On the *Continuum of Educational Philosophy*, the curriculum, pedagogy, and purpose of education have moved closer to a place where objective, universal knowledge and values meet current social and economic needs. The curriculum is fixed in great part by identifying essential knowledge all students should know, but somewhat flexible by incorporating new knowledge as it emerges. Student interests do not drive the change, however, as others continue to hold the position of authority on what content is included in the curriculum and how learning is assessed.

How Do Your Prior Observations and Experiences Relate to a Curriculum Designed to Teach Essential Knowledge?

How has the curriculum in schools you have observed or attended represented essential knowledge? Has core content been required that all students should learn? How does that content reflect an interest in developing cultural literacy?

Is the knowledge the school provides open to scrutiny? Can a student dispute knowledge offered as accepted facts or assumptions?

In what ways does the educational program prepare one for college and career, as well as for participation in society as a citizen? What distinctions can be made between one's civic responsibilities and productively contributing to the economy?

How Do Your Prior Observations and Experiences Relate to a Pedagogy Designed to Teach Essential Knowledge?

How has instruction you have observed or experienced centered on acquiring essential content? Was mastery a goal? Was memorization a means to achieving mastery? How was literacy, competence, or mastery assessed?

How Do Your Prior Observations and Experiences Relate to a School Designed to Teach Essential Knowledge?

Have you observed or taught in schools that explicitly state the purpose of education is to learn essential or core knowledge? How does this affect the organization or administration of the school? Were curricular decisions made by others and mandated to teachers? Or were teachers involved in the development of the curriculum? Did teachers, individually or collaboratively, make decisions about instructional methods, or did the school impose expectations about instruction that were appraised by a standardized evaluation system?

Did teachers choose their own assessment methods or did the school, local school system, or state school system determine the assessment process and how results would be used? Did the assessment methods align with the purpose of learning essential knowledge to become culturally literate? Did student achievement relate to college or career preparation, or to other goals?

How Do Your Own Practices and Beliefs Relate to the Purpose of Education as Learning Essential Knowledge?

You may have been a student or taught in a school that followed a core curriculum and assessed achievement through standardized testing. Were your educational beliefs compatible with this purpose of education? In what ways would you have preferred to learn or to teach that would have been compatible with this purpose of education? Did you agree with the school's perspective or detect discrepancies between your views and the school's priorities? Do you find any differences between how a student perceives this purpose of education and how teachers view it? Would one's perspective change from being a student in this system of education to becoming a teacher?

In Part II, we have asked the wonder question, *"What if . . . the purpose of education were to learn objective and universal knowledge?"* Three purposes of education relate to that overarching question: 1) learning enduring ideas and eternal truths, 2) learning structure and principles, and 3) learning essential knowledge. In general, all three purposes detect a rational order to existence that assumes objective, universal knowledge can be discovered and identified. The differences concern what sources of knowledge are trusted and valued, what instructional methods best direct the learner to attaining this knowledge, how learning this knowledge can be assessed, and the role of the teacher and the student engaged in this process. All three purposes fall within a range on the left-hand side of the *Continuum of Educational Philosophy*, which values ideas as expressed by an education in the liberal arts.

Alfred North Whitehead (1929/1949) states that the aim of education is "the apprehension of general ideas, intellectual habits of mind, and pleasurable interest in mental achievement" (p. 18). Ultimately, the perspectives we have investigated would agree. As Robert M. Hutchins (1952), founder and editor of the *Great Books*, declares, "The aim of liberal education is human excellence" (Vol. 1, p. 3).

References

Bagley, W. C. (1938). An essentialist's platform for the advancement of American education. *Educational Administration and Supervision, 24*, 241–256.

Bloom, B. S. (1968). Learning for mastery. *Evaluation Comment, 1*(2), 1–12.

Bloom, B. S. (1971). Mastery learning. In J. H. Block (Ed.), *Mastery learning: Theory and practice* (pp. 47–63). New York, NY: Holt, Rinehart & Winston.

Bloom, B. S. (1974). An introduction to mastery learning theory. In J. H. Block (Ed.), *Schools, society and mastery learning* (pp. 3–14). New York, NY: Holt, Rinehart & Winston.

Core Knowledge Foundation. (2013). *Core knowledge sequence: Content and skill guidelines for grades K–8.* [PDF file]. Charlottesville, VA: Core Knowledge Foundation. Retrieved from http://www.coreknowledge.org/mimik/mimik_uploads/documents/480/CKFSequence_Rev.pdf

Department of Education. (2009). *Race to the top program executive summary.* [PDF File]. Washington, DC: U.S. Department of Education. Retrieved from http://www2.ed.gov/programs/racetothetop/executive-summary.pdf

Eggen, P. D., & Kauchak, D. P. (2006). *Strategies and models for teachers: Teaching content and thinking skills* (5th ed.). Boston, MA: Allyn & Bacon.

Estes, T. H., Gutman, C. J., & Harrison, E. K. (1988). Cultural literacy: What every educator needs to know. *Educational Leadership, 46*(1), 14–17.

Fisher, D., & Frey, N. (2008). *Better learning through structured teaching: A framework for the gradual release of responsibility.* Alexandria, VA: ASCD.

Hirsch, E. D. (1987). *Cultural literacy: What every American needs to know.* Boston, MA: Houghton Mifflin.

Hirsch, E. D., Kett, J. F., & Trefil, J. (1988). *The dictionary of cultural literacy.* Boston, MA: Houghton Mifflin.

Hirsch, E. D. (Ed.). (1993). *What your fifth grader needs to know: Fundamentals of a good fifth-grade education.* New York, NY: Doubleday.

Hirsch, E. D., Kett, J. F., & Trefil, J. (2002). *The new dictionary of cultural literacy: What every American needs to know* (3rd ed.). Boston, MA: Houghton Mifflin.

Hirsch, E. D. (2004). *The new first dictionary of cultural literacy: What your child needs to know* (3rd ed.). Boston, MA: Houghton Mifflin.

Hirsch, E. D. (2009–10, Winter). Creating a curriculum for the American people: Our democracy depends on shared knowledge. *American Educator, 33*(4), 13.

Honey, M., Pearson, G., & Schweingruber, H. (Eds.) (2015). *STEM integration in K-12 education: Status, prospects, and an agenda for research.* Washington, DC: National Academies Press.

Hunter, M. (1994). *Enhanced instruction.* New York, NY: Macmillan.

Hunter, M. (2004). *Mastery teaching: Increasing instructional effectiveness in elementary and secondary schools.* (Revised and updated by R. Hunter). Thousand Oaks, CA: Corwin.

Hutchins, R. M. (Ed.). (1952). *Great books of the western world.* Chicago, IL: Encyclopedia Britannica.

Joyce, B., Weil, M., & Calhoun, E. (2014). *Models of teaching* (9th ed.). Upper Saddle River, NJ: Pearson.

Kendall, J. (2011). *Understanding common core state standards.* Alexandria, VA: ASCD.

Liberty Common School. (n.d.). Home page. [Website]. Retrieved from http://www.libertycommon.org

National Commission on Excellence in Education. (1983). *A nation at risk: The imperative for educational reform.* Washington, DC: The Commission.

National Council for the Social Studies. (2013). *The college, career, and civic life (C3) framework for social studies standards: Guidance for enhancing the rigor of K–12 civics, economics, geography, and history*. [PDF file]. Silver Spring, MD: National Council for the Social Studies.

National Governors Association Center for Best Practices, & Council of Chief State School Officers. (2010). Common Core State Standards for mathematics. [Website]. Retrieved from http://www.corestandards.org

NGSS Lead States. (2013). Next generation science standards: For states, by states. Appendix C: College and career readiness. [Website]. Retrieved from http://www.nextgenscience.org/next-generation-science-standards

No Child Left Behind. (2002). *A desktop reference*. [PDF file]. Washington, DC: US Department of Education. Retrieved from https://www2.ed.gov/admins/lead/account/nclbreference/reference.pdf

Partnership for 21st Century Skills. (P21) (n.d.) Framework for 21st Century Learning. [Website]. Retrieved from http://www.p21.org/about-us/p21-framework

Paul, R. W. (2012). Critical and cultural literacy: Where E. D. Hirsch goes wrong. In J. Willsen & A. J. A. Binker (Eds.). *Critical Thinking: What every person needs to survive in a rapidly changing world* (pp. 527–533). Tomales, CA: Foundation for Critical Thinking.

Pearson, P. D., & Gallagher, M. C. (1983). The instruction of reading comprehension. *Contemporary Educational Psychology, 8*, 317–344.

Reinhartz, J., & Van Cleaf, D. (1986). *Teach-practice-apply: The TPA instruction model, K-8*. Washington, DC: National Education Association.

Whitehead, A. N. (1949). *The aims of education and other essays*. New York, NY: New American Library. (Original work published 1929.)

Part III

What If . . . The Purpose of Education Were to Learn Subjective, Changing Knowledge?

Part III asks, "*What if . . . the purpose of education were to learn subjective, changing knowledge?*" Related to this overall wonder question, the chapters investigate purposes of education based on the natural development of the child, a child's interests and needs, solving practical problems, learning as a community, transforming society, developing one's self-identity and exercising personal freedom.

In Part II, we investigated educational philosophies associated with learning objective, universal knowledge. These perspectives hold a rational, objective view of reality based on absolute ideas, universal principles, and essential knowledge. Even empirical observations of nature (advocated by Aristotle, Bacon, and others) place great emphasis on deriving universal principles.

In contrast, Part III examines the point of view that the purpose of education is to learn to adapt to changing situations and construct knowledge based on subjective, personal experience. These perspectives consider multiple possible interpretations of reality and accept socially and individually constructed sources of knowledge. Empirical observation takes precedence over pure rational reasoning, no longer seeking to ascertain the existence of general or universal principles. Truth and values may be relative, depending on the social and cultural context and one's personal, subjective experiences. By valuing the individual perceptions of the learner, we begin to move from an ideas-focused, teacher-directed perspective on education to a process-oriented, child-centered perspective.

The educational philosophies in Part III place less emphasis on mastering an established body of knowledge than on learning a flexible, ever-evolving curriculum. Student-centered instruction begins to replace teacher-directed methods, with the process of learning becoming as (or more) important a priority as measuring and reporting achievement of pre-determined outcomes. Students may explore in a more open-ended fashion, providing an increasing level of responsibility and exercising greater choice in the topics of study, kinds of learning activities, and types of assessment. The school takes into account individual differences and modifies instruction to adapt to learners' needs and interests.

6 What If . . . The Purpose of Education Were to Learn According to Natural Development?

Wonder

Chapter 6 poses the wonder question, *"What if . . . the purpose of education were to learn according to natural development?"*

On the *Continuum of Educational Philosophy* (Figure 6.1), we begin to explore philosophical perspectives that view reality as based on personal experience and subjective interpretation. Rather than seeking absolute or universal knowledge, we shift to learning based on context. Prescribed, standardized outcomes are replaced by a focus on the individual child's interests, needs, and growth.

Observe

Classroom Vignette: Free Play

On a crisp autumn morning, students sprint down the slope and into the woods. Twigs snap beneath their footsteps. Immediately, a half-dozen students drag fallen limbs to construct a fort. Limbs are wedged diagonally between the crooks of standing trees to form the frame while rocks and dry

EDUCATIONAL PRACTICES

RATIONAL	EMPIRICAL
Ideas-Focused	Experience-Focused
Content-Oriented	Process-Oriented
Fixed Curriculum	Flexible Curriculum
Teacher-Centered	Student-Centered
Teacher-Directed	Self-Directed
Pre-Determined Outcomes	Open-Ended Exploration
Whole-Class Activities	Differentiated/Individualized Activities

Objective External Reality	Internal Subjective Reality
Absolute Universal Truth	Changing Relative Truth
Pre-Existing Knowledge	Constructed Knowledge
Knowledge Independent of Experience	Knowledge Dependent on Experience
Autonomous Knowledge	Interdependent Knowledge
Absolute Universal Values	Relative Local Values
Values Independent of Experience	Values Dependent on Experience

PHILOSOPHICAL PERSPECTIVES

Figure 6.1 Continuum of Educational Philosophy (Natural Development)

leaves are piled in front to make a wall. The enormous hollowed-out stump of an ancient oak tree is incorporated into the design. Once completed, a red flag is affixed to a tree to mark the fort. Delegations from neighboring forts visit, bearing goods to barter and trade in the fort economy. Stones of various shapes and colors are swapped for nuts, berries, wild apples, and other found natural objects. All agree to comply with a "fort treaty" that stipulates guidelines for conduct in the culture of the fort community.

Other children use the wooded area for different pursuits. A group builds a dam in the stream, hauling logs and rocks to the construction site. A pair of children lifts stones searching for salamanders, one group tracks animal prints in the mud, while two other children speculate that bats reside in the hole of a tree. Children forage for acorns, spot different species of birds, or simply toss stones in the water to watch them splash. One child sits alone digging in the dirt with a stick, laying out a make-believe city.

Shouts and cheers careen across the basketball court where a friendly game ensues. On the adjacent playground, younger students scramble up the ladder to the spiral slide, crawl through the large concrete pipe, hang from the monkey bars, or swing on the swings. Two children shriek with delight as they run with a bubble wand. Sunlight dances off the floating spheres as another child leaps trying to catch each one before it pops. Some children organize games, such as kickball or tag. Others create original games of pretend. On the periphery, pairs or small groups of children engage in quieter activities. Some play with the buckets and shovels in the sandbox while others draw with sidewalk chalk. Students may bring their own toys or choose from a bin of various-size balls, Frisbees, plastic baseball bats and balls, a bowling set, and a host of other colorful objects. In addition to commercially manufactured playthings, the playground includes items such as an old tractor tire, wooden boards, a discarded hose, and sundry yard and garden implements.

Outdoor play is more than recess for these children. Rather than a break from learning, the school considers the outdoors part of the learning environment and free play a component of the curriculum. While some schools have reduced recess or eliminated it altogether, all of the students in this school play outside twice a day, and again in the after-school program. The sustained blocks of unstructured time allow students to experience diverse play activities as well as become occupied in complex and imaginative games. Teachers observe the younger children at play and record notes on their development. These observations provide valuable information on children's motor skills, social interactions, problem-solving skills and strategies, use of language and nonverbal communication, decision-making, types of conflict resolution, and other physical and emotional responses to the rich variety of stimuli outdoor play offers. The teachers regard outdoor playtime as an opportunity to identify student needs and interests, helping them plan learning activities and modify assessment methods.

Investigate

As the vignette illustrates, this perspective values free outdoor play and interacting with nature in an unstructured manner. To examine philosophies that have influenced this view of the purpose of education, we will investigate the following inquiry questions:

- What Do Teachers Teach? Questions about the Curriculum
- How Do Teachers Teach? Questions about Pedagogy
- How Are Schools Organized? Questions about the Role of the School

What Do Teachers Teach? Questions about the Curriculum

"Observe nature and follow the path she marks out."

(Rousseau)

French philosopher Jean-Jacques Rousseau (1712–78) denies a rational, single source of all knowledge and rejects absolutes. "We can never know absolute good or evil," Rousseau (1762/1962) claims. "Everything in this life is mixed" (p. 34). Neither does he accept the concept of innate or latent knowledge. "We are born with a capacity for learning, but know nothing and distinguish nothing" (p. 21). Instead, Rousseau identifies three sources of knowledge: other people, physical things, and nature. Education from others and education from experience with things in the physical environment often draw us in different and competing directions. Rousseau insists that education follow nature's order, which arises from the inclinations of the individual. Therefore, children should be educated according to natural stages of development. "Observe nature and follow the path she marks out," Rousseau advises (p. 17).

From this perspective arises an emphasis in education on the developmental stages of a child (such as in the learning theories of Piaget) and developmentally appropriate instruction and materials. Rousseau recommends treating children according to their age level. Rousseau held a keen distrust of social institutions and cautions not to impel children to conform to social expectations early in their development. "Everything is good as it comes from the hand of the Maker of the world," he says, "but degenerates once it gets into the hands of man" (p. 11).

In his book *Emile* (1762/1962), Rousseau invents a fictitious child to illustrate his concepts about education. Emile learns in a natural environment, away from the corrupting influence of social institutions. In the book, Rousseau acts as a tutor for Emile, whose natural interests guide his learning. His first impulse is to learn through the senses. "The first reason of man is a reason of the senses," Rousseau insists (p. 54). "It is through the senses that we come to the intellect" (p. 72). Rousseau describes four stages in Emile's education, from infancy and childhood to adolescence and into young adulthood. Only after age twelve does a child develop the capacity for reason.

In childhood, Rousseau eschews having Emile learn abstract concepts and generalizations, believing detached facts difficult for a child to grasp and retain. Instead, he favors concrete activities. "Reading is the greatest plague of childhood," Rousseau remarks (p. 51). A child "reads better in the book of nature" (p. 66). Students should be free to discover through open exploration. Emile learns in an open-ended, non-prescriptive manner, through spontaneous actions in direct contact with the natural environment. "You can be sure that he will learn more from an hour's work than he would remember after a day's explanations" Rousseau observes (p. 86).

Rousseau complains that learning by habit or through a systematic process prepares the child to enter society and assume a role determined by others. An inherent source of tension in education is whether to educate according to the needs and interests of society or for the needs and interests of the individual. One direction leads to conformity and domination, the other to personal freedom. Rousseau's perspective shifts the focus from the interests of society to the natural inclinations of the individual. A child's education should lead to harmony with the natural world rather than serving the will of society. Rousseau seeks to liberate the child from the constraints of society, to fulfill obligations to social life in a way that preserves the individual's natural sense of independence and integrity.

Stages of Development

Johann Pestalozzi (Swiss, 1746–1827) expresses similar beliefs in his approach to education. "From the moment in which his mind can receive impressions from Nature," Pestalozzi (1951) remarks, "Nature teaches him" (p. 57). Education through the senses should be the initial source of learning. Education should focus on the child gaining "intelligent sense-impressions of all things" (p. 58). Sense-impressions of nature are the true foundation of human knowledge; all other knowledge follows as a result.

Living things in nature grow in stages, Pestalozzi observes. A child should flourish in the same way a tree gradually sprouts from a shoot to a fully developed trunk with branches and leaves.

Human nature, Pestalozzi reasons, follows the same laws as the physical world. Therefore, all learning connects to the senses. Nature is the source of all knowledge and the foundation of all learning principles. From the senses, ideas and understanding grow. The child's learning should proceed in stages from simple tasks to complex reasoning.

Voicing a sentiment resembling Rousseau's, Pestalozzi (1951) states, "Nature only does us good; she alone leads us uncorrupted and unshaken to truth and wisdom" (p. 65). Therefore, books and verbal sources of information should not be foisted upon a child. "Not art, not books, but life itself is the true basis of teaching and education" (p. 36). Our perceptions of reality are shaped by experiences in nature, not by words. Experience is the source of truth. Children should gain knowledge through direct observation, interaction with objects, and physically productive activities.

Friedrich Froebel (German, 1782–1852), who studied under Pestalozzi, founded the first kindergarten (translated as "child's garden"). In the metaphorical sense, Froebel considers children to be growing things that require nurturing and cultivating. He also literally proposes that schools maintain outdoor gardens for children to raise plants and tend flowers (and provides specifications for laying out the garden area).

Knowledge and skills should be developed "in the necessary succession in which they come forth in the child" (Froebel, 1827/1885, p. 23). Froebel's (1840/1914) aim is "to make it possible for man freely and spontaneously to develop" (p. 9). A true education regards the whole child. "Because all life rests in one unity," Froebel believes, a school should also be "a living whole" founded on principles derived from nature (pp. 13–14). Such a school provides opportunities for outdoor activities and for play.

Children naturally express themselves through play and creative activities. Froebel (1827/1885) calls play "freely-active representation and exercises of every kind" (p. 159). Play possesses great meaning for the child and is crucial to developing and exercising a number of significant skills. Play indeed lays the foundation for the type of person the child will become, not only engendering enthusiasm and joy but also fostering patience, diligence, endurance, dependability, clear-mindedness, compassion, and other favorable qualities.

Materials for play (which Froebel calls *gifts*) should be presented to children in order: the ball, sphere, cylinder, cube, cone, cube divided into eight cubes, rectangular blocks or prisms, and triangular blocks or prisms. Froebel advises to begin with simple things and move sequentially and progressively to the more complex. Each gift comes with directions for a variety of activities. All gifts are presented in boxes and many connect to or nest within one another to preserve the sense of unity upon which Froebel bases all of his educational philosophy.

In addition to the gifts, Froebel designed tasks for children to engage in, such as working with solids (e.g., clay, cardboard, wood), surfaces (e.g., paper-folding and cutting), lines (e.g., lacing, weaving, threading, embroidery), and points (e.g., stringing beads and buttons). These practical activities (or *occupations*) permit the child to represent the world, express creativity, be productive, and develop skills and traits required for later accomplishments in life.

Children engage in play and physical activities with meaningful purpose. "Play has for the child the greatest earnestness and attracts the little one like a business" (1899, p. 214). Play and outdoor activities should place demands on the child—physically, mentally, and spiritually. The goal is for complete development, and for self-development, to result. "The law of connection is the most important law of the universe" (p. 203).

Maria Montessori (Italian, 1870–1952) established *Casa dei Bambini* ("Children's House") in 1907. Montessori (1949) describes four planes of development through which a child progresses. In infancy, a child has an "absorbent mind" (p. 35), forming basic human abilities and skills as an "unconscious creator" (p. 235). In the toddler years, a child becomes a "conscious creator," willfully attempting to master the immediate environment (p. 235). From ages six to twelve, a child enters the period where abstract thinking develops. In adolescence, a child gains independence and transitions to young adulthood. "These conquests of independence are in the beginning the different steps of what is generally known as natural development," Montessori explains. "In other words, if we examine natural development closely, we can describe it as the conquest of successive degrees of independence" (p. 123).

Montessori (1946) believes one can better help a child learn if conscious of "sensitive periods" when the child is ready for learning a new skill (p. 53). Montessori describes instructional materials to develop motor skills, sensory learning, and intellectual or academic skills. Montessori classrooms feature materials for children to lace, fasten, tie, and button; objects of various shapes, sizes, colors, and textures to handle, sort, stack, and count; and materials for reading, writing, and arithmetic. In addition, Montessori advises that children spend as much time outdoors in the "open air" as possible (1914/1964, p. 10). Montessori education includes plenty of opportunities for movement, play, and manual work such as gardening.

Montessori (1914/1964) calls the second plane of development, "the blessed age of play" (p. 239). A child learns "by means of his experience, first through play, then through work" (1946/1963, p. 37). Education is not a matter of imparting knowledge, but a "natural process spontaneously carried out by the human individual, and is acquired not by listening to words but by experiences upon the environment" (p. 3). Play performs a critical function in refining a child's skills and abilities, as well as fostering social and moral development.

The founder of Waldorf education, Rudolf Steiner (Austrian, 1861–1925), refers to play as "the awakening of what is actually there within the human being" (Steiner, 1967, p. 23). Play stimulates the imagination or fantasy of the child, as well as including practical outdoor experiences such as tending a garden or caring for animals. Play for a child is a form of reality, reproducing or reenacting life experiences. The play of children "is in one respect based upon their desire to imitate," (Steiner, 2001, pp. 216–17). However, play takes on a social aspect as children grow older. Steiner sees this as preparation for roles to be assumed later in life. Play helps children prepare for transformations that will occur as they mature.

In the Children's Garden at a Waldorf school, learning materials and toys are made of natural materials such as wood and cloth (like Pestalozzi's objects and Froebel's gifts). Young children tend to imitate; therefore, Steiner cautions giving children elaborate or realistic toys that prescribe how they should be used and stifle the imagination (Steiner, 2004). Waldorf education bases its design on the natural development of children and rhythms found in nature. Because Waldorf schools do not emphasize reading or technology in the early years, play represents an integral part of the early childhood curriculum. (Chapter 7 examines Waldorf education and the philosophy of Rudolf Steiner in greater depth.)

Loris Malaguzzi (Italian, 1920–94) opened the first municipal pre-schools in Reggio Emilia, Italy in 1963. The network of schools expanded, and added infant-toddler centers in 1971. Reggio Emilia schools emphasize student self-expression through words, movement, song, art, dramatics, and play. Malaguzzi calls the many symbolic ways children communicate "the hundred languages of children" (Edwards, Gandini, & Forman, 1998, pp. 9, 12). Spontaneous, unstructured free play, in indoor and outdoor spaces, is one of the languages children use to explore their environment and express their growing understanding. Interacting with nature, and with natural objects and materials, is an active part of the learning experience.

For example, at Young School locations, children ages 2–5 learn according to a Reggio Emilia-inspired curriculum, featuring spontaneous learning as well as long-term projects. The Young School pioneered the Cottage, a unique learning environment fostering independent exploration and creative problem solving. The North America Reggio Emilia Alliance connects early childhood educators to resources and support for Reggio Emilia-inspired education.

Another school model whose philosophy values play is Sudbury education. Sudbury schools permit free play among children throughout the day, in keeping with a philosophy based on natural development. "Nature has arranged matters in such a way that play is the chief, overridingly absorbing, activity of human young" (Greenberg, 1994, p. 45). Society tends to consider play frivolous, an activity that must cease when it is time to begin or resume serious work. At a Sudbury school, play is considered an integral part of the curriculum and of the child's total learning experience. "Play itself is educational," Greenberg (2000, p. 8) explains. "Curiosity drives play, and play feeds on curiosity" (p. 12). Play is part of human nature, a universal activity that can be observed in all cultures, to which people freely devote time, effort, and attention.

According to this view of education, play is a highly effective means of accelerating learning. Play is not only physically active, but an imaginative and creative way to build mental models of how the world works. Play involves formulating rules, hypothesizing, organizing, innovating, adapting to new situations, and testing different models of reality. Play also provides an outlet for feelings and emotions. Play fosters independence as well as experiencing social interaction. "Suppressing play in children means suppressing the expression of their imagination and creative impulses" (Greenberg, 1994, p. 47). Rather than attempt to reduce the amount of time allotted to play from the schedule, or remove it altogether, a Sudbury school encourages play. Greenberg (2000) proposes, "Giving children the freedom to play is giving them the freedom to explore the nature of the innovative process first-hand" (p. 29). (Chapter 11 examines Sudbury education in greater depth.)

One of the most influential philosophers of education, John Dewey (American, 1859–1952) strongly supports the role of play in the curriculum. He observes that play, games, and other physical activities tend to find their way into the school day only as "relief from the tedium and strain of 'regular' school work" (MW 9:202). He laments the separation between the official educational program and the child's natural affinity for creative and productive exploration. Play is rarely "mere physical exuberance," but is often organized by children and "made to cohere in connected ways" (LW 8:284–5). Adults often mistake play for only that which they externally observe. Play involves all dimensions of a child's learning—mental, psychological, emotional, and physical. "It is the free play, the interplay, of all the child's powers, thoughts, and physical movements (MW 1:82). Dewey notes even the freest of play observes rules or principles that children apply to the activity. "To the child," Dewey explains, "play is his activity, his life, his business" (MW 1:339). Play is more than a mere diversion. Play stimulates the imagination and has practical, social, and moral benefits that schools overlook or disregard. The teacher should ask how play activities can both appeal to the child and develop capacities and abilities. Play should be purposely incorporated into the curriculum, with its outcomes recognized and supported by the school.

Every philosopher presented in this chapter has emphasized play and outdoor activities, including tending a garden. Montessori (1914/1964) concedes, "In considering an ample playground with space for a garden as an important part of this school environment, I am not suggesting anything new" (p. 80). Dewey includes gardening in the curriculum, not with the goal of necessarily preparing for a future career, but as a way to study natural processes, environmental issues, and social studies topics. He puts forth similar arguments to justify the inclusion of activities such as woodworking and cooking. These subjects involve more than mere movement. They are purposeful activities that require elaborative skills, such as planning, designing, constructing, combining, repurposing, revising, refining, cooperating, evaluating, persisting, and other critical, creative, and social skills.

How Do Teachers Teach? Questions about Pedagogy

"The pedagogical world is guided by human logic, but nature has other laws."

(Montessori)

The pedagogy of Naturalism turns away from Socratic questioning and discussion. "Avoid verbal lessons with your pupil," Rousseau proposes (1762/1962). "The only kind of lesson he should get is that of experience" (p. 40). Pestalozzi (1951) agrees, maintaining that "all educated instruction must be drawn out of the children themselves" (p. 44). He recommends starting to teach first with objects and pictures rather than with words. Pestalozzi describes placing a "capable child between two less capable ones" and watching them learn from one another (p. 44). In turn, the teacher learns from the children and develops his methods. A teacher-directed education has many disadvantages and may actual hinder learning. A child "learns by action," Pestalozzi states (p. ix). A teacher should allow the child to experience the "charm of self-activity" (p. 60).

Choosing to "respect the unity of Nature," Pestalozzi (1898) establishes an educational method in harmony with the natural course of a child's development (p. 127). He cautions teachers not to have their instruction outpace the natural development of the child, calling such instruction "overhasty" (p. 319). Pestalozzi lists a number of guidelines for instruction, among them to make natural connections among things, subordinate unessential thing to essentials, arrange objects by likeness (as they are arranged in nature), allowing learning of new things through different senses, teach knowledge in gradual steps, and start with the simple and build to the complex. Above all, remain constantly aware of the "proportion of nearness or distance between the object and our senses," realizing children will learn and understand those things closest to their sense-impressions rather than those things more distant and removed from the sense experiences (p. 321). We can teach by first naming the object and then studying it, or begin with the thing itself and then learn its name. Pestalozzi prefers the second approach.

For Froebel (1827/1885), the aim of instruction is to "bring the child to an insight into the unity of all things" (p. 79). Froebel instructs teachers to be observant for moments where the child exhibits a readiness to learn a new topic or skill. "Of course the indication for this is often very slight, like the desire of a new bud to sprout forth," he explains (p. 174). Therefore, all the teacher's attention should be directed toward noticing when these instances appear and seize upon each opportunity. Every teacher strives not to overlook "the moment of sprouting" and the implications these have for instruction (p. 175).

Montessori education draws no division between instruction and play, between learning time and free time. Children are free to choose objects and activities, organize their time, and move about as they wish. Learning can occur individually and in small groups, among children of different ages. The teacher, however, organizes activities to encourage specific learning and conducts lessons on how to use specific objects before the child may use them on her own. "All the activities we have described," according to Montessori (1914/1964), "are due to active preparation and guidance of the teacher" (p. 86). She (1909/1964) calls the set of instructional materials a "didactic system" because each object has been designed for a specific use (p. 169). However, once instructed in their use, children may handle the objects independently and self-correct their own errors. "The method used by me," she explains, "is that of making a pedagogical experiment with a didactic object and awaiting the spontaneous reaction of the child" (p. 167).

The Montessori teacher provides opportunities, resources, and assistance, but should "never be the obstacle between the child and his experience." Montessori teachers spend a great deal of time observing the children rather than directing them. "It is necessary for the teacher to guide the child without letting him feel her presence too much" (Montessori, 1914/1964, p. 77). Montessori (1946/1963) believes that as children freely and independently explore within the school environment, their nature will be revealed. "Life is activity," she writes (p. 35).

Types of Play

The children in the vignette engaged in a variety of outdoor activities. Researchers have identified several different types of play (Anderson-McNamee & Bailey, Fox, Miller, & Almon, 2009). Large-motor play involves running, climbing, swinging, and other types of movement that develop coordination, balance, and strength. Small-motor play develops dexterity, such as putting together puzzles, stringing beads, or sorting objects. In sensory play, children develop the senses by running sand through their hands, digging in dirt, splashing in water, or building with mud. Many types of play test a child's physical abilities, challenge their nerves, push their boundaries, or even assume taking risks, such as wrestling, scaling walls, or jumping from heights.

Constructing forts, dams, and boats are forms of construction play. Make-believe play uses the imagination to pretend. Symbolic play converts or transforms found objects to new uses, inventing a toy or tool needed in the moment.

In mastery play, children repeat an action until they improve, such as tying knots or balancing on a beam. For rules-based play, children organize games that follow existing rules, adapt or modify rules, or create new rules. Children engaged in language play make up songs, chant rhymes, tell stories, or role-play by inventing dialogue. In artistic or expressive play, children draw, paint, dance, play an instrument, or otherwise perform.

Play may be solitary or social. Children may play alone with an object, even talking aloud to themselves as they coach themselves or develop a scenario. Many children will watch and observe other children play before joining in, play together with different toys in no organized manner, or play alongside others in separate activities.

What Is the Role of the Teacher to Teach According to Natural Development?

TEACHER AS FACILITATOR

A teacher in this pedagogy is a facilitator of exploration, discovery, creativity, self-expression, and play. As a facilitator, the teacher does not direct student activity according to a fixed set of procedures but mediates between the child and the learning environment. Pestalozzi (1951) believes, "All instruction of man is then only the Art of helping Nature to develop in her own way" (p. 57).

TEACHER AS OBSERVER

The teacher also acts in the role of Observer. Froebel (1827/1885) instructs, "Teaching should in the first characteristics necessarily be passive, watchfully and protectively following, not dictatorial, not invariable, not forcibly interfering" (p. 4). Teachers should recognize and choose instructional methods that naturally and spontaneous arise from the conditions.

Montessori (1914/1964) refers to the teacher as "guardian and custodian of the environment" (p. 87). The teacher prepares the learning environment and provides resources, then observes the students and assists when needed. "Experience has shown that the teacher must withdraw more and more into the background," she explains, "only preparing for the children to work by themselves" (p. 68). As much as possible, the children act in a spontaneous manner, as the teacher observes. Montessori calls this "the Method of Non-Intervention" (p. 67). The teacher's role is indirect, leaving the child free to experience. Montessori's motto is, "Wait while observing" (p. 78).

THE TEACHER AS GARDENER

A third metaphor that emerges from this view is Teacher as Gardener. Children must be permitted to grow naturally, as plants do. The teacher's role is to tend to this growth in a caring manner. A teacher should educate the whole child, cultivating the heart as well as the physical and the intellect. "Teaching is by no means the essence of education. It is love that is its essence," Pestalozzi (1951) maintains. "What [an educator] really needs is a sense of love and happiness" (p. 33). "Be virtuous and good yourselves," Rousseau (1764/1962) advises, "and the examples you set will impress themselves on your pupil's memories, and in due season will enter their hearts" (p. 46).

What Is the Role of the Student to Learn According to Natural Development?

STUDENT AS INITIATOR

In this perspective, the student is in the role of Initiator. Learning according to natural stages of development emphasizes spontaneity and self-initiated activity. Curiosity, discovery, and creativity are highly valued. The students should have input and choice in activities. Montessori (1909/1964) reasons, "The children work by themselves, and, in doing so, make a conquest of active discipline, and independence in all the acts of daily life" (p. 374). When a child becomes interested in an object or activity, and encounters a difficulty, she should struggle through that challenge without interference or intervention.

Reggio Emilia schools refer to the child as "protagonist" and "co-constructor" (Edwards, Gandini, & Forman, 1998, p. 457). The student as protagonist speaks out for herself and has a voice in the direction of her own growth. A co-constructor perceives the environment and constructs meaning through a "synthesis of all the expressive, communicative, and cognitive languages" (p. 457).

STUDENT AS FLOWER

The actions of the teacher do not cause a child to grow. Growth is a natural process that a teacher nurtures. Montessori (1946) explains, "It is nature that is giving to the child the opportunity of growing, gives him independence and at the same time leads him to freedom" (p. 127). In an atmosphere that permits freedom to move and experience, a child's "spontaneous manifestations will become more clear, with the clearness of truth, revealing his nature" (1909/1964, p. 95).

Design

How Are Schools Organized? Questions about the Role of the School

Montessori Schools

According to Montessori (1914/1964), a school should be a place where "free children develop with the help of material designed to bring about development" (p. 140). The physical environment should aid in the natural development of children. This includes the way spaces are arranged, the kinds of furniture selected, the materials designed, and the decor. The school Montessori envisions "ought to be a real house," with a set of rooms and a garden that creates a home-like environment (p. 9). She recommends the houses consist of a main room and a parlor or sitting room, dining room, kitchen, bathroom, and other spaces as can be provided (such as a clubroom, music room, and gymnasium). The rooms are furnished with child-sized furniture (such as low tables and small wooden chairs) and a cupboard for storing materials that the students can access on their own. A chest of drawers contains a drawer for every child to store personal belongings. Pieces of different-colored carpet are to be used by children to spread on the floor to work on tasks. Montessori also insists on "an artistic environment" containing "things of beauty" (p. 147). Works of art, plants, and flowers should decorate the rooms. She suggests:

> There is no limit to the equipment of the 'Children's House,' because the children themselves do everything. They sweep the rooms, dust and wash the furniture, polish the brasses, lay and clear away the table, wash up, sweep and roll up the rugs, wash a few little clothes, and cook eggs.
>
> (p. 14)

Montessori schools have been established all over the world, with more than 4,000 in North America (American Montessori Society, 2015). Modern Montessori classrooms are usually large, open spaces, with low shelves and child-sized furniture. Children do not sit in rows or assigned seats for whole-class instruction, but retrieve their materials and work at tables or on pieces of carpet on the floor in small groups, pairs, or alone. Despite this child-centered environment, students learn in an orderly atmosphere using specialized materials and following specified procedures. The teacher and an assistant observe and guide the children, circulating within the classroom to work with one child or a small group. Students convene in a large open area for circle time, which includes songs, games, and stories.

Montessori (1914/1964) states that her approach "transforms the school itself in action into a kind of scientific laboratory" (p. 125). Montessori schools provide teacher training in the skills and application of observation, as well as in the methods of instruction. "The teacher must not limit her action to observation, but must proceed to experiment," Montessori (1909/1964) explains. "In this method the lesson corresponds to an experiment" (p. 107).

Jemicy School

The Jemicy School, a suburban founded for students with dyslexia and related language-based learning differences, regards outdoor play as "an essential part" of the Lower and Middle School curriculum (Jemicy School, 2014, Jemicy Facts section, para 3). In addition to a playground area and athletic fields, the school has constructed an Outdoor Learning Center to extend learning beyond the walls of the classroom. The school grounds feature a two-acre wooded area bounded by a stream that features a small waterfall. Here, students construct forts, build dams, tend gardens, and observe wildlife such as turtles, frogs, and salamanders. Faculty members unobtrusively monitor the students, who develop a culture of interaction with nature and each other.

The Jemicy School philosophy states, "A school should be designed for its children" (Stanley, 2010, p. 227). Such a school provides "a well-planned physical setting . . . which promotes the healthy, vigorous, joyful growth of its children" (p. 227). Learning experiences that develop competence and adaptability offer the best preparation for children, fostering intellectual curiosity, creativity, and flexibility. Like in Rousseau's *Emile*, the unstructured play of children represents a major aspect of their learning experiences, with the outdoors functioning as another classroom. This creates a seamless continuity between indoor and outdoor learning activities and integrates valued knowledge and skills.

The Jemicy School cites numerous benefits to encouraging and facilitating outdoor play.[1] Physical activities promote health and wellness, as well as providing multisensory and mental stimulation. Children at play form new friendships, initiate diverse social relationships, and create strategies for interacting with peers. As they play, students exhibit independence, problem solving, rule-making, and other skills. They also practice skills learned in the classroom, such as manipulating objects, combining materials, and using symbols. Values such as responsibility, fairness, and cooperation are reinforced. Play unleashes imaginations and builds creativity. Children role-play, dramatize, invent, and take risks. Students involved in outdoor play explore their environment, pursue their curiosity, construct meaning, and produce understanding in ways that structured class time is unable to foster.

A school designed to teach according to the natural development of the child (Table 6.1) would create a variety of learning opportunities, allowing students the choice to engage in solitary activities, to observe and learn from others, and to cooperate with peers. Instruction would include individual, small-group, and whole-group experiences. Exploring and discovering on one's own initiative would be encouraged. Movement would be incorporated into lessons in all subject areas. Student input would be valued and ample choices would be offered. The education program would place a priority on self-expression and creativity. The school would provide access to an array of learning supplies and objects of different sizes, colors, textures, and materials. Learning outcomes and assessment methods would extend beyond cognitive processes. Some goals would be emergent and even co-constructed by the teacher and student.

Table 6.1 Design a School (Natural Development)

Purpose of Education	Learning according to natural development
Curriculum	Flexible, direct experiences, process-oriented
Instruction	Structured and unstructured play, explore, create
Role of Teacher	Facilitator, observer, gardener
Role of Student	Initiator, flower
Role of School	Natural environment and materials

How Does a School Designed to Teach According to Natural Development Define an Educated Person?

In a school designed to teach according to the natural development of the child, the definition of an educated person is one who initiates spontaneous activity, including free play. The child would creatively express her imagination, explore based on curiosity, and display independence.

Evaluate

Consistency

Student-centered education that emphasizes the importance of play exhibits varying degrees of structure. For example, in a Sudbury school, students choose what they wish to learn and how and when they wish to learn it. Therefore, play might constitute much or all of the day for children in that kind of school. In Montessori schools, teachers organize the learning environment, offer choices of what to learn, and provide materials to facilitate instruction, while allowing students to decide when they may wish to learn and in what groupings. What may look like play to an observer would be considered a learning activity in a Montessori classroom. Waldorf schools incorporate play in the school day as an essential part of the curriculum. However, classes in the middle and older grades run on a schedule and follow a curriculum.

In many of the examples we have examined, children are encouraged to experience natural, spontaneous, and free play. Even in an organized game, students may invent or modify the rules. However, play may be organized by the teacher to achieve specific learning goals. To be consistent, play in all instances would not be considered a frivolous break from learning. Play would be recognized and valued for contributing to the development of knowledge and skills in a child. Use of play inconsistent with this perspective would schedule a brief recess to offer a respite from academics. Physical education classes could be considered as opportunities for play. However, if the teacher makes all the decisions, requires students to follow directions, and complies with external standards of performance, this would be inconsistent with a student-directed approach. Also, if the subject is regarded as less than equal to learning experiences provided in other classes then that viewpoint would clash with the purpose of regarding natural development as the purpose of education.

Rousseau shuns a specialized education, promoting a well-rounded education that develops the whole child. This view echoes claims by Perennialists, such as Hutchins, who define a liberal arts education in terms of its relevance beyond vocational utility (see Chapter 3). However, Perennialists seek to teach a permanent body of knowledge that time has determined possesses redeeming value. Rousseau's concern is less on society's interest in the worth of an individual's education and more on the child experiencing the world of the present. Curiosity and discovery direct the child's learning, developing abilities that may prove beneficial in future situations. The purpose of education is not to preserve the traditions of the past but to prepare the child to encounter and adjust to changing social and environmental conditions. The difference lies in the intent. Rousseau would rebel against the idea that a general education compels students to conform to society's expectations.

Compatibility

Froebel seeks to create unity, arguing that education should comply with the unity found in nature. This may seem to correspond to the sense of unity that Aristotle perceived in the natural world. However, the two positions are not compatible. Aristotle seeks to divine the essence of each thing to discover universal principles. Froebel wishes to educate the whole child to expand the definition of an educated person beyond only the rational.

Montessori (1912/1964) asserts her approach is "a pedagogical method informed by the high concept of Immanuel Kant, 'Perfect art returns to nature'" (p. 374). The claim that she and Kant share a similar philosophy about education is only partially convincing. One finds it difficult to imagine that a school run by Kant would resemble a Montessori school. Much of what one observes in a Montessori classroom—students working with natural materials on concrete learning activities (such as lacing, tying, and buttoning) under a teacher's supervision—Kant might consider training rather than education. Kant (1803/1900) distinguishes between play and work, viewing play as leisure time recreation and work as productive activity with a specified goal in mind. Kant and Montessori do hold similar views about the child developing self-discipline and initiative. Montessori education, however, institutes much of the direction by preparing the environment and selecting the materials.

Lastly, Kant (1803/1900) focuses on developing rational understanding, and dismisses amusements that distract from cultivation of the intellect. Spontaneous, unstructured free play would appear to fall into this category. "It is necessary to have rules for everything which is intended to cultivate the understanding," he writes (p. 75). For example, although Kant believes the imagination should not be entirely neglected, he demands it be brought under control, not indulged. Education fosters the intellect, which "aims at skills and perfection, and has not for its object the imparting of any particular knowledge, but the general strengthening of the mental faculties" (p. 77). Kant's view on education consistently stresses understanding, judgment, and reason. Montessori, on the other hand, believes a child can grow into independence following natural inclinations.

Coherence

A coherent school program would provide an environment that nurtures exploration and a growing sense of independence. Frequent opportunities for unstructured free play would be incorporated into the schedule. Physical activity would occur throughout the school day across subject areas. The layout of the school and classrooms would feature open spaces suitable for movement and interaction with a variety of objects. Student choice of materials and activities would be encouraged.

Outdoor spaces would offer a variety of choices as well. Natural objects and settings would inspire imaginative play and student-directed games. Many different types of play would be observed, developing large- and small-motor and sensory skills and promoting construction, make-believe, creative rule-making, and inventiveness. Children would engage in both solitary activity and social interaction. Students would have ample time to participate in several activities or become immersed in a single pursuit.

The teacher would monitor play for safety and the well-being of children, but not supervise with the intention of imposing rules or structure on the process. Teacher observations would provide input on decision-making about a child's development and instructional needs.

Reflect

To reflect on the philosophical concepts, compare your prior observations and experiences in schools and classrooms to the vignette, descriptions, and examples we have examined.

How Do Your Prior Observations and Experiences Relate to a Curriculum Designed to Teach According to Natural Development?

You may have observed play in a school during recess or physical education classes. How often were children provided opportunities for free play during the school day? How long were the play periods? Was play considered part of the learning process, or a respite from academics? In what ways did children direct their own play and manage their own use of time?

In what grades or at what age levels did you observe play? Did the amount of time and types of play change as children advanced in age or grade level?

What indoor and outdoor spaces, equipment, and materials did the school provide to foster play?

How Do Your Prior Observations and Experiences Relate to a Pedagogy Designed to Teach According to Natural Development?

How did teachers facilitate play among children? Did the teacher organize the process, and observe as children created their own structure? Were students directed to engage in certain types of play or were they free to choose their own activities? How did teachers integrate play into instruction? How did teachers incorporate observations of student play into their planning of lessons and assessments?

How Do Your Prior Observations and Experiences Relate to a School Designed to Teach According to Natural Development?

Have you observed schools where play was highly valued and featured as part of the education program? Have you observed play being restricted, or the amount of time for play limited? Was play offered as a reward for proper conduct and/or withheld as a punishment for disruptive behavior or poor academic performance? If so, have you observed a school where another subject (such as reading, math, or science) was offered as a reward or withheld as punishment, or was participation in those subjects required for all students as part of the comprehensive curriculum?

How Do Your Own Practices and Beliefs Relate to the Purpose of Teaching According to Natural Development?

In this chapter, the educational practices observed have moved past the mid-point on the *Continuum of Educational Philosophy*. Education is more student-centered, and the process of learning is valued as greatly as or even more than evidence of achieving pre-determined outcomes.

From your own point of view, should students be permitted greater latitude in pursuing their own interests and choosing their own activities? Is the purpose of school to direct student learning or to guide students in following their natural inclinations? Would play be a regular aspect of your instruction or a distraction from learning? What benefits can children realize from free play that complement their overall educational experience?

A student-centered education suggests far more than occasions to engage in free play. In this chapter, play has been portrayed as a means to contrast the perspectives in Part III with the rational, structured approaches described in Part II. Experience as a source of knowledge begins to usurp the cognitive or intellectual domain. Rousseau (1762/1962) establishes the outlook that influences these perspectives. "Let us lay it down as an incontestable principle," he writes, "that the first impulses of nature are always right" (p. 40).

Note

1 Additional sources describing the role of outdoor play at the Jemicy School: 1) Chawla, L., Keena, K., Pevec, I., & Stanley, E. (2014). Green schoolyards as havens from stress and resources for resilience in childhood and adolescence. *Health & Place, 28*, 1–13; 2) Stanley, E. (2009). Replaying recess: An inquiry into the value of outdoor play in school. *Thresholds in Education, 35*(3), 37–44; and 3) Stanley, E. (2011). The place of outdoor play in a school community: A case study of recess values. *Children, Youth and Environments, 21*(1), 185–211.

References

American Montessori Society. (2015). Home. [Website]. Retrieved from http://amshq.org/Montessori-Education/Introduction-to-Montessori/Montessori-Schools

Anderson-McNamee, J. K., & Bailey, S. J. (2014). The importance of play in early childhood development [PDF file]. Bozeman, MT: Montana State University. Retrieved from http://store.msuextension.org/publications/HomeHealthandFamily/MT201003HR.pdf

Dewey, J. (1976). School and society. In J. Boydston (Series Ed.), *The middle works of John Dewey, 1899–1901: Vol. 1* (pp. 1–109). Carbondale, IL: Southern Illinois University Press.

Dewey, J. (1976). Play and imagination in relation to early education. In J. Boydston (Series Ed.), *The middle works of John Dewey, 1899–1901: Vol. 1* (pp. 339–343). Carbondale, IL: Southern Illinois University Press.

Dewey, J. (1980). Democracy and education: An introduction to the philosophy of education. *The middle works of John Dewey, 1916: Vol. 9* (pp. 192–361). Carbondale, IL: Southern Illinois University Press.

Dewey, J. (1986). How we think: A restatement of the relation of reflective thinking to the educative process. In J. Boydston (Series Ed.), *The later works of John Dewey, 1933: Vol. 8* (pp. 105–352). Carbondale, IL: Southern Illinois University Press.

Edwards, C., Gandini, L., & Forman, G. (1998). *The hundred languages of children: The Reggio Emilia approach – Advanced reflections* (2nd ed.). [E-book] Greenwich, CN: Praeger.

Fox, J. E. (n.d.). Back-to-basic: Play in early childhood. Retrieved from http://www.earlychildhoodnews.com/earlychildhood/article_view.aspx?ArticleID=240

Froebel, F. (1885). *The education of man.* (J. Jarvis, Trans.). New York, NY: A. Lovell & Company. (Original work published 1827.)

Froebel, F. (1899). *Education by development.* (J. Jarvis, Trans.). New York, NY: D. Appleton & Company. (Original work published n.d.)

Froebel, F. (1914). *Pedagogics of the kindergarten.* (J. Jarvis, Trans.). New York, NY: D. Appleton & Company. (Original work published 1840.)

Greenberg, D. (1994). *Worlds in creation.* Framingham, MA: Sudbury Valley School Press.

Greenberg, D. (1995). *Free at last: The Sudbury Valley school.* Framingham, MA: Sudbury Valley School Press.

Greenberg, D. (2000). *A clearer view: New insights into the Sudbury school model.* Framingham, MA: Sudbury Valley School Press.

Kant, I. (1900). *Kant on education.* (A. Churton, Trans.). Boston, MA: D.C. Heath. (Original work published 1803.)

Miller, E., & Alom, J. (2009). Twelve key types of play [PDF file]. *Alliance for Childhood.* Retrieved from http://www.allianceforchildhood.org/sites/allianceforchildhood.org/files/file/12_types_of_play.pdf

Montessori, M. (1964). *Dr. Montessori's own handbook.* Cambridge, MA: Robert Bentley, Inc. (Original work published 1914.)

Montessori, M. (1964). *The Montessori method.* (A. E. George, Trans.). New York, NY: Shocken Books. (Original work published 1909.)

Montessori, M. (1963). *Education for a new world.* Madras, India: Kalakshetra Publications. (Original work published 1946.)

Montessori, M. (1949). *The absorbent mind.* Madras, India: Theosophical Publishing House.

Pestalozzi, J. H. (1898). *How Gertrude teaches her child, and An account of the method.* E. Cooke, (Ed.). (L. E. Holland & F. C Turner, Trans.). Syracuse, NY: C. W. Bardeen.

Pestalozzi, J. H. (1951). *The education of man: Aphorisms.* New York, NY: Philosophical Library. (Original work published n.d.)

Rousseau, J. (1962). *The Emile of Jean-Jacques Rousseau: Selections* (10th ed.). W. Boyd (Trans. & Ed.). New York, NY: Teachers College Press. (Original work published 1762.)

Stanley, E. (2010). *Monkey brains and monkey bars: An ecological approach to the values of school recess.* (Electronic Thesis or Dissertation). Retrieved from https://etd.ohiolink.edu/

Steiner, R. (1967). *Discussions with teachers.* London: Rudolph Steiner Press.

Steiner, R. (2001). *The renewal of education.* Great Barrington, MA: Anthroposophic Press.

Steiner, R. (2004). *On the play of the child: Indications by Rudolf Steiner for working with young children.* F. Jaffke (Ed.). Spring Valley, NY: Waldorf Early Childhood Association of North America.

7   What If . . . The Purpose of Education Were to Learn According to Feeling and Imagination?

Wonder

In Chapter 6, we investigated schools that teach according to the natural development of a child. In this chapter, we focus on a type of school whose curriculum, instruction, and school organization center on clearly defined and articulated stages of development. To examine one stage in particular, we ask the wonder question, *"What if . . . the purpose of education were to learn according to feeling and imagination?"*

Observe

Classroom Vignette: Sixth-Grade Lesson on Mediaeval History

As the students arrive in the classroom, Ms. S individually greets each one by name with a handshake and a friendly "Good morning." The students take their places, standing quietly behind their desk chairs. On a cue from the teacher, they recite in unison a "Good Morning" verse, followed by a song sung from memory.

EDUCATIONAL PRACTICES

RATIONAL   EMPIRICAL

RATIONAL	EMPIRICAL
Ideas-Focused	Experience-Focused
Content-Oriented	Process-Oriented
Fixed Curriculum	Flexible Curriculum
Teacher-Centered	Student-Centered
Teacher-Directed	Self-Directed
Pre-Determined Outcomes	Open-Ended Exploration
Whole-Class Activities	Differentiated/Individualized Activities

Objective External Reality	Internal Subjective Reality
Absolute Universal Truth	Changing Relative Truth
Pre-Existing Knowledge	Constructed Knowledge
Knowledge Independent of Experience	Knowledge Dependent on Experience
Autonomous Knowledge	Interdependent Knowledge
Absolute Universal Values	Relative Local Values
Values Independent of Experience	Values Dependent on Experience

PHILOSOPHICAL PERSPECTIVES

Figure 7.1 Continuum of Educational Philosophy (Feeling and Imagination)

The day begins with a brief music lesson. As the students put away their recorders and sheet music, they sing another song (*a cappella* from memory) until each student has returned to standing behind his or her desk. The group then recites three homilies in unison, stressing character-building and providing inspiration ("You Can Never Tell What a Word May Do" and "Look to this Day").

For the main lesson of the morning, the students arrange their desks in a U-shaped pattern facing the teacher. The chalkboard displays a large, colorful, hand-drawn map of Europe, with different-colored arrows depicting invasions of the Roman Empire by Huns, Goths, Vandals, Angles and Saxons, and Franks. To review a previous lesson on the fall of the Roman Empire, Ms. S asks students recall questions, followed by probing questions seeking elaboration. She refers to the map to reinforce certain points, such as an invasion of barbarians from the north. Infrequently, she writes a note or two on the large front board to illustrate a concept (such as the increments of time between generations) or to relay a fact (such as the date of a particular invasion).

A key theme of the lesson on the fall of the Roman Empire is the decadence of the society, when reliance on slave labor and an increase in resources caused complacency and lethargy. Ms. S pauses at critical points in the story to identify these aspects of Roman life and associate them with society today, and with the culture of this classroom of students in particular. "Through unity," she emphasizes, "different civilizations or different groups were able to rise. But when that unity left them, they disintegrated. That's a truth that lives today, and into the future."

This portion of the lesson ends with a prompt for student reflection, "What can we learn from the fall of the Roman Empire that can help us today?"

Transitioning to a new topic, Ms. S slides the section of chalkboard to one side, revealing another chalk-drawn map depicting Europe after the fall of the Roman Empire. She begins to tell a story from memory, without resorting to notes, books, or technology. The students listen in rapt attention as the teacher masterfully narrates the story.

The classroom setting reflects the theme. Examples of the teacher's talent in chalk-drawing are evident at different locations in the classroom. In addition to the map of Europe, a mediaeval stained-glass rose window is displayed on an easel to the side of the front chalkboard. Mounted on a second easel near the windows is a small chalkboard drawing of a mediaeval lion, while on another easel at the front of the room rests an outline map of Europe on paper.

Three tapestries hang on the walls: one a knight fighting a dragon, one a scene of a village burning, and the third a battle scene. Student-rendered sketches of shield designs, patterned after examples Ms. S has provided, line the bulletin board at the side of the room. The bulletin board also displays black-and-white diagrams of mediaeval costumes, with descriptions of the various features of each one. A globe sits on a counter below the bulletin board. A costume, a purple cloak, covers a dress form in the back of the room.

Framed examples of calligraphy (such as poems and sayings) are on display on a back wall, and a collection of books provides examples of mediaeval manuscripts (including styles of illustration, decoration, bordering, and calligraphy). On a small chalkboard beside the door are written the dates of two upcoming school events: the mediaeval Feast and Play, and the May Faire.

Mrs. S stresses to the class that the fall of the Roman Empire is an important period in history because, from this clash of cultures, a new Europe emerged and a transition occurred in the development of civilization. The students conclude the lesson by reciting the poem, "O Roma Nobilis" (O Noble Rome).[1]

Investigate

In the vignette above, content is represented in a variety of ways: music, singing, group-recitation, creative writing, drawing, and oral story-telling. This approach to education represents the philosophy of Waldorf education (introduced in Chapter 6), which focuses on the development of the whole child. To examine the philosophy that supports this purpose of education, we will investigate the following inquiry questions:

- What Do Teachers Teach? Questions about the Curriculum
- How Do Teachers Teach? Questions about Pedagogy
- How Are Schools Organized? Questions about the Role of the School

What Do Teachers Teach? Questions about the Curriculum

"The true curriculum results from an understanding of the stages of human life."

(Rudolf Steiner)

In 1919, the Austrian scientist and philosopher Rudolf Steiner (1861–1925) established the Free Waldorf School (*Die Freie Waldorfschule*) for the children of the Waldorf-Astoria cigarette factory workers in Stuttgart, Germany. Steiner, former general secretary of the German branch of the Theosophical Society in Berlin, brought his personal philosophy to the design of the school. Anthroposophy, from the Greek *anthropos* ("human being") and *sophia* ("wisdom"), means "human wisdom" (Steiner, 2002, p. 8). Anthroposophy views the human being as a "threefold social organism" of spirit, soul, and body who develops in three stages from childhood to adulthood (Steiner, 1995, p. 7). Although this philosophy forms the basis of the Waldorf educational approach, it is not explicitly taught in Waldorf classrooms to students.

Waldorf education proceeds according to the pattern of human development espoused by Anthroposophy. "The true curriculum," Steiner (1995) explains, "results from an understanding of the stages of human life. The children themselves tell us, if we can really observe them, what they want to learn in a particular stage of life" (p. 42). Steiner departs from the position of educating a child for the future requirements of adulthood and focuses instead on needs that appear in each stage of a child's development.

According to Waldorf education, the stage of early childhood (to about age seven years) is the stage of *imitation* and the *will*, when learning occurs primarily through physical activity in the child's immediate surroundings. Teachers de-emphasize academics during this stage of development. For example, reading is not taught in kindergarten, but is gradually introduced in the first grade. Middle childhood (from age seven to about fourteen years) is the stage of *feeling*, when imagination and experience are the strongest factors in learning. Finally, adolescence and young adulthood (from age fourteen) begins the stage of the *intellect*, when a sense of independence emerges and intellectual thinking occurs (Almon, 1992; Barnes, 1980, 1991; Easton, 1997; Kotzch, 1990; Uhrmacher, 1993, 1995).

The Waldorf curriculum is designed to be appropriate for each of the three developmental stages, presenting content based upon prior knowledge and prior learning experiences.

Organized as an ascending spiral, many themes of the curriculum are repeated at varying degrees of depth and complexity at subsequent grade levels (Barnes, 1980, 1991). Repetition and a deliberate sense of rhythmic pattern are part of the curriculum and the daily routine in a Waldorf classroom. Steiner (2001) observes, "The entirety of human life is based upon rhythm" (p. 125).

Waldorf education embodies the philosophical vision to educate the whole child—which Steiner (1995) alternately refers to as "physical, emotional and mental," "thinking, feeling and willing," or "body, soul and spirit" (pp. 17–18, 42). The developmental approach strives to depart from a strictly intellectual education. Educating the whole child involves exposing students to many forms of content and types of skills. In addition to the more traditional subjects of reading, writing, and arithmetic, the visual and performing arts, and practical skills such as woodworking, knitting, and gardening, are fundamental aspects of the curriculum considered essential to the development of the child. Special classes include eurythmy (movement), handwork (such as knitting), and woodworking.

Especially in the elementary grades, Waldorf lessons often revolve around folk tales, legends, mythology, parables, and pictures. The use of the tales, legends, and parables addresses both the *feeling* and *imagination* aspects of the children in this stage of development. Steiner recommends preparing students in middle childhood by telling stories, creating art, performing drama, and offering other activities that connect history to their present experiences. The experiences should also connect to a shared sense of human nature. "A true living consideration of history," Steiner (2001) says, "requires that people understand external events as symptoms of something hidden within" (p. 209).

The oral tradition is highly valued in the Waldorf classroom. The teacher asking students questions, engaging them in discussions, and participating in the daily review creates a dialogue between teacher and students. In the vignette, Ms. S conveys content through story-telling. During her stories, the students are attentive listeners. They do not take notes during the story, nor do they read passages aloud or follow along in a book. The stories live through the expressive telling by the teacher.

Story-telling, in particular, is intended to accomplish this goal of connecting the information of the lesson to the stage of imagination. Facts such as historical names and dates, or specific literary techniques, are not presented to the students for the primary purposes of memorization or comprehension, but to enhance the authenticity and appeal of the story. Students are not taught about characters, setting, and plot as discrete elements. Using the imagination, they are to experience how those they listen and read about feel and what it means to live through these events.

Ms. S relates instances in the stories to the students' background experiences or prior knowledge. In one analogy, she compares the competing forces vying for resources at that time in history to the children's playground game of four-square. "If someone took the ball away during the game," she asks, "how would you feel? How would you react?" Because Ms. S has taught most of these students since the first grade, she also has them recall earlier learning pertaining to the lesson, often from units taught to the children several years ago.

Instances of written work do not assume the form of note-taking, homework assignments, essays, or tests. Student lesson books contain samples of expository and creative writing that expand upon the themes of the lesson, such as reports, original stories, and poems. Some poems and passages have been transcribed from primary sources. Usually the written text is illustrated, or the page decorated or colored in around the writing.

In one example, the students take dictation about mediaeval history. Ms. S carefully enunciates each word and indicates each punctuation mark. Afterwards, the students check their accuracy as Ms. S writes the sentences on the board for correction. The written activity is not turned in for evaluation and a grade, however, nor does it conclude with the transcriptions. Instead, the students refer to the framed examples of calligraphy displayed in the room and to the books about mediaeval manuscripts to recopy the dictated passage into their lesson books in the mediaeval style, embellished with appropriate calligraphy, borders, decorations, and illustrations. The forms Ms. S introduces to the students during the lessons serve as archetypes for students to recreate and embellish. Their work connects to the theme of the lesson block, and simulates the activity and experience representative of the period being studied.

Student artwork is incorporated into the lessons, which the students usually complete in their lesson books. In one lesson, Ms. S has the students color-code and label a map depicting Charlemagne's Empire (identical to a paper map displayed at the front of the room). As mentioned above, students have also designed drafts of shield diagrams, the final versions to be completed on larger paper. Student lesson books contain drawings, sketches, diagrams, notes, and creative writing assignments on Roman and mediaeval history, as well as products completed for prior lessons on astronomy, geology, and mineralogy. Ms. S purposefully instructs students in using each form, directing their practice and development as she models technique and style and furnishes ample examples for student reference.

Singing and reciting are routine transition exercises between lessons and other parts of the day, and reinforce not only content from the lessons but themes about cooperation, unity, and responsibility within the school culture and society. Aesthetics relate to the philosophical dimension of Axiology, which asks questions about artistic values (as well as moral and ethical virtues). An extensive incorporation of the visual image is to be found throughout the Waldorf learning environment in the presentation of the content by the teacher and in the response to the content by the students. The integration of artistic forms into the curriculum aims to extend and deepen the intellectual experiences of the students, stimulating the senses, enriching the imagination, and cultivating feeling.

The significance of preparing for the play, feast, and faire culminating in the lesson block exemplifies the Waldorf approach to imagination, feeling, and experience. Many of the learning tasks in the lessons relate to these closing events: songs and recitations to be performed, drawings to decorate the setting, costumes the students are to design and wear, and food prepared for the occasions. The synthesis of the various tasks into a grand finale unifies the diverse learning experiences of the lesson block, appealing to the imagination while relying upon active involvement. Ms. S tells the students, "The rehearsal of the play is far more important than the public performance on stage. It's how you work together to make it happen that's important."

The central role of the play, feast, and faire also reinforces the Waldorf emphasis on rhythms and cycles, symbolized by festivals, rituals, and ceremonies. Rather than ending the lesson block with a cumulative examination or some other summative assessment, the students engage in a group effort, integrating various forms of representation that address the objectives of feeling, imagination, and experience.

How Do Teachers Teach? Questions about Pedagogy

> "We cannot begin with a pedagogy of rules, but with a feeling."
>
> (Steiner)

In Waldorf education, daily instruction centers on the "main lesson," an in-depth, uninterrupted two-hour lesson each morning (Steiner, 1997, p. 22). Steiner dispenses with a standard schedule consisting of periods devoted to separate subjects, fearing students moving from a relatively brief lesson on one subject to the next would lose whatever learning occurred in the process. Main lessons are organized into integrated, interdisciplinary units (or blocks) lasting two to four weeks focused on a principal theme.

The lesson depicted in the vignette presents topics in a block on mediaeval history. Ms. S bases the ways she represents this topic on the belief that the child is in the stage of imagination and feeling. Hence, her goal is for the students to connect to the information in a way that relies on imagining what it was like to live in the Middle Ages and how the people would feel being in those conditions. Ms. S values her students attaining a sense of the experience as greatly as acquiring factual knowledge about the period. Accordingly, she represents content in ways she hopes convey experiences, reveal feelings, and inspire imagination. Story-telling, visual arts, writing, music, singing, and reciting are some of the forms used to accentuate the feeling and imagination qualities of the learning experience. The use of many forms of representation during the lesson block creates a multi-layered experience to reenact the period. Teachers should "give children living concepts and feelings" (Steiner, 2001, p. 225).

Ms. S, who completed a three-year Waldorf education teacher-training program, places great emphasis on the philosophical bases underlying Waldorf education. She expresses her goal as "bringing the content on a feeling level rather than on a thinking level, particularly with this age child, and making learning as much of an experience as possible." Although Ms. S does not teach Anthroposophy to students as part of the curriculum, its tenets guide her instruction. As a result, Ms. S concentrates on making each lesson a living experience for her students. "On the surface I'm teaching mediaeval history," she explains, "but there's another reason for teaching mediaeval history, and that has to do with Steiner's philosophy of where the children are. At this particular age, they really are in that middle ages place in their lives."

What Is the Role of the Teacher in a School Designed to Teach According to Feeling and Imagination?

TEACHER AS NURTURER

A Waldorf teacher should focus on how the developing child wants to learn, according to the stages of human development. The teacher seeks to educate the whole child, demonstrating a genuine compassion for each individual student. "This understanding of humanity, this understanding of the growing child," Steiner (1995) effuses, "should so saturate the teachers that a love of humanity enters the teaching" (p. 60). Steiner says the teacher "acts as a kind of physician for the development of the human spirit" (2001, p. 243). Therefore, the metaphor Teacher as Nurturer can be proffered as one way to represent the teacher in this educational philosophy.

TEACHER AS ARTIST

Waldorf education also views teachers as artists in their role as educators. "Instruction in the Waldorf School begins from a purely artistic point of view" (Steiner, 2001, p. 91). Waldorf teachers literally produce works of art in the classroom as part of their pedagogical skills. Teacher preparation in Waldorf education includes training in music, singing, speech, drama, painting, drawing, form drawing, and other art forms.

TEACHER AS GUIDING AUTHORITY

Despite the emphasis on a child-centered learning experience, the role of the teacher is tantamount. In the stage of early childhood, the child seeks to imitate the adult. In middle childhood, the child looks to the teacher for direction. Steiner (1995) asserts that "the teacher who faces us is the world" (p. 58). By that, Steiner means that the teacher provides the guidance children need before entering a later stage when they can learn directly from experience. Until children reach adolescence, "there is an abyss between ourselves and the world," Steiner claims. "The teacher should bridge that gulf for us" (p. 58).

Ideally, the classroom teacher remains with the same students from grades 1 through 8. Ms. S has been teaching the majority of her sixth-grade students since the first grade, remaining with them for each successive grade. According to the Waldorf philosophy, children have a need for adult direction and supervision, though not a strict, authoritarian style of enforcement. The teacher maintains a close relationship with the students, characterized by guidance and rules. The teacher's role is one of guiding authority, trusted and respected by the students.

Steiner (2001) maintains that, in addition to the intellect, children "must be educated in feelings," which includes their ethical and moral development (p. 122). This requires connecting to the whole child. "We cannot begin with a pedagogy of rules, but with a feeling" (p. 81). During the lesson block on mediaeval history, each activity contains within it a moral lesson. Reciting and singing in unison, for example, is intended to foster the values of group cooperation, unity, and moral responsibility, a theme of the lesson block and an important aspect of Waldorf schooling. Story-telling also imparts moral lessons, with each story punctuated by moral admonitions.

Ms. S stresses the moral truth embedded in each lesson, which also helps link the lessons into a thematic whole. Discovering and sharing these moral truths is at the heart of Waldorf education, regardless of the subject area.

What Is the Role of the Student in a School Designed to Teach According to Feeling and Imagination?

STUDENT AS IMITATOR

In the stage of early childhood, the metaphor for the role of the student is Imitator. Steiner (1995) believes children at this age "learn everything through imitation" (p. 106). The student mimics adults, older children, and peers, and relies on the teacher as a model, support, and authority figure.

STUDENT AS CREATOR

In the stage of middle childhood, the stage of feeling and imagination, the student as Creator is an apt metaphor. Steiner believes art can cultivate the will. Drawing, painting, music, movement, drama, and other artistic forms stimulate the senses and activate thinking. "We must derive the whole education from the child's artistic capabilities," Steiner explains. "The children's artistic capabilities touch their entire being. They touch the child's will and feeling, and then, through will and feeling the intellect" (p. 91).

STUDENT AS THINKER

In the stage of adolescence, the student as Thinker emerges. The student makes connections, begins to generalize, can grasp abstract concepts. This is a natural progression from the stages of willing and feeling. Only in adolescence does the learner have the capacity to impact his environment, adapt to circumstances, and make conscious decisions that instill meaningful direction to his life.

Design

How Are Schools Organized? Questions about the Role of the School

The first Waldorf school in North America, the Rudolf Steiner School of New York, was founded in 1928. The Waldorf movement has since grown to more than 900 independently administered schools in 83 countries, 160 member schools and fourteen teacher-training institutes in the United States (Association of Waldorf Schools of North America, n.d.). In a Waldorf school, the purpose of education is to develop all capacities of every individual (Table 7.1). Therefore, all students participate in every subject. Language arts, mathematics, natural and earth sciences, social sciences and history are taught in main lesson blocks of three to five weeks. Special subjects include handwork (e.g., knitting, crochet, sewing, cross-stitch, weaving, and woodworking), music (instrumental and vocal), art, drama, and movement (including eurythmy). Foreign languages are offered beginning in the early grades.

Learning in early childhood relies on story-telling (such as fables and folk tales), pictorial representations, numbers, movement, play, interactions with nature (such as gardening), and practical skills such as preparing snacks and cleaning up. In middle childhood, students begin to read and write, studying literature, poetry, drama, myths, and legends. In addition to mathematics, students study geography, botany, and zoology. The Waldorf high school curriculum includes literature, speech, foreign languages, math, introduction to computer education, sciences, and U.S. and world history. Music classes may include performing choir, orchestra, and band. Arts and handwork continue to be offered, as well as physical education and eurythmy.

Table 7.1 Design a School (Feeling and Imagination)

Purpose of Education	*Learning according to willing, feeling, and thinking*
Curriculum	Primary sources, art, music, drama, eurythmy (movement), handwork
Instruction	Story-telling, art, movement, handwork, practical skills (and other multi-sensory experiences)
Role of Teacher	Nurturer, artist, guiding authority
Role of Student	Imitator (early childhood), creator (middle childhood), thinker (adolescence)
Role of School	Whole child (willing, feeling, thinking)

The physical design of Waldorf schools reflects the philosophy. Walls are rich with color and artwork, artwork is made from natural materials, and objects include real tools and implements (such as knives, spades, hoes, and cooking utensils). Outdoor spaces provide access to nature, including gardens and pens for animals (such as rabbits and chickens).

The Alliance for Public Waldorf Education (n.d.) lists forty-two member schools in twelve U.S. states. Although the Alliance does not accredit schools, the organization provides support and resources to help establish Waldorf-based or Waldorf-oriented public schools (most as charter schools). The Urban Waldorf School in Milwaukee, Wisconsin opened in 1991 as the first public school offering a Waldorf education (Easton, 1997; Prager, 2004). The elementary school provides a similar curriculum found in independent Waldorf schools while complying with the standards of a public school, including requiring standardized state assessments. The George Washington Carver School of Arts and Sciences is a "Waldorf-inspired" public high school in Sacramento, California. The school philosophy is based on "critical thinking (head), creative expression (heart), and wholesome action (hands)" (George Washington Carver School of Arts and Sciences, n.d., Home page section, para 2). The academic program integrates experimentation and arts instruction into the comprehensive college-preparatory curriculum. The high school offers a two-hour main lesson in a three to four-week block to delve deeply into a subject. Students create their own textbooks and engage in artistic projects in every main lesson.

How Does a School Designed to Teach According to Feeling and Imagination Define an Educated Person?

A child educated according to the philosophy of Waldorf schools would use all senses in learning, engage in experiences that stimulate the imagination (such as play, role-playing and drama, movement, music, and artistic forms of expression), and demonstrate practical life skills (such as cooking, sewing, knitting, gardening, and woodworking).

Evaluate

Consistency

The emphasis of the Waldorf philosophy on willing, feeling, and thinking (or hands, heart, and head) endeavors to educate the child in a learning atmosphere conducive to a more holistic interpretation of how students experience content (Easton, 1997; Kotzsch, 1990; Schwartz, 1992). For Ms. S, studying the Middle Ages engenders more for students than the act of supplying a set of correct answers on a test or researching a term paper that cites information compiled from secondary sources. She uses different forms of representation to transform the historical period into a backdrop for a range of activities involving active student participation. By coming to know the era from the perspective of those who lived it, the students do not read about who was and what was, but hear and experience how it was. The layers of experience provide equal emphasis on the acquisition of knowledge, the practice of skills, the fostering of creative ability, the stimulation of the imagination, the nurturing of feelings of empathy and understanding, the importance of social responsibility, and the value of moral principles.

Waldorf schools exhibit remarkable consistency. The threefold view of human development permeates teaching in all subjects and disciplines. Waldorf instruction adheres to principles that embody Steiner's educational philosophy. For example, listening to oral story-telling enlivens an event from history for middle-grade children in a way that reading from a textbook does not. "Children want to take stories in through feeling," Steiner observes (1995, p. 38). This may be especially true for a story recounted from memory by a teacher who has taught the child every school year from the first grade to the sixth. By illustrating the stories, the teacher not only demonstrates her drawing skills and helps foster an appreciation of the visual arts, she also aims to invoke in the students a personal, genuine connection to the topic under study by engaging in authentic practices. Reciting passages, poems, or proverbial sayings from memory differs from writing and memorizing notes for a test or completing worksheets for independent seatwork. The motivation behind presenting the content orally, as a whole-group activity, relates to an underlying philosophical and moral dimension integral to the experience of the Waldorf classroom community.

Classes in other subjects follow the Waldorf philosophical approach. For example, in a middle school science class, the teacher uses a chalk drawing of the skeletal system during an anatomy lesson. Instead of reading from a textbook, students draw and label the diagram in their lesson books. Movement is incorporated into lessons about functions of the body. Natural materials are used and no technology is employed to view information or research details about the topic. The rhythms and cycles of life, beliefs that underlie Anthroposophy, are represented in the curriculum and observed in instruction. The lesson begins and ends with recitations about truth, which the teacher associates with learning about the human body.

Compatibility

The philosophy of Anthroposophy, focused on the threefold aspects of human nature, "penetrates into the teacher's will and into his work, and becomes the impulse for all that he does in the classroom" (Steiner, 1968, p. 59). The Waldorf philosophy enacted by Ms. S in her classroom seems to embrace that concept. Use of the visual arts, recitation, story-telling, singing, music, creative writing, and physical movement, together and independently, serves to engage the various senses and modes of thinking of the students. Integrated into a thematic unit, the different forms of representation create multi-dimensional kinds of activities, often employing many symbol systems simultaneously. Ms. S relies on her formal training, her collegial relationships with other Waldorf teachers, and her interpretation of Steiner's philosophy to support the meanings she ascribes to the different forms of representation selected. Her choices demonstrate a belief in learning and development compatible with the school's philosophy, fostering the construction of meaning and understanding through multiple layers of feeling, imagination, and experience.

The three stages of life reflected in the curriculum and pedagogy of a Waldorf school do not, however, relate to learning theories that describe natural stages of development. Steiner bases his educational approach on the philosophical teachings of Anthroposophy, not psychological studies. The stages of willing, feeling, and thinking do not align with Piaget's four stages of development: sensorimotor, preoperational, concrete operational, and formal operational (Wadsworth, 1996). Neither do they correspond to the three stages of representation Bruner defines (1966): enactive (i.e., physical action such as moving, touching, and feeling), iconic (i.e., visual images), and symbolic (i.e., words and symbols). The three stages of development in Waldorf education have a spiritual basis.

Coherence

Waldorf schools straddle a teacher-directed and student-centered education, especially in the stage of middle childhood. On the *Continuum of Educational Philosophy* (Figure 7.1), the school's practices range from a fixed curriculum and teacher-directed methods to student-centered practices based on experience. Waldorf offers a range of traditional academic content matter from practical skills to artistic expression. Despite this variety, the curriculum is fixed in that the same subjects are offered to all students and the overall structure has remained essentially unaltered since Steiner founded the first school in 1919. Despite the emphasis on child-centered experience, the stage of middle childhood is predominantly a teacher-directed phase. The classroom teacher of this age group remains with the same students from grades 1 through 8 as a "loving authority" figure (Almon, 1992, p. 77).

The spiritual aspect of Anthroposophy anchors the school on the ideas-oriented side of the Continuum even as it extends into the process-oriented side in many of its practices. The view of reality Steiner espouses connects observations of natural development with a metaphysics that transcends purely physical, empirical explanations. Those who choose to become Waldorf teachers accept the tenets of Anthroposophy as well as the pedagogy. "Spiritual knowledge must be the foundation of a real art of education and instruction," Steiner asserts (1995). "Understanding of spiritual knowledge leads to an understanding of human nature" (p. 165). As with many of the philosophers we have encountered thus far in our inquiry, Steiner's belief in a spiritual essence ultimately tethers his educational practices to a divine nature while at the same time reaching beyond a purely rational and intellectual approach to meet the needs of children in a practical and developmentally appropriate way.

Reflect

How Do Your Prior Observations and Experiences Relate to a Curriculum Designed to Teach According to Feeling and Imagination?

You may not have experience observing in a Waldorf school. However, many curricula emphasize a developmentally appropriate sequence for introducing content and skills and using developmentally appropriate materials for presenting content. In what ways has the curriculum you have experienced or observed been designed to align with stages of development? In what ways can you relate the stages to the Waldorf stages of willing and imitation, feeling and imagination, and thinking?

In what other ways is the curriculum you have observed similar to or different from Waldorf education? Does the curriculum incorporate the arts (e.g., visual arts, music, drama) in all subjects? Do all students participate in movement as a subject? What practical skills does the curriculum include? Is handwork such as knitting, sewing, and woodworking part of the curriculum? At what grade level does the school begin to offer the study of foreign languages?

Waldorf education stresses spiritual development and learning moral truths. How do schools integrate character lessons into the curriculum? In what ways are these lessons explicit or implicit? Do schools you are familiar with ask students to recite sayings or sing songs that reinforce a moral or ethical point of view or otherwise express a particular set of values? How are the values taught in a Waldorf school similar to or different from values emphasized by other philosophies of educational, such as Perennialism (Chapter 3) or Essentialism (Chapter 5)?

How Do Your Prior Observations and Experiences Relate to a Pedagogy Designed to Teach According to Feeling and Imagination?

The pedagogy of Waldorf education stems from the beliefs of Anthroposophy and the three stages of development at the center of that philosophy. How is teaching with which you are familiar depend on a system of propositions concerning the development of the child? How does the teacher implement practices that address those stages? Are teaching practices modified or altered to adjust to an individual child's development or are all students taught in the same way according to assumptions about how all children develop?

In what ways is a teacher able to express talents in arts, singing, movement, and other skills and incorporate those forms into instruction? To what degree does a teacher create in the classroom or does a teacher reproduce methods of instruction prescribed by others?

How is the role of the teacher similar to or different from the teacher as a guiding authority? How would having a teacher follow the same group of students through a series of grade levels affect the teacher-student relationship?

In what ways does a teacher nurture a child's natural development or expect the child to conform to the school's expectations of achievement at each level of education?

How Do Your Prior Observations and Experiences Relate to a School Designed to Teach According to Feeling and Imagination?

All Waldorf schools follow the same curriculum and train teachers in the same set of methods. How do these practices create an environment that matches the purpose of the school to teaching according to the stages of development? What aspects of a Waldorf school produce a learning climate similar to or different from school where you have attended, observed, or taught?

The interior of a Waldorf school features open spaces, soft natural colors, and natural lighting. Outdoor spaces encourage play, exploration, interaction with natural objects and materials, gardens, and animals such as chickens and rabbits. How are these elements of design similar to or different from schools you have experienced?

Waldorf schools explain the philosophy behind their practices to families and hold workshops and study groups for families to become more acquainted with the school's purpose and practices. In what ways do schools you have experienced inform families of the school's purpose? How do they involve families in learning more about the philosophy that supports the school's practices?

How Do Your Own Practices and Beliefs Relate to the Purpose of Education as Learning According to Feeling and Imagination?

Reading about Waldorf education may have raised interest about its practices. You may wish to visit a Waldorf school and observe in classrooms to see the practices in action. What aspects of the Waldorf teacher do you find intriguing and would perhaps wish to implement in your own classroom? Do you believe it is possible to incorporate elements of Waldorf education in the classroom without completing Waldorf training and becoming a teacher in a Waldorf school?

The purpose of Waldorf education is to educate the whole child. Steiner (1995) describes "a pedagogy that results from a true understanding of the whole person, that is, the body, soul and spirit of human beings" (p. 128). He believes, "We should always emphasize the need to educate people as whole beings" (p. 45).

Note

1 Portions of this chapter have been adapted from "Layers of Experience: Forms of Representation in a Waldorf School Classroom" by David W. Nicholson, 2000, *Journal of Curriculum Studies, 32*(4), 575–588. © 2000 by Routledge. Adapted with permission.

References

Alliance for Public Waldorf Education. (2015). Home page. Retrieved from http://www.allianceforpub licwaldorfeducation.org

Almon, J. (1992). Educating for creative thinking: The Waldorf approach. *Revision, 15*(2), 71–78.

Association of Waldorf Schools of North America. (n.d.). [Website]. Retrieved from http://www.whywal-dorfworks.org

Barnes, H. (1980). An introduction to Waldorf education. *Teachers College Record, 81*(3), 323–336.

Barnes, H. (1991). Learning that grows with the learner: An introduction to Waldorf education. *Educational Leadership, 49*(2), 52–54.

Bruner, J. S. (1966). *Toward a theory of instruction.* New York, NY: W. W. Norton.

Easton, F. (1997). Educating the whole child, "head, heart, and hands": Learning from the Waldorf experi-ence. *Theory into Practice, 36*(2), 87–94.

George Washington Carver School of Arts and Sciences. (n.d.). Home page. Retrieved from http://www.carverartsandscience.org

Kotzsch, R. E. (1990, July/August). Waldorf education: Schooling the head, hands, and heart. *Utne Reader, 41,* 84–89.

Prager, D. R. (2004). Learning through creating an urban Waldorf elementary school background. *Online Yearbook of Urban Learning, Teaching, and Research,* 19–26.

Schwartz, E. (1992). Holistic assessment in the Waldorf school. *Holistic Educational Review, 5*(4), 31–37.

Steiner, R. (1968). *The roots of education.* London: Rudolf Steiner Press.

Steiner, R. (1995). *The spirit of the Waldorf school.* (R. F. Lathe & N. P. Whittaker, Trans.). Hudson, NY: Anthroposophic Press.

Steiner, R. (1996). *The education of the child: And early lectures on education.* Hudson, NY: Anthroposophic Press.

Steiner, R. (1997). *Discussions with teachers.* Hudson, NY: Anthroposophic Press.

Steiner, R. (2001). *The renewal of education.* Great Barrington, MA: Anthroposophic Press.

Steiner, R. (2002). *What is Anthroposophy? Three perspectives on self-knowledge.* (C. Bamford & M. Spiegler, Trans.). Great Barrington, MA: Anthroposophic Press.

Uhrmacher, P. B. (1993). Coming to know the world through Waldorf education. *Journal of Curriculum and Supervision, 9*(1), 87–104.

Uhrmacher, P. B. (1995). Uncommon schooling: A historical look at Rudolph Steiner, anthroposophy, and Waldorf education. *Curriculum Inquiry, 25*(4), 381–406.

Wadsworth, B. J. (1996). *Piaget's theory of cognitive and affective development* (5th ed.). Boston, MA: Allyn & Bacon.

8 What If . . . The Purpose of Education Were to Learn to Solve Practical Problems?

Wonder

In the two previous chapters, we investigated educational philosophies based on the natural development of the child. Another aspect of a student-centered education focuses on learning knowledge and developing skills to solve authentic, practical problems. The wonder question asks, *"What if . . . the purpose of education were to learn to solve practical problems?"*

On the *Continuum of Educational Philosophy* (Figure 8.1), student experiences in the process of learning become as important as acquiring knowledge of the subject area content. This perspective emphasizes making learning relevant and applicable to the needs and interests of students.

Observe

Classroom Vignette: A Third-Grade Problem-Based Math Lesson

"Mrs. K needs your help!"

The class comes to attention as their teacher opens the school day with a plea to her third-grade class.

EDUCATIONAL PRACTICES

RATIONAL	EMPIRICAL
Ideas-Focused	Experience-Focused
Content-Oriented	Process-Oriented
Fixed Curriculum	Flexible Curriculum
Teacher-Centered	Student-Centered
Teacher-Directed	Self-Directed
Pre-Determined Outcomes	Open-Ended Exploration
Whole-Class Activities	Differentiated/Individualized Activities

Objective External Reality	Internal Subjective Reality
Absolute Universal Truth	Changing Relative Truth
Pre-Existing Knowledge	Constructed Knowledge
Knowledge Independent of Experience	Knowledge Dependent on Experience
Autonomous Knowledge	Interdependent Knowledge
Absolute Universal Values	Relative Local Values
Values Independent of Experience	Values Dependent on Experience

PHILOSOPHICAL PERSPECTIVES

Figure 8.1 Continuum of Educational Philosophy (Practical Problems)

"Field Day is coming up, and the teachers in the third grade are planning a scavenger hunt."

As yelps of excitement burst forth from the students, Mrs. K writes the third-grade class sizes on the whiteboard at the front of the room:

Mrs. K's class = 24 students
Ms. W's class = 24 students
Mr. S's class = 32 students

"What do you notice? What do you wonder?" Hands shoot up. Mrs. K points to a student.

"Mr. S's class has more students," Jordan notices.

"So, what do you wonder?" More hands rise.

"How can you make an even number of teams in all classes?" Michael responds.

"Is having an equal number of teams from each class important?" Mrs. K asks.

After some murmuring, a student volunteers an answer.

"Not if only one team wins the scavenger hunt out of the whole third grade," Carly reasons. "But if a team wins, does that count as that class winning?"

"Then it's not fair!" Rob chimes in.

"What's not fair?" Mrs. K asks.

"If a class has more teams, they have a better chance of winning."

"So we need to decide the best way to make teams so the scavenger hunt is fair. What else do you wonder?"

Mrs. K lists the students' responses on the board:

How many items in the hunt?
What is the time limit?
What is the size of the area where items will be hidden?
Is there a prize for the winning class? Or only for the winning team?
Will there be different prizes, such as first place, second place, third place depending on how many items your team finds?
How many students per team? How many teams per class?
How to make the teams fair?
Is an equal number of students on each team fair?

"This is an amazing set of questions!" Mrs. K tells her students. "I knew you could help me to solve this problem."

The students beam with pride.

"I notice that you ask about the scavenger hunt being fair," Mrs. K observes. "Does fair mean that each class has an equal number of teams or that each team has to have an equal number of people?"

"I think I know!" Janel calls out. More students begin raising their hands.

"I am so glad that you are already thinking about how to solve the problem," Mrs. K announces. "I have a plan."

Mrs. K asks her students to work in groups to propose a solution. She writes on the board the following three directions:

1   Make fair teams.
2   Represent the problem using pictures, words, number sentences, and/or manipulatives.
3   Construct an argument for your choice. Be prepared to defend your solution.

"Show your group's thinking on a whiteboard," Mrs. K instructs. "Be able to explain how you solved the problem. I will be circulating the room to see how your groups are working and ask questions about your ideas."

A member from each group grabs a portable whiteboard as teams gather at tables and on the floor. One student in each group writes the class sizes on the board. Then the brainstorming begins. One group adds all the class sizes to arrive at a total of 80. They divide the sum by the number of classes. Already, they begin to puzzle.

A team searches for a factor that will divide the number of students in each class evenly, to suggest how many teams each class might contain. They start with 2, then try 3, 4, 6, and 8. All of these factors work for each class.

Mrs. K moves to observe another group. They arrange blue blocks into a square representing a large field, and orange blocks into a smaller square. They lay their teams onto the "fields" using counting blocks that accurately depict the team sizes. They argue that a larger field requires more teams.

"The size of the field makes a big difference," Mariya insists. "It's easier to find stuff in a smaller area. If you hide things all over the playground and even inside the school too then bigger teams can spread out."

"Smaller teams can communicate better," Morgan points out. "They can shout out to each other."

"But large teams can still pair up and go out and search," Sarah suggests. "They can even send one person from each pair to a certain place, like the swing set, to check in every once in a while and find out what they have so far."

Mrs. K approaches another group in the midst of their deliberations.

"All teams don't have to be exactly even," Sam explains. "Let's just set a minimum and a maximum and people can team up with whoever they want."

The group began by marking the class sizes on the whiteboard using symbols for tens and ones. A nearby team uses a similar approach, but has brought a container of counting blocks to the table. They lay out 10-base blocks and cubes to represent the number of students in each class and begin to arrange these manipulatives to form teams.

Another group has drawn circles to represent each group. The circles are color-coded, and the group has provided a "key" (Green=Mrs. K's class, Orange=Ms. T, Red=Mr. S, and Yellow=Ms. W). Dots have been drawn within each circle to represent the number of students on a team, and they have placed a star beside any unequal or uneven groups. Below the representations, the group has written out their comments.

"Groups of two are too small," Jenny explains. "Four still seems too small. Eight works for all three classes but that seems too big."

"I like six," Amber interjects, "but that doesn't work for Mr. S's class."

"Then they can have bigger teams of eight," Brittany suggests.

"That isn't fair," Andrew complains.

"Why is that not fair?" Mrs. K asks the team.

Amber replies, "If your team has more kids, you have more chances to find things. Your team might win over a team with fewer kids."

"There's no way each class can have both an equal number of teams and the same number of kids on each team," Rob declares. "It's impossible!"

Mrs. K recommends they get a second whiteboard and propose an alternative solution. "Show one solution on one whiteboard," she suggests, "and another solution as a back-up plan."

As Mrs. K circulates, she overhears various arguments to solve the problem.

"Can we mix all the classes up?" Blake asks her group. "Why does it have to be one class against another? How about just make even teams out of everybody in the third grade and whatever team finds the most stuff wins?"

When all groups have finished their representations and solutions, the groups prop their whiteboards up around the room and students take a "gallery walk." Mrs. K asks each group to notice which solutions are similar to theirs and which are different.

Josh volunteers, "At first I felt confused because I wasn't sure how we were going to make teams fair. But then we decided that each group had to be equal so we decided on groups of 4."

"I wanted to just divide it up so we mixed with other classes," Blake shares, "but my team didn't like that idea. They convinced me to make sure that the groups were divided equally in each class."

"As usual, Mrs. K didn't give us all the information so we had to find several different solutions for different situations," Aleisha explains. "We came up with a couple of ideas just in case."

"We were worried that you would ask us if we were sure we had found all the possible group sizes," Angie says. "This helped us feel sure about the group size we decided on."

Mrs. K smiles, "You all worked very hard on this problem and I can see several different solutions. Let's see if we understand all the mathematics."

Mrs. K points to the class sizes written on the board. "What are all the group sizes you found for each class?"

Carly goes to her group's whiteboard. "For a class of 24, we found, 2, 3, 4, 6, and 8."

Mrs. K writes the group sizes on the board beside Mrs. K's class.

"We found 12, too!" Michael calls out. Mrs. K writes 12 next to the 8.

"Now, how about for a class of 32?" Mrs. K asks.

Janel says, "We found 2, 4, 8, and that's it!"

"Are you sure you found all the group sizes?" Mrs. K asks.

The groups start talking and looking at their boards again.

"Yes, that is it!" Blake confirms.

"So, what is the mathematics we used today to solve this problem?"

Nicole says, "We divided."

Mrs. K asks, "How did you divide?"

Brandon responds, "Well, we found equal groups and we took the class amounts and divided them up."

"Any other mathematics?"

"We kind of multiplied," Rob explains. "We guessed a group size and then just started making groups until it added up."

"So, we used division and multiplication," Mrs. K confirms.

"And addition!" Kelsie interrupts.

"And addition, good." Mrs. K then asks, "Why do you think multiplication and division worked for this problem?"

"Because multiplication and division both work with equal groups," Michael explains.

"Okay, so what are equal groups called?"

"Sometimes we've called them groups but other times we called them arrays," Janel determines.

"Very nice, Janel. Thank you for remembering the vocabulary word 'array.' I am going to introduce you to new mathematics vocabulary to describe what you did today."

Mrs. K points to the list the students generated on the board. "When you found all the group sizes, you actually found all the factors for each number." She writes the word "factor" on the board.

"Tomorrow, we will use our work today to see if we can figure out a way to define the mathematics vocabulary word, 'factor.' Also, we are going to use our work to make proposals about the scavenger hunt group sizes to the other teachers."

"I can't wait to show the teachers your hard work and great thinking."

Investigate

The students in the vignette devise strategies and test ideas to suggest practical solutions to an authentic, relevant problem. To examine philosophical perspectives that support this purpose of education, we will investigate the following inquiry questions:

- What Do Teachers Teach? Questions about the Curriculum
- How Do Teachers Teach? Questions about Pedagogy
- How Are Schools Organized? Questions about the Role of the School

What Do Teachers Teach? Questions about the Curriculum

"All genuine education comes about through experience."

(John Dewey)

In the vignette, students do not learn new math content and procedures, then practice solving sample problems contained in a textbook or workbook. The teacher does not list several similar problems on the board for individual students to solve for the correct answer in front of the class. Students do not complete independent seatwork that repeats operations required to demonstrate mastery. Instead, the teacher describes a real-life problem the students need or want to solve, which involves using math as a tool for arriving at possible solutions.

Problem-Based Learning

In problem-based learning (PBL), students are presented with an "ill-structured problem" to solve prior to the teacher introducing new content (Stepien, & Gallagher, 1993, p. 26). The teacher does not model the steps or procedures for solving the problem and typically does not furnish all the information needed at the outset. In PBL, the problem functions as a tool to learn new knowledge and skills (Dochy, Segers, Van den Bossche, & Gijbels, 2003). The teacher asks questions that prompt students to examine their thinking as they engage in the activity. Students interpret the problem, gather needed information, identify possible solutions, evaluate options, and present conclusions (Jyeong Ha Roh, 2003).

Learners approach the problem by accessing prior knowledge, testing ideas, and constructing understanding. They may struggle at first and need to collaborate with peers to make decisions and take action. Initial efforts to solve the problem may not work, requiring multiple attempts. Students represent the problem in different ways to analyze the factors involved. The problem may need to be redefined and additional questions may emerge. More than one possible solution may exist. In the absence of a single, correct answer or method, PBL does not seek universal, objective knowledge, but searches for knowledge applicable in the context of the situation.

In this perspective, the curriculum is flexible, not fixed, and outcomes are not pre-determined. The curriculum adapts to needs and uses. The content of the curriculum includes contemporary problems and issues, which may vary according to conditions. In this approach, the process is equally as important as the product. Knowledge is constructed as learners share their experiences. Assessment strives to indicate growth, rather than meeting a set of objective, external standards, and includes affective, psychological, and emotional dimensions as well as subject area content.

Pragmatism

The philosophical perspective associated with learning practical knowledge and skills is known as Pragmatism. Pragmatism comes from the Greek word *pragma*, meaning "action." Pragmatic is also defined as "practical." Three American philosophers (Charles Sanders Peirce, William James, and John Dewey) conclude that education should focus on learning how to solve practical problems.

Charles Sanders Peirce (1839–1914) defines beliefs as habits of mind formed through investigation. Peirce (1905) argues that these habits of mind inform future action. "Reflection," he writes, "is part of the self-preparation for action on the next occasion" (p. 169). True knowledge is determined by experience and confirmed by practical consequences. The effects of ideas verify their veracity. According to this perspective, the scientific method does not seek to discover eternal Forms or universal truths but to obtain practical results that have immediate application. General meanings are merely propositions, hypotheses requiring testing and verification.

"The rational meaning of every proposition lies in the future," Peirce claims (p. 173). The purpose of inquiry is to find practical solutions to problems encountered in everyday circumstances.

The philosopher and psychologist William James (1842–1910) distinguishes between a rational perspective, which seeks unity of all things into a whole, and an empirical one. "Empiricism means the habit of explaining wholes by parts," James (1908/1977) writes, which thereby "inclines to pluralistic views" (p. 9). This perspective rejects a single objective view of reality that exists external and independent of human experience. We live in an open, dynamic universe, constantly changing and evolving. Interpretations of reality depend on human experience, with no single view offering the final version of truth. A pluralistic universe suggests many possible ways to view reality. Pragmatism does not view the universe as fixed or closed, with an absolute Form for everything arising from definite origins. The metaphysical quest for truth and reality is restless, and can never land upon any one definitive answer.

In questions about reality, all that matters are the practical consequences. "The whole function of philosophy," James (1907/1991) argues, "ought to be to find what definite difference it will make to you and me" (p. 25). The various meanings that may be ascribed to different viewpoints only come down to that which is practical. "It is astonishing," James writes, "to see how many philosophical disputes collapse into insignificance the moment you subject them to this simple test of tracing a concrete consequence" (p. 25).

Speculation about the nature of reality should not offer final metaphysical results, with the goal of discovering first principles and ultimate causes, but only recommend pragmatic solutions based on first-hand facts. Scientific discoveries, even those touted as facts, are only tentative. They have the appearance of truth only so far as they relate to our experiences. Pragmatism does not seek to unify all of reality under a single explanation. The value of truth rests only in its ability to explain how things work in practical experience. James (1907/1991) contends, "The pragmatist clings to facts and concreteness, observes truth at its work in particular cases, and generalizes" only insofar as those explanations continue to hold true in different circumstances under varying conditions (p. 33). "This is an instrumental view of truth," he explains, "the view that truth in our ideas means their power to 'work'" (p. 28).

The work of Charles Darwin (British, 1809–1882) concerning natural selection and evolution greatly influenced these educational thinkers. Darwin's theory dispels antiquated notions of an immutable structure to the universe. Natural development implies constant change, and represents a departure from the belief in detached abstractions and other absolute explanations about the universe that appear remote from experience. James (1907/1991) claims, "Darwinism has once and for all displaced design from the minds of the scientific" (p. 34). Darwin (1859/2009) himself anticipates resistance to his research from "experienced naturalists" who will continue to present "unity of design" as fact rather than as a point of view (p. 482).

John Dewey (1859–1952) agrees that the findings of Darwin refute the existence of fixed forms and final causes existing in nature. As a result, philosophy will need to abandon the search for the ideal and the absolute "in order to explore specific values and the specific conditions that generate them" (MW 4:10). Dialectic arguments concerning the nature of reality must be replaced with methods that subject hypotheses to testing. Science investigates the concrete and particular, deriving meaning from direct observation and experiment. According to Peirce (1905), "What will remain of philosophy will be a series of problems capable of investigation by the observational methods of the true sciences" (p. 171).

The sense of an evolutionary nature to reality dates to before Darwin. Auguste Comte (1798–1857), a French philosopher and scientist, explains that civilization has gone through three stages. In the first stage, the Theological (the religious or the "fictitious"), humans seek absolute knowledge about the origin and purpose of all (Comte, 2000, p. 27). This first state attributes all phenomena to supernatural causes, and is a necessary phase for beginning to comprehend existence. In the second stage, the Metaphysical (philosophical or "abstract"), reasoning replaces belief in the supernatural, and supposes that abstract forces produce all phenomena (p. 27). The third stage, the Scientific (or "positive"), represents the final and definitive state, in which the search for absolute causes is abandoned (p. 27). Instead, humans focus on detecting and understanding physical laws that govern observable phenomena. Further, Comte argues that every individual passes through these same three phases, progressing from a Theological state (in childhood) to a Metaphysical phase (in youth) to the Scientific stage (in maturity).

According to Comte, this evolution in human understanding is a natural process, culminating in the current era of science wherein observations and experiments investigate claims about truth and explain reality. The incompatibility of the three states (Theological, Metaphysical, and Scientific) to co-exist in society creates instability and crises. Scientific methods should be applied in all fields of education to solve problems, including social problems. The Scientific is the one state that will prevail, producing order and advancing society.

In the classroom vignette, the students worked together to solve a practical problem using mathematics. Comte (2000) calls mathematics "the most ancient and the most perfect science of all" (p. 56). Mathematics is the basis for all scientific inquiry, Comte reminds us. "The Greeks had no other, and we may call it *the* science; for its definition is neither more nor less . . . than the definition of all science whatsoever" (p. 60). The application of mathematics and science has no limits, and all matters can fall within their domain. Hence, Comte envisions an era of social reorganization based on scientific solutions. The same principles that govern nature will regulate the evolution of modern society. This extends to moral and ethical issues, which should move past the theological and metaphysical stages to be solved by practical, social methods.

Dewey argues that traditional education is subject-matter oriented, with the aim of transmitting knowledge and skills to students. Knowledge is taken to be "objective in character . . . without any particular reference to the individual" (EW 5:164). Sources of information exist outside of one's experience. This perspective artificially delineates bodies of knowledge into distinct disciplines and separates content from the processes of learning. Teaching within this system is autocratic and didactic, dependent on textbooks and conforming to prescribed standards. The school exhibits a "pattern of organization" characterized by "time-schedules, schemes of classification, of examination and promotion, of rules and order" that separates it from other social institutions (LW 13:5). The presumed goal, to prepare students for future responsibilities by means of acquiring "organized bodies of information and prepared forms of skill," imposes routine learning on passive, docile students (LW 13:6). Moreover, knowledge is represented as fixed, delivered as a "finished product" that appears to assume the future will be much like the past in a society that will fundamentally not change (LW 13:7).

However, Dewey shuns simply opposing traditional education and rejecting its methods. Instead, he asks how organized subject-matter may be attained based on the learner's experiences within a flexible curriculum that allows for both learning from the past and living in the present. He does not believe all experiences have equal educational value. Were that the case, any experience that occurs within the paradigm of traditional education would be of equal value with any other proposed learning experience. Dewey distinguishes between experiences that hinder a child's development and experiences that enrich one's life and enhance the possibility for growth.

Dewey calls for "a philosophy of education based upon a philosophy of experience" (LW 13:14), asserting that "all genuine education comes about through experience" (LW 13:11). He proposes a "newer education" that values individual expression, recognizes the need to accept change, and encourages learning through activity and experience (LW 13: 7). Dewey concludes that "conditions founds in present experience should be used as sources of problems" within the curriculum (LW 13:52).

In Dewey's definition, the philosophy of Pragmatism maintains "the continuity of knowing" that has been accumulated from past thinkers and doers to apply to present-day circumstances (MW 9:353–4). Pragmatism as a way of thinking encourages activity that "purposely modifies the environment" (MW 9:354). This perspective views knowledge as a means to "adapt the environment to our needs and adapt our aims and desires to the situation" (MW 9:354). Knowledge has practical implications that directly connect to our experiences. Furthermore, Pragmatism focuses on progress. Education, in turn, should provide activities that give direction and meaning to everyday life, and emphasize the practical usefulness of learning.

Reminiscent of Rousseau, James (1899/1958) declares that "there is nothing absolutely ideal" (p. 186). The truth of an idea is not an inherent quality or trait, but a proposition that is shown to be true through verification. Truth is a process. Meaning is relative, based on the experiences of the individual. When new ideas enter a person's consciousness, old ones are often discarded. We can change our mind about the ideals that form the basis for living one's life. "Education," James supposes, "is a means of multiplying our ideals, of bringing new ones into view" (p. 186). Therefore, the mere possession of ideas is an insufficient definition of an educated person. Intelligence is characterized by intelligent progress. The significance of education is to enhance our ability to recognize new ideas, to combine ideas, and to continually develop and grow.

A basic fact of psychology, James explains, is that "some kind of consciousness is always going on" (p. 28). He argues a child's consciousness "has two functions that are obvious: It leads to knowledge, and it leads to action" (p. 32). A philosophy of education based on purely rational thinking ignores the application of knowledge to useful purposes. James suggests that the study of psychology has transferred emphasis from the abstract to the practical. The epistemological implication is that knowledge has value when it leads to practical action. In contrast to philosophers who define humans as rational beings, James declares, "Man, whatever else he may be, is primarily a practical being, whose mind is given to him to aid in adapting him to this world's life" (p. 34).

James argues that abstract thinking and dwelling on metaphysical, ethical, aesthetic, and logical matters invariably affect our behavior and produce practical results. "We cannot escape our destiny," he concludes, "which is practical" (p. 35). He admonishes teachers to avoid abstract lessons full of teacher talk. He advises teachers to refrain from implementing teacher-directed activities and instead to wait for opportunities where they can enable students "to think, to feel, and to do" (p. 60). Humans by nature react to the environment and make associations between responses and their effect. The purpose of education is to guide a child's responses to the environment. The teacher's responsibility is to observe a child's reactions and turn those reactions to productive ends, to "build up useful systems of associations in the pupil's mind" (p. 68).

A philosophical system that best serves education is one in accordance with natural laws of human behavior. The teacher's task is to train a child's behavior in the broadest sense. "Education, in short," James asserts, "cannot be better described than by calling it the organization of acquired habits of conduct and tendencies to behavior" (p. 36–7). A consequence of shaping a child's behaviors and helping students make associations is the acquisition of ideas and concepts. Strive to make abstract topics more attainable through using familiar analogies and concrete examples. Engage students in practical activities that involve objects and physical materials. Educate the child through experiences, and meaningful intellectual learning will follow. The attainment of knowledge can only be of value, however, if it manifests itself in useful, practical action.

How Do Teachers Teach? Questions about Pedagogy

"Problems are the stimulus to thinking."

(John Dewey)

In the classroom vignette, the teacher does not present a mathematical principle or axiom that the students must then apply to different problems. Nor does the teacher offer a formula that the students are expected to follow to arrive at a solution. The students themselves do not ask for a formula that produces a correct answer. The students struggle with the problem of creating groups needed in this particular situation. A single correct procedure for creating equal groups in all situations is not proposed. On the contrary, some students argue that not all groups need to be equal for the whole of the third grade, much less the whole of the universe. They grapple with a practical problem that requires a workable solution to satisfy their immediate goals. For the students, the goal is not to learn mathematics. Mathematics is a tool used to solve a problem. From James's perspective, they are not looking at the parts to unify their learning into an absolute whole, but are learning more about the whole (mathematics) through experience with the parts. The students experience mathematics on the concrete level and assess its worth in a particular case. They come to value mathematics when it demonstrates practical value that serves their purposes. In other words, the students are not learning math for its own sake, but learning how to solve practical problems using available tools. Math is not taught as preordained truth, but as a means for finding a truth. Math, or any subject, "becomes true" (James, 1907/1991, p. 28) by justifying its instrumental value.

In the pragmatic philosophy, a person is confronted with a situation that requires a solution. Through examination and analysis of the factors present, one infers possible alternative actions. Thinking involves "a jump from the known into the unknown," Dewey explains, arguing that there is no thought without inference and no proof without testing (LW 8:191). Thinking arises only out of direct experiences. One should be puzzled or perplexed by a situation and engage in active inquiry to discover a solution.

Dewey proposes five steps or phases to solving a problem: 1) encountering a situation that causes the mind to leap forward to possible solutions, 2) framing the situation as a problem to be solved, 3) formulating an hypothesis to initiate and guide inquiry, 4) reasoning that leads to inferences, and 5) testing the hypothesis (LW 8:200). This process closely parallels the steps of the scientific method: 1) pose a question or define a problem, 2) make a prediction or state a hypothesis, 3) conduct an experiment and collect data, 4) analyze and interpret the findings, 5) state a tentative conclusion.

"To appreciate a problem as such, the child must feel it as his own difficulty, which has arisen within and out of his own experience" (EW 5:145). A problem must present a dilemma, an ambiguous situation that requires considering alternatives. He emphasizes the need for learners to formulate their own purposes and direct their own activities within the learning process. In this sense, a purpose involves a plan of action. Purposes are formulated from observing one's surroundings, recalling knowledge gained in similar situations, and making a judgment on how to act under the circumstances. "The material of thinking is not thoughts," Dewey contends, "but actions, facts, events, and the relations of things" (MW 9:163). Through observation and the collection and analysis of data, the learner forms inferences. "Ideas," Dewey conjectures, "are anticipations of possible solutions" (MW 9:167).

Education should be a reconstruction of real-life experience. Experiential and experimental methods, such as trial and error, characterize problem solving in daily life. Ideas or truths are merely propositions or hypotheses that must be tested and verified in the natural or social world. Learning consists not only of ideas, but of actions and consequences. Learning requires interpreting meaning of events and consequences in context. That knowledge is valued that achieves desired ends. In other words, practical knowledge is knowledge of what works.

What Is the Role of the Teacher in Learning to Solve Problems?

TEACHER AS FACILITATOR

In problem solving, the teacher acts as Facilitator. A problem is identified and a process must be determined to solve the problem. A teacher may begin by modeling the process, or establishing the conditions for students to collaboratively decide for themselves. The teacher prompts the students by asking questions about the nature of the problem, factors related to the problem, and possible strategies, solutions, and consequences. In addition, the teacher asks questions that explicitly probe student thinking during the problem-solving process.

TEACHER AS COACH

The teacher may be viewed as a Coach, offering advice and suggestions, encouraging effort, coaxing alternative thinking, and supporting decision-making. The teacher may also function as a member of the problem-solving team. Dewey observes, "The teacher loses the position of external boss or dictator but takes on that of leader of group activities" (LW 13:37).

What Is the Role of the Student in Learning to Solve Problems?

STUDENT AS PROBLEM-SOLVER

The student acts in the role of Problem-Solver. Students learn to recognize, define, and frame problems that arise from their own experiences. Working with peers, they develop strategies and devise methods for analyzing and solving problems, including posing alternative solutions and anticipating consequences. The teacher guides and assists the process, but the students assume greater responsibility for directing their own learning.

STUDENT AS EXPERT

In problem-based learning, students assume the roles of professionals such as mathematicians, scientists, historians, and others who deal with real-life, complex problems. A goal of PBL is to gain expertise in problem-solving skills and specialized knowledge. The student becomes a developing expert in the field of study.

Design

How Are Schools Organized? Questions about the Role of the School

University of Chicago Laboratory School

In 1896, Dewey founded the Laboratory School at the University of Chicago. Still in operation today, the school serves as a setting to implement and test innovative teaching and learning methods. The basis of the school is experiential and experimental in nature, from the organization of the school to the curriculum and instruction. From the outset, the school's aim was "to subordinate the amassing of facts and principles to the development of intellectual self-control and of power to conceive and solve problems" (Mayhew & Edwards, 1936/1965, p. 33–4). All grade levels participate in problem-solving learning activities in different subject areas, focusing on current issues present in everyday life.

From its founding, the school focused on "various forms of practical and constructive activity" (Mayhew & Edwards, 1936/1965, p. 32). The curriculum included practical skills such as cooking, sewing, carpentry, and woodworking. Activities conducted in the kitchen permitted testing different cooking techniques, as well as learning to weigh, measure, and perform computations. Students worked with materials such as wood, textiles, and metals in construction projects. Children at the school made their own materials, such as pencil boxes, notebooks, towels, and utensils. They also role-played various jobs and occupations. One child gathered props, made a costume, and play-acted as a postal worker. Another became a grocer. A third group assembled a streetcar from chairs and acted as the conductor.

Reggio Emilia Schools

In the Reggio Emilia approach to early childhood education (introduced in Chapter 6), "classrooms are organized to support a highly collaborative problem-solving approach to learning" (Edwards, Gandini, & Forman, 1998, p. 7). No formal curriculum is prescribed. Instead, children

are provided a resource-rich environment encouraging exploration. Students ask questions, speculate, and test their initial hypotheses. In this system of learning, "children try to figure out how
something happens rather than try to describe how something looks" (p. 373). Understanding is
not limited to definitions; rather students engage in an active search for explanations.

For example, in one Reggio Emilia school, a group of five- and six-year-olds was curious about
the sizes of dinosaurs. After deciding to build a scale model of Tyrannosaurus Rex, the children
needed to calculate measurements and select materials. Dividing into two smaller groups, one
group built a four-foot-high model using Styrofoam while another fashioned a body from metal
and wire. Still not satisfied, the children wished to construct something that would show the true
dimensions of a life-size dinosaur. Consulting a diagram as a guide, they established that the
animal was twenty-seven meters long by nine meters tall. Using meter-length plastic rods (used
for hanging posters), the children laid out a rectangle in the athletic field. They converted these
dimensions to graph paper to draw the dinosaur within the rectangle, then returned to the athletic
field to mark out gridlines. When told they could no longer hold up activities on the athletic field,
the students reduced the size once more and fit a scaled-down version in the courtyard. Each step
of the problem-solving process was documented and the class presented an exhibit to the rest of
the school (Edwards, Gandini, & Forman, 1998).

Sammamish High School

Sammamish High School in Bellevue, Washington, has integrated PBL into its curriculum. The
school states that "real learning only happens when we are confronted with a problem that we need
to solve" (Sammamish High School, n.d., p. 1). Students work collaboratively on authentic problems inside and outside of the classroom on real-world challenges. A teacher may create a problem
that has a correct solution, offering students flexibility in determining how to solve the problem.
In other instances, the teacher and students identify a problem that requires an original solution.
Students define and represent the problem, develop the method, research sources of information,
suggest and test solutions, and communicate the results. Professionals in the community are often
consulted and the results presented for feedback. Students reflect on the process as part of the
learning cycle.

The characteristics of PBL at Sammamish High School (2013) include identifying authentic
problems "relevant to the lives of students, teachers, and/or to a professional field or discipline"
(p. 1). Problems are complex, multi-faceted and multi-layered, and ill-structured. Authentic
assessments reflect performance in the various tasks required to solve the problem and present
one or more viable solutions, emphasizing "growth over time" and developing expertise (p. 1).
Students engage in collaboration and academic discourse.

Examples of PBL in the school include agricultural and land use solutions developed by the
AP Human Geography class, students working with University of Washington researchers to
develop a cancer drug delivery system, the Honors English 10 class gaining analytic writing
skills at the Seattle Art Museum, and the AP Government class working on election campaigns.

Junior Achievement Programs

Junior Achievement is an organization that offers experiences and resources for students in
grades K-12 to develop financial, workplace, and entrepreneurial skills. Their experiential,
hands-on activities provide students with authentic challenges: "Our programs help prepare
young people for the real world" (Junior Achievement Programs). Students can launch a start-
up business or begin an enterprise in the classroom. In addition, students can participate in

programs at on-site virtual communities. During a day-long visit to JA Biztown, a simulated city, elementary and middle school students elect a local government and operate all the businesses (such as a bank, restaurant, radio station, and package delivery service). At JA Finance Park, middle school and high school students participate in a budgeting simulation implemented in a PBL format.

In all these examples, solving practical problems forms the basis of the curriculum and pedagogy (Table 8.1).

How Does a School Designed to Teach How to Solve Practical Problems Define an Educated Person?

The examples we have examined would define an educated person as one who can recognize, define, and solve practical, real-life problems. Such problems would be complex, ill-structured, and require testing various methods and suggesting alternative solutions.

Evaluate

Consistency

A school designed to teach practical problem solving would integrate these skills and knowledge into the entire educational program. Sources of the curriculum would include real-life problems and the pedagogy would facilitate students developing problem-solving methods. Rather than restricting the approach to any particular discipline (such as science), problem solving would permeate all subject areas. Daily instruction would consist of encountering problems, defining and framing them, devising strategies, and proposing solutions. Problem-solving activities would not be offered sporadically but constitute the pedagogy of the school.

How does this problem-solving process differ from the scientific method of Realism (described in Chapter 4)? Realism employs the scientific method to search for definitive answers that formulate and verify generalized principles. The end-product of problem solving is not to discover and codify a single, unified solution that applies in all cases. The goal of problem-solving is to engage in the process and develop habits of mind about interacting with one's immediate surroundings. "Ideas, then, are not genuine ideas unless they are tools with which to search for material to solve a problem," Dewey explains (LW 8:222).

Dewey is as influential a figure in advocating use of the scientific method in education as Descartes and Bacon. The distinctions between these philosophers are in the purposes of education. Descartes and Bacon, for all their differences, share as a common goal the search for principles. Dewey focuses on practical knowledge useful in the context of the situation and does not promote the scientific method for the pursuit of generalizations. For Dewey, change is the only constant.

Table 8.1 Design a School (Practical Problems)

Purpose of Education	Practical problems
Curriculum	Relevant, real-life needs and interests
Instruction	Problem-solving, problem-based learning
Role of Teacher	Facilitator, coach, resource
Role of Student	Problem-solver, expert
Role of School	Practical knowledge and skills

Compatibility

In a philosophy that emphasized practical knowledge and skills, one might ask: What subjects are practical? What subjects are impractical? For example, is how to read a practical skill? If so, what content matter is practical to read? Is learning how to read poetry practical? Pragmatism is concerned with navigating both the physical and social worlds of the individual. In answering questions about what knowledge and skills to deem practical, context matters. The knowledge and skills one needs and values at any given time and location may vary. Perennialism (Chapter 3) identifies a body of knowledge that applies to everyone and endures for all time. Essentialism (Chapter 5) describes a body of knowledge necessary to participate as a responsible, productive citizen and literate member of a defined national culture, resting firmly on tradition. For Pragmatists, all knowledge is open to scrutiny based on its immediate usefulness.

Dewey repudiates claims of universal objective knowledge. The assumption that "facts and principles exist in an independent and external way" separates knowledge from its uses (EW 5:165). For most teachers and students, subjects are required without discussion about how they earned their place in the curriculum or their value to the student. Dewey asks how the study of any body of knowledge functions "as a mode or form of experience" (EW 5:168).

Dewey rejects learning knowledge of the past merely as an end in itself. However, past knowledge can serve as a tool for understanding the present and informing future decisions and actions. "A knowledge of the past and its heritage is of great significance when it enters into the present," Dewey concedes, "but not otherwise" (MW 9:81). The present links to the past and the future, forming a single continuity. The products of the past should not be the focus of education. Their value resides in how they contribute to solving problems in the present.

How might problem solving be compatible with other methods of instruction? Might teachers use problem-solving activities as a means to master content (as described in Chapter 5)? Understanding of content should indeed result from PBL. However, occasional problem-solving activities offered as a diversion from established teacher-directed methods of transmitting content would be incompatible with the purpose of developing problem solving as a way of learning. For example, a teacher brings in M&Ms for a counting activity, believing she is implementing PBL. However, when this brief detour into hands-on learning ends, the teacher returns to drilling students with the goal of mastering content for a test. If the students do not collaborate in trial-and-error testing of methods and ideas, suggest alternative strategies, pose multiple possible solutions, evaluate consequences, and reflect on the process, they have not participated in PBL. Assessment should likewise be authentic, focused on participating in the activity, contributing to the solution, reflecting on the results, and communicating the results. Objective-style assessment methods intended to ascertain recall of facts or mastery of a prescribed procedure would contradict the philosophical underpinnings of the pedagogy.

Coherence

How does this PBL differ from other student-centered perspectives on education? PBL is an interdisciplinary approach integrating curriculum design and pedagogy rather than a method of teaching (Savery, 2006). The problem is the topic of learning, not simply one of several instructional options for studying a subject. The entire learning experience revolves around PBL, from the introduction of the topic to participation in the process to assessment and reflection. A coherent school program designs all instruction around PBL. Problem-solving activities may be found in other school designs, incorporated into an otherwise teacher-directed curriculum, but this approach does not accurately reflect a PBL environment. "Problem-based learning must be the pedagogical base in the curriculum," Savery writes, "and not part of a didactic curriculum" (p. 14).

How does a Pragmatic, problem-based school differ from other schools that develop practical skills? The practical skills that can be observed in a Montessori or Waldorf share many similarities with Pragmatism. Both schools teach young children to prepare meals or snacks, clean up their work spaces, handle and manipulate objects to explore their uses, and discover their environments. Montessori recalls that Dewey searched New York City stores in vain looking for child-sized furnishings and useful objects (such as small brooms) for children to use. Montessori schools place real objects in the hands of children to develop independence. Learning activities must have a useful purpose. By carefully preparing the learning environment, Montessori (1909/1964) claims "to apply, in a practical way, the fundamental principles of scientific pedagogy" (p. 64). Montessori requires instruction on the use of specially designed instructional materials before students are permitted to learn with them. The approach also limits how students use each object based on its intended function. PBL, on the other hand, presents students with ill-structured problems and allows them to exercise ingenuity in arriving at a solution.

Steiner (1995) argues a conventional liberal arts education creates a gulf between what school teaches and what one needs in real life. He believes schools should "remove all abstractions so that the teaching would come from the practical" (p. 89). Steiner also states, however, that "true spirituality affects practical life" (p. 97). The focus on the spiritual dimension is not always compatible with a Pragmatic view to solving current problems in a scientific way.

Would Pragmatism accept any method of understanding as long as it "works" in a practical sense? For example, for centuries, the sun and all celestial bodies were believed to revolve around the Earth. Aristotle (*On the Heavens*) describes a system with all astronomical objects attached to concentric spheres that rotate around the Earth. Based on empirical observations, this model operates according to eternal, unchanging principles. The sun rises in the east and sets in the west, and all visible planets and stars move across the sky in regular, predictable patterns of motion. For all practical purposes, this system would still "work" today from the perspective of one standing on the surface of the planet gazing skyward. One could attend to daily activities with a belief in this system and not be affected.

Pragmatism, however, emphasizes the scientific method. Therefore, hypotheses must be tested and verified. Alternative explanations should be pursued until discredited. A scientific approach also extends to educational practice. A teacher should seek out research-based methods and materials. What Works Clearinghouse, for example, offers a database of educational products and programs vetted using scientific findings. "Focusing on the results from high-quality research," the site states, "we try to answer the question 'What works in education?'" with the goal of enabling educators to make informed decisions based on empirical evidence (What Works Clearinghouse, n.d., Home section, para 2). The site provides a wide variety of resources, however, not specifically PBL products. *The Interdisciplinary Journal of Problem-based Learning* (IJPBL), a peer-reviewed open-access journal, publishes "relevant, interesting, and challenging articles of research, analysis, or promising practice related to all aspects of implementing problem-based learning (PBL) in K-12 and post-secondary classrooms" (*The Interdisciplinary Journal of Problem-based Learning*, n.d., Home section, para 1).

Reflect

How Do Your Prior Observations and Experiences Relate to a Curriculum Designed to Teach How to Solve Practical Problems?

How does the curriculum you have observed or experienced reflect the real-life experiences of students? What practical skills and knowledge does the curriculum emphasize? How can each subject and topic in the curriculum be described as having practical use?

In what ways have you observed problems to be the source of knowledge in the curriculum?

How would you define a traditional math "problem" in a teacher-directed classroom? How does PBL define a "problem"?

How Do Your Prior Observations and Experiences Relate to a Pedagogy Designed to Teach How to Solve Practical Problems?

How has the instruction you have observed or experienced centered on problem solving? In what subject areas does problem solving occur?

How does problem solving develop practical skills? In what subjects are practical skills not applicable?

What aspects of PBL did the students implement? How did the teacher guide the process?

How Do Your Prior Observations and Experiences Relate to a School Designed to Teach How to Solve Practical Problems?

Have you observed or experienced a school that emphasizes solving practical problems? How did the curriculum differ from other schools? How was instructional time organized? What kinds of resources does a school need to provide to facilitate PBL?

How Do Your Own Practices and Beliefs Relate to the Purpose of Education as Learning How to Solve Practical Problems?

On the *Continuum of Educational Philosophy*, PBL and using the scientific method to solve practical problems values the contributions of students in the learning process. Students are encouraged to engage in open exploration and trial and error to construct understanding. Activities promote creativity and inventiveness. Ideas must demonstrate their usefulness. Dewey writes:

> Thoughts just as thoughts are incomplete. At best they are tentative; they are suggestions, indications. They are standpoints and methods for dealing with situations of experience. Till they are applied in these situations they lack full point and reality.
>
> (MW 9:168)

The purpose of education is to develop practical skills in authentic situations under real-life conditions. The philosophical perspective supporting this approach considers experience the most important source of knowledge. "Indeed," Dewey concludes, "the business of education might be defined as an emancipation and enlargement of experience" (LW 8:277–8).

References

Aristotle. (1984). *The complete works of Aristotle: The revised Oxford translation*. J. Barnes (Ed.). Princeton, NJ: Princeton University Press.

Comte, A. (2000). *The positive philosophy of Auguste Comte, Vol. 1*. (H. Martineaue, Trans.). Kitchener, ON: Batoche Books.

Darwin, C. (2009). *The annotated Origin: A facsimile of the first edition of* On the origin of species. (J. T. Costa, Annot.) Cambridge, MA: Harvard University Press. (Original work published 1859.)

Dewey, J. (1972). The psychological aspect of the school curriculum. In J. Boydston (Series Ed.), *The early works of John Dewey, 1895–1898: Vol. 5* (pp. 164–176). Carbondale, IL: Southern Illinois University Press.

Dewey, J. (1977). The influence of Darwinism on philosophy. In J. Boydston (Series Ed.), *The middle works of John Dewey, 1907–1909: Vol. 4* (pp. 3–14). Carbondale, IL: Southern Illinois University Press.

Dewey, J. (1980). Democracy and education: An introduction to the philosophy of education. *The middle works of John Dewey, 1916: Vol. 9* (pp. 192–361). Carbondale, IL: Southern Illinois University Press.

Dewey, J. (1988). Experience and education. In J. Boydston (Series Ed.), *The later works of John Dewey, 1938–1939: Vol. 13* (pp. 5–62). Carbondale, IL: Southern Illinois University Press.

Dochy, F, Segers, M., Van den Bossche, P., & Gijbels, D. (2003). Effects of problem-based learning: a meta-analysis. *Learning and Instruction, 13*, 533–568.

Edwards, C., Gandini, L., & Forman, G. (1998). *The hundred languages of children: The Reggio Emilia approach – Advanced reflections* (2nd ed.). [E-book]. Greenwich, CN: Praeger.

Interdisciplinary Journal of Problem-based Learning. (n.d.) Home page. [Website]. Retrieved from http://docs.lib.purdue.edu/ijpbl/

James, W. (1958). *Talks to teachers.* New York, NY: W. W. Norton. (Original work published 1899.)

James, W. (1977). *A pluralistic universe.* Cambridge, MA: Harvard University Press. (Originally published 1908.)

James, W. (1991). *Pragmatism.* New York, NY: Prometheus Books. (Original work published 1907.)

Junior Achievement USA. (n.d.). Junior Achievement programs. [Website]. Retrieved from https://www.juniorachievement.org/web/ja-usa/programs-info

Mayhew, K. C., & Edwards, A. C. (1965). *The Dewey school: The laboratory school of the University of Chicago, 1896–1903.* New York, NY: Atherton Press. (Original work published 1936.)

Montessori, M. (1949). *The absorbent mind.* Madras, India: Theosophical Publishing House.

Montessori, M. (1964). *The Montessori method.* (A. E. George, Trans.). New York, NY: Schocken Books. (Original work published 1909.)

Peirce, C. S. (1905). What pragmatism is. *The Monist, 15*(2), 161–181.

Roh, K. H. (2003). Problem-based learning in mathematics. ERIC Digest # EDO-SE-03–07. Washington, D.C.: Office of Educational Research and Improvement.

Sammamish High School. (2013). Key elements of a Sammamish classroom. [PDF File]. Retrieved from http://www.bsd405.org/Portals/22/documents/Key%20Elements%20of%20a%20Sammamish%20Classroom.pdf

Sammamish High School. (n.d.). Problem based learning at Sammamish High School. [PDF file]. Retrieved from http://www.bsd405.org/Portals/22/documents/pbl-at-sammamish.pdf

Savery, J. R. (2006). Overview of problem-based learning: Definitions and distinctions. *Interdisciplinary Journal of Problem-Based Learning, 1*(1), 9–20.

Steiner, R. (1995). *The spirit of the Waldorf school.* (R. F. Lathe & N. P. Whittaker, Trans.). Hudson, NY: Anthroposophic Press.

Stepien, W., & Gallagher, S. (1993) Problem-based learning: As authentic as it gets. *Educational Leadership, 50*(7), 25–28.

What Works Clearinghouse. (n.d.). Home page. [Website]. Retrieved from http://ies.ed.gov/ncee/wwc/

9 What If . . . The Purpose of Education Were to Learn as a Community?

Wonder

Our inquiry continues to proceed along the *Continuum of Educational Philosophy* (Figure 9.1). The perspectives in Part III emphasize the process of learning and the ways in which interdependent knowledge is constructed through experience. In this chapter, the wonder question asks, *"What if . . . the purpose of education were to learn as a community?"*

Observe

Classroom Vignette: Fourth-Grade Interdisciplinary Project on Immigration

The room buzzes with activity. Small groups congregate in various places in the classroom working on different parts of the project. Four groups sit at round tables, one group sits on the floor on a rug, and another group has pulled beanbag chairs into a huddle. On the whiteboard, Ms. T has written the following guiding questions: "What is the American Dream? What drives immigration to the United States? How is life for an immigrant different from life as a refugee?"

RATIONAL	EMPIRICAL
Ideas-Focused	Experience-Focused
Content-Oriented	Process-Oriented
Fixed Curriculum	Flexible Curriculum
Teacher-Centered	Student-Centered
Teacher-Directed	Self-Directed
Pre-Determined Outcomes	Open-Ended Exploration
Whole-Class Activities	Differentiated/Individualized Activities

Objective External Reality	Internal Subjective Reality
Absolute Universal Truth	Changing Relative Truth
Pre-Existing Knowledge	Constructed Knowledge
Knowledge Independent of Experience	Knowledge Dependent on Experience
Autonomous Knowledge	Interdependent Knowledge
Absolute Universal Values	Relative Local Values
Values Independent of Experience	Values Dependent on Experience

PHILOSOPHICAL PERSPECTIVES

Figure 9.1 Continuum of Educational Philosophy (Community)

Large pieces of easel paper taped to the walls display long-term and short-term Learning Targets for each unit. One asks, "What Have We Learned?" and a second, "What Are We Learning?" Below the heading "Expedition Learning Targets," several "I can" statements list the targets for the project:

- I can display my hopes and dreams for the Fourth Grade.
- I can use writing and/or pictures to show my favorite things.
- I can write an "I am" poem.
- I can create a "recipe" of me.
- I can research my family background.
- I can choose symbols to represent parts of my family culture.
- I can use an artifact to explain something important about my family.
- I can give and receive feedback on my artifact presentation.

A drawing of a target hangs on the wall. Each concentric circle indicates a student's level of progress on the lesson's target objective. The outermost circle contains phrases such as "I have no idea" and "I can never do this." The next circle states, "I don't really know yet" and "I need some help." The third circle reads, "Just need a little more practice" and "I'm almost there!" Inside the bull's-eye is written, "I am an expert!" Students have written their names on post-it notes and stuck them at different locations on the target.

Exhibits of student work cluster around the target poster, such as "I am" poems, "recipes" of individual students, and family coats of arms. On another large piece of easel paper, students have written responses to the prompt, "What are different ways someone can show where they are from?"

Today, each group examines primary sources. One table group analyzes diary entries, another group interprets political cartoons, a third notes their observations of photographs of arrivals being processed at Ellis Island, while the fourth inspects artifacts and jots down their inferences about the purpose of each one and what it reveals about the home country of the immigrants. The group on the beanbag chairs moves to the floor to study maps tracking the movement of immigrants from different countries. The remaining group has converged at the listening station, wearing headphones to hear audio recordings of immigrants describing their experiences and noting the challenges they faced. Student groups become "experts" on a specific question, which they will later report and share with the entire class.

Ms. T circulates among the groups, monitoring their progress, answering questions, and offering advice. One student struggles to record answers about a reading on her sheet.

"I don't care if you get the answers right the first time," Ms. T reassures him. "The important thing is that you persevere and keep thinking."

"Be confident, Dion!" a classmate urges.

"Yes, be confident, Dion!" Ms. T repeats.

Ms. T call the students' attention to a list of "Expedition Words" displayed on the wall, and adds new vocabulary words students have discovered.

When the timer bell sounds, Ms. T calls the class together at the front of the room. Each student grabs a square of colored carpet and sits in a circle on the floor around their teacher. She asks questions about what they have gathered so far from their research, where each group is in relation to their targets, and what their next steps will be.

"Now, remember," she says. "Tomorrow, we make bread!"

A cheer arises from the class.

"From scratch!" one child shouts with excitement.

"Yes," Ms. T replies. "I will bring all the ingredients. First, we will do an experiment to see how yeast makes bread rise. Then we will measure each ingredient very carefully and mix them together in a big bowl. The fun part will be kneading the dough!"

The children murmur in anticipation.

"When the dough is ready," Ms. T continues, "we will take it to the kitchen. The staff has agreed to bake our bread in the oven. The whole wing of the building will smell like freshly baked bread."

"Then we can eat it?" a student asks.

"Hot right out of the oven!"

More cheers ring out, followed by clapping. Ms. T leads the class in a song about the different languages to say bread all over the world. To end the school day, she plays a pop song and joins the students in an improvised round of energetic dancing.

Investigate

What Do Teachers Teach? Questions about the Curriculum

"Education being a social process, the school is simply that form of community life."

(John Dewey)

The vignette depicts instruction based on Expeditionary Learning (EL), a model that emerged from the Outward Bound program (Expeditionary Learning, 2011–2014). Ten EL schools opened in 1993, expanding to over 160 schools in thirty-three states (Expeditionary Learning, 2011–2014). In EL schools, learning is active, challenging, meaningful, collaborative, and public. Students engage in projects, called *expeditions*, "investigating real community problems and collaborating with peers to develop creative, actionable solutions" (Expeditionary Learning Outward Bound, 2011, p. 1). Students assume the roles of "scientists, urban planners, historians, and activists," applying their skills and knowledge to "real-world issues [to] make positive change in their communities" (p. 1). Fieldwork cultivates a direct relationship with the natural environment and the surrounding community. Students present their learning through presentations and public exhibitions, offering opportunities for self-critique as well as public feedback. EL instills in students qualities of "trust, respect, responsibility, and joy in learning" (p. 1).

Expeditions investigate topics situated in the surrounding community. These can include the natural environment (such as the habitats of local wildlife, types of indigenous plants, the local watershed, and the geology of the area), cultural history (such as local Native American tribes and nearby battlegrounds of the American Revolution), or even the school itself (such as first graders mapping the school for kindergarteners and producing a public service announcement on bullying).

The EL motto states, "We are crew, not passengers" (p. 2). In learning conditions that offer students a primary role in discovery, learning becomes an "adventure" (p. 2). Engaging in the challenging, real-world learning research tasks of an expedition requires curiosity and imagination, self-discipline and cooperation, and perseverance and persistence. The role of the teacher is to provide students with time to experiment, opportunities to collaborate, and tools and resources to investigate and explore. The goal is to increase student responsibility for directing their own learning, as individuals and as part of an interdependent social group. Opportunities for both communal and solitary reflection are built into the learning model.

In "My Pedagogic Creed," John Dewey (American, 1859–1952) maintains that participation in the social community is the source of all education. Through demands encountered in social situations, a child is stimulated to act as part of the larger community. A child's own natural instincts serve as the starting point for learning, which is formed and given meaning through education. Learning activities have value in terms of their social context. Formal education cannot depart from this process, only help organize and guide it. Objective, external knowledge imposed upon a child by a teacher may provide certain measureable results, "but cannot truly be called educative" unless teaching connects to activities initiated by the child "independent of the educator" (EW 5:85).

"School is primarily a social institution," Dewey explains. "Education being a social process, the school is simply that form of community life" (EW 5:86–7). Learning activities must have a practical function occurring within social conditions and social relationships. Because education cannot prepare a child in advance for every possible set of conditions, education prepares a child to act under ever-changing circumstances. If schooling focuses on a remote future that does not relate to the child's experiences, the child does not grasp the value or relevance. A genuine education is grounded in the background of the child, building continuity between familiar activities and new ideas presented in school. "Education, therefore, is a process of living and not a preparation for future living" (EW 5:87).

Dewey expresses a democratic vision of schooling and education. A citizen's responsibility is to participate in society, share knowledge, and create community. These democratic values should be reinforced in school. Values are created by exchanging diverse perspectives within a community of learners, rather than relying on absolute knowledge or inerrant principles based on tradition, custom, hierarchy, or the status quo.

School subjects should arise from the child's own experiences and social activities. Owing to the influence of Pragmatism, a curriculum based on learning as a community is flexible, emphasizes relevant topics and issues, adjusts to individual interests, adapts to social interest needs and uses, and varies according to context. "The scheme of a curriculum," Dewey writes, "must take account of the adaptation of studies to the needs of the existing community life" (MW 9:199).

Dewey proposes three levels to the curriculum. The first stage involves teaching "how to do" through the direct use of materials in activities and projects (MW 9:192). The second stage introduces informational knowledge, which includes "the body of facts and truths ascertained by others" (MW 9:193–4). Dewey cautions that this second-hand information overly influences our view of what constitutes knowledge. The various disciplines or branches of learning should not be regarded as knowledge in and of themselves but as the basis for further inquiry. Finally, the curriculum consists of organized sciences or "rationalized knowledge" that has been tested experientially (MW 9:196). This level represents "what we think *with* rather than what we think *about* [emphasis added]" and is distinguishable from "opinion, guesswork, speculation, and mere tradition" by testing hypotheses through systematic procedures and methods to produce verifiable results (MW 9:196).

Subject-matter that has the greatest practical application to the widest segment of democratic society is considered the most significant, with specialized and technical subjects of secondary importance. Rather than presenting subjects as remote from everyday experience, connections should be made between the topics of study and the learner. Subjects should be taught in context, "to enrich and liberate the more direct and personal contacts of life" and reveal interdependence between the individual and society (MW 9:218). For example, geography connects facts of nature with its social implications. History describes events that have political, economic, and other connections to current life. "The true starting point of history is always some present situation with its problems" (MW 9:222). Science serves to test and verify knowledge and "to revise current beliefs" (MW 9:227). The study of science is not pursued as "an end in itself" but to connect the findings to everyday encounters with familiar objects and experiences (MW 9:227). Beyond that, science is "the agency of progress in action," a way to further society (MW 9:231). The goal of education is not simply to acquire and retain a fixed body of knowledge, but to actively engage in activities that have a direct relevance to one's experience and effect change.

The Progressive Education Association, founded in 1919, adopted seven principles of progressive education:

1   *Freedom to Develop Naturally*. The conduct of the pupil should be governed by himself according to the social needs of his community, rather than by arbitrary laws. Full opportunity for initiative and self-expression should be provided, together with an environment rich in interesting material that is available for the free use of every pupil.

2   *Interest, the Motive of all Work*. Interest should be satisfied and developed through: (1) Direct and indirect contact with the world and its activities, and use of the experience thus gained. (2) Application of knowledge gained, and correlation between different subjects. (3) The consciousness of achievement.

3   *The Teacher a Guide, not a Task-Master*. It is essential that teachers should believe in the aims and general principles of Progressive Education and that they should have latitude for the development of initiative and originality. Progressive teachers will encourage the use of all the senses, training the pupils in both observation and judgment; and instead of hearing recitations only, will spend most of the time teaching how to use various sources of information, including life activities as well as books; how to reason about the information thus acquired; and how to express forcefully and logically the conclusions reached. Ideal teaching conditions demand that classes be small, especially in the elementary school years.

4   *Scientific Study of Pupil Development*. School records should not be confined to the marks given by the teachers to show the advancement of the pupils in their study of subjects, but should also include both objective and subjective reports on those physical, mental, moral, and social characteristics that affect both school and adult life, and which can be influenced by the school and at home. Such records should be used as a guide for the treatment of each pupil, and should also serve to focus the attention of the teacher on the all-important work of development rather than on simply teaching subject-matter.

5   *Greater Attention to All that Affects the Child's Physical Development*. One of the first considerations of Progressive Education is the health of the pupils. Much more room in which to move about, better light and air, clean and well-ventilated buildings, easier access to the outdoors and greater use of it are all necessary. There should be frequent use of adequate playgrounds. The teachers should observe closely the physical condition of each pupil and, in cooperation with the home, make abounding health the first objective of childhood.

6   *Cooperation Between School and Home to Meet the Needs of Child-Life*. The school should provide, with the home, as much as is possible of all that the natural interests and activities of the child demand, especially during the elementary school years. These conditions can come about only through intelligent cooperation between parents and teachers.

7   *The Progressive School a Leader in Educational Movements*. The Progressive School should be a leader in educational movements. It should be a laboratory where new ideas, if worthy, meet encouragement; where tradition alone does not rule, but the best of the past is leavened with the discoveries of today, and the result is freely added to the sum of educational knowledge (Park School, 2015, The Principles of Progressive Education section, paras 3–9).

How Do Teachers Teach? Questions about Pedagogy

"The learning in school should be continuous with that out of school."

(John Dewey)

The project method encourages students to work as a learning community on problems and issues in long-term, interdisciplinary, problem-solving inquiry. Thomas H. Kilpatrick (American, 1871–1965) expresses suspicion of fundamental principles, instead seeking a way to engage learners in processes that unify individual needs with social aims. Kilpatrick (1918) defines a project as a "purposeful act" that occurs in a social environment while serving the student's interests and goals (p. 319). He argues that "projects may present every variety that purposes present in life" (p. 321). He equally emphasizes both the social aspect and the requirement that the activity fulfill a purpose. Kilpatrick claims, "As the purposeful act is thus the typical unit of the worthy life in a democratic society, so it also should be made the typical unit of school procedure" (p. 323).

Like Dewey, Kilpatrick maintains, "Education should be considered as life itself and not as a mere preparation for later living" (p. 323). On this basis, school should only be constructed of purposeful acts rather than exercises in acquiring a fixed set of knowledge or arbitrary skills. Schools should offer students a wide variety of learning opportunities that correspond to authentic situations. Successful outcomes are those that fulfill practical, useful ends and achieve the desired purpose. Kilpatrick cautions that projects should not cater to every "childish whim," but guide the student to investigate interests that help foster growth (p. 328). The teacher's role is to plan experiences that combine the child's motives with the proper situation matched with appropriate procedures and resources.

Dewey proposes that a child's four "native impulses" guide development of learning activities and projects: 1) social, 2) constructive, 3) investigative or experimental, and 4) expressive (Mayhew & Edwards, 1936/1965, p. 40). He proposes projects meet four criteria: 1) be of interest to the learner, 2) be intrinsically worthwhile, 3) "present problems that awaken new curiosity and create a demand for information," and 4) "involve a considerable time span" for completion (LW 8:291–2). A project should be based on an enduring interest that requires in-depth investigation into a real-world problem that develops knowledge and skills in new areas. Rather than "a succession of unrelated acts," a project requires continuity that progresses in a cumulative way toward a coherent product (LW 8:292).

In many ways corresponding to Dewey's four native impulses, Kilpatrick recommends four types of projects: 1) creative (construction) projects, such as building a boat, writing a letter to the editor, or producing and performing in a play, 2) appreciation (enjoyment or aesthetic) projects, such as touring a museum, attending the theater, or listening to a story, 3) problem (issue) projects, such as investigating a social issue or conducting a science experiment, and 4) specific learning projects, wherein the student acquires new knowledge or skills (such as learning irregular verbs). Creative and problem-solving projects should be interdisciplinary and involve experiential, problem-solving activities. In Kilpatrick's approach, students should be given autonomy to collaboratively choose, plan, direct, implement, and evaluate their own work as much as possible. The teacher's role is to "steer" the child, not prescribe, direct, and assess each step (p. 333). Even in specific learning projects, the teacher must be careful not to substitute drill exercises for activities involving student engagement and participation.

A progressive pedagogy consists of real-world, authentic learning activities or projects, what Dewey refers to as "expressive or constructive activities" (EW 5:90) or "occupations" (MW 1:92). Dewey distinguishes these activities from the kinds of "busy work" intended to keep children occupied in their seats so they stay out of mischief. Occupations reproduce or parallel the kinds of work or actions that one carries on in social life outside of school. These are not occupations in the sense that they train students only in skills for a trade or vocation. Projects strike a balance between intellectual (or traditional areas of academic study) and practical learning through physical as well as mental exertion. Topics in formal subject areas should be taught through experiential learning activities or take the form of projects that reflect a child's interests and represent social activities encountered outside of school. Dewey recommends, "The learning in school should be continuous with that out of school" (MW 9:368).

The design of project-based learning embodies the following eight elements (Larmer, Mergendoller, & Boss, 2015):

1 *Key Knowledge and Understanding, and Success Skills.* Developing key concepts and funda-mental understanding of disciplinary content lies at the center of the design of project-based learning. Students should delve deeply into a topic, emphasizing what students learn as a result of the process. In completing projects, students activate prior learning, analyze issues, solve problems, collaborate, and manage time and resources.

2 *Challenging Problem or Question.* Projects are structured around a challenging problem or question, giving learning a purpose. New knowledge should be applied to the immediate situ-ation and connected to future circumstances.

3 *Sustained Inquiry.* As Dewey suggests, a project should involve a long-term investment of time, effort, and focus. Problems or issues should be complex enough to require more than a lesson or a few class sessions to investigate. The process should develop in phases over several weeks.

4 *Authenticity.* The context and tasks of a project should be authentic, using tools and proce-dures that simulate real-world, professional conditions. The results of the project should have an impact on the world outside of the classroom, as well as reflect the interests, concerns, needs, and values of the students participating.

5 *Student Voice and Choice.* Students should have the opportunity to contribute to the design and structure of the project, exercising judgments and making decisions that affect the pro-cess. The degree of student autonomy depends on the nature of the issue or problem and the complexity of the tasks. Even so, students should assume a great deal of responsibility in determining their actions and assessing their own performance.

6 *Reflection.* Reflection occurs throughout the project. Students consider what problems or issues they may have confronted in the past that relate to the current challenge, propose strate-gies that may have been useful in similar situations, predict the consequences of their actions, exhibit awareness of their own thinking processes as they progress, and express how the pro-ject experience is impacting the development of knowledge, skills, confidence, and abilities.

7 *Critique and Revision.* Strategies and actions should be assessed during each phase of the project, with modifications being suggested and tested, errors corrected, or even entire steps discarded and redone. The teacher, other experts or mentors, and peers should provide con-tinual feedback. Checkpoints or deadlines at intervals, and reference to a rubric, can aid in organizing formative assessment.

8 *Public Product.* The project should culminate in a tangible product that can be presented or exhib-ited. An audience beyond the classroom should view the product and offer real-world feedback. The product may even have authentic application in the community that can be demonstrated.

One viewpoint on education, "situated learning," regards learning in the context of authentic social relationships (Lave & Wenger, 1991, p. 30). Learners participate in a "community of practice," comparable to apprenticeships, internships, and service learning projects (p. 29). These activities apply knowledge under specific circumstances in collaboration with others, learning from more experienced practitioners who guide the learner into greater degrees of involvement. Learning is a social practice, involving membership in a community. The situation in which learning occurs is an integral part of the process. "Situations might be said to co-produce knowledge through activ-ity" (Brown, Collins, & Duguid, 1989, p. 32). In authentic situations, learning involves negotiating meaning and socially constructing understanding.

What is the Role of the Teacher in Learning as a Community?

TEACHER AS MEMBER OF LEARNING COMMUNITY

Students construct knowledge and create understanding in a collaborative social environment. "The teacher is not in the school to impose certain ideas or to form certain habits in the child,"

Dewey declares, "but is there as a member of the community" (EW 5:88). Projects should be planned and implemented cooperatively by the teacher with the students, to avoid activities that "express the teacher's purpose rather than that of the pupils" (LW 13:46). Student input and suggestions should contribute to the design of the project, "organized into a whole by the members of the group" (LW 13:46).

As an institution, the school should reproduce a simplified version of social life. The teacher's role is to establish a community of learners within the classroom. As such, Dewey refers to the teacher as a "social servant" (EW 5:95). EL refers to students as members of a "crew" and to teachers as "crew leaders."

TEACHER AS GUIDE OR MENTOR

The teacher as guide or mentor helps students complete projects, instructing in an indirect manner. Depending on the level of structure and degree of student autonomy in the project, this role may range from "senior partner" to coach (Larmer, Mergendoller, & Boss, 2015, p. 28). The teacher may design the project and gradually hand over greater responsibility to the students.

TEACHER AS TRANSLATOR

In an EL school, goals for learning are expressed as learning targets rather than objectives. Objectives reflect the teacher's intended outcomes. Objectives are commonly written in the form, "The student will be able to . . . " Learning targets, on the other hand, are "written for – and owned by – students" (Berger, Rugen, & Woodfin, 2014, p. 21). Learning targets are written in the form of "I can . . . " statements. For example, "I can use important details from a person's life to support my idea" or "I can explain my reasons for sorting and classifying insects" (pp. 25, 27). Using learning targets, students can assess their own progress toward a specific goal. Long-term targets are divided into supporting targets. Learning targets shift the focus from what the teacher will teach to what the students will learn. Students accept greater responsibility for their own learning and gain confidence in their own ability when they can state their learning using "I can."

Writing a learning target is "an act of translation," by wording a standard in a form that students can understand (Berger, Rugen, & Woodfin, 2014, p. 47). Translating involves selecting the right way to communicate and convey meaning. Composing learning targets that build student ownership takes practice. Merely posting objectives for students to see may result in the teacher owning the outcomes rather than the students. In expressing the goals of instruction as learning targets, the teacher acts in the role of translator.

What Is the Role of the Student in Learning as a Community?

STUDENT AS COLLABORATOR

Students belong to a community of learners, collaborating on projects. EL refers to students as members of a "crew" on an expedition. As mentioned previously, the level of structure and degree of student autonomy on a project may vary. The teacher may begin directing the project, but as they gain experience and develop skills, students assume the role of "project manager" (Larmer, Mergendoller, & Boss, 2015, p. 28).

STUDENT AS EXPLORER

Children possess a natural inclination to learn about the world around them. Progressive education focuses on the intrinsic motivation of children to explore their environment and discover information, and formulate explanations. The role of the student also overlaps with that of problem-solver (Chapter 8), applying the scientific method or inquiry approach to investigate a challenge, problem, or question; collect information; analyze, evaluate, and interpret sources of information; critique the results, findings, or product; and evaluate and reflect on the process.

Design

How Are Schools Organized? Questions about the Role of the School

"I believe that education is the fundamental method of social progress and reform."

(John Dewey)

University of Chicago Laboratory School

The laboratory school at the University of Chicago was designed as an experiment, a "working hypothesis" of what a school could be (Mayhew & Edwards, 1936/1965, p. 365). Principles of education were to adapt to actual conditions as they occurred, rather than adapting conditions to fit a preconceived program. Teachers worked cooperatively to develop the curriculum and select instructional methods. Meetings and conferences coordinated the efforts, and consensus emerged as ideas were put into practice. Many meetings functioned as "seminars in method," exploring questions about the purpose of the school, the curriculum, instruction, the role of the teacher and student, and the organizational structure of the school (p. 368). "Cooperative social organization applied to the teaching body of the school as well as to the pupils" (p. 371). Teacher collaboration substituted for formal supervision by a team of administrators. However, as enrollment grew, the need for administration increased. Departments formed and students were grouped by age to add levels of structure. Nevertheless, flexibility remained a priority.

As a long-term project, the students at the lab school constructed a model farm. A farmhouse, barn, chicken coop, and stone fence were erected, and land was divided into field for raising crops and pastures for grazing. Students tested different types of soil, plowing methods, and other conditions for growing plants. In another project, the students built a wooden boat. They designed a pointed bow and stern to overcome drag, figured out the best shapes and configurations of sails, designed a buoy, learned to measure speed by knots and sounding for depth of water, and in every way possible recreated the process of ship making. The experience led to learning navigation and map-making skills.

Geography, history, and social studies reconstructed living conditions of different civilizations, including shelter, transportation, means of communication, and methods of trade. Student groups reenacted cave dwelling, early agrarian settlements and herding livestock, different eras of exploration and voyages of global discovery, colonial life, forts and log cabins, and other periods of society. Field trips examined local history, geography, and economics, as well as geology and earth sciences.

"In the first place, the school itself must be a community life in all which that implies" (MW 9:368). As a democratic community, the school not only represents a microcosm of society but should also help change society, rather than reproduce the existing social order. Schools should not adjust students to society, but adapt education to the students. Schools can help individuals develop while also sharing in the responsibility of reforming society. "I believe that education is the fundamental method of social progress and reform," Dewey writes (EW 5:93). Students should emerge from schools prepared to engage in and serve society.

Hull-House

Another early experiment in putting progressive principles into practice is Hull-House, founded by Jane Addams (1860–1935) in Chicago in 1889. Addams (1935) established Hull-House as a "social settlement" to serve the local community (p. 115). Beginning with a kindergarten, Hull-House offered classes, lectures, and learning activities for both children and adults. The project expanded to provide a number of services, such as a public kitchen, playground, gymnasium, swimming pool, theater, and juvenile court. Hull-House became a center for social programs, actively cooperating with local agencies and civic organizations to initiate social reform efforts.

Current events formed the basis for much of the education at Hull-House. Addams believes local issues can inspire learning, leading to new educational opportunities. "At such a moment," she writes, "it seemed possible to educate the entire community by a wonderful unification of effort" (p. 381). The settlement took pride in educating those who otherwise would be left out of the social and economic life of society, such as recent immigrants. Education based on the genuine interests of the individual could help reform society at the local level and beyond. Hull-House emphasized connecting education to occupational training, to assist those experiencing economic hardship. In addition, the settlement stressed play and the arts, offering courses in art, music, drama, and dance.

Bank Street School

In 1916, Lucy Sprague Mitchell established the Bureau of Educational Experiments (BEE) in New York. The Bureau founded a laboratory nursery school in 1919 and a teacher training school in 1930, which became Bank Street College. Bank Street Graduate School of Education continues to operate today and Bank Street School for Children became a full-scale elementary school in 1954. The school functions as a demonstration school for the Graduate program, following principles of progressive education. The school focuses on educating the whole child in an experience-based environment. The missions of both the Graduate School and the elementary school connect teaching and learning to the life of the community. Sprague writes, "Our work is based on the faith that human beings can improve the society they have created" (Bank Street, n.d., Mission and Credo section, para 4).

Mitchell published a book of children's stories titled *Here and Now Story Book* (1921) for use in the nursery school of the BEE. Mitchell calls the stories "experiments," because they are based on the interests of the children in the school (p. 1). Mitchell expresses disappointment in fables and fairy tales typically found in classrooms, believing children should listen to and read stories related to their experiences. Stories should capture children's curiosity and raise questions about the world around them. The content of the stories begins by exploring the child's immediate environment and gradually expands beyond familiar surroundings. Early stories engage the senses and describe physical activities. Later stories examine relationships and explain the social significance of actions. This approach is in keeping with a philosophical perspective to base education on children's experiences and follow their natural development.

Park School

The Park School was founded in 1912 in Baltimore, Maryland. The first headmaster, Eugene Randolph Smith, served as president of the Progressive Education Association. The Park School models the principles of progressive education, believing "authentic learning flourishes when people work, think and collaborate within a diverse community" (Park School, 2015, Philosophy section, para 1). Learning should not be an alienating process performed under strict supervision, but an opportunity to grow by encountering challenges, taking initiative, accepting responsibility, and applying self-discipline. The Park School believes children possess the ability to assert their own capacities for self-governance and express themselves naturally in interactions with others. Therefore, the school is based on a "cooperative sense of community" that is pluralistic, interdependent, and democratic (Park School, 2015, Objectives section, para 2). Learning activities stress participation in the larger community to address social problems.

Monarch Academy

The classroom vignette that opens this chapter represents observations at Monarch Academy in Glen Burnie, one of three Monarch Academy public charter schools in Maryland. Entering the building, one is greeted by the sight of an enormous Monarch butterfly hanging from the ceiling. A huge poster displays a compass with the quote, "Logic Can Get You From A to B; Imagination Will Take You Everywhere (Albert Einstein)." Stenciled on the wall in bright colors are the words: "Struggle, Enlightenment, Transformation." Emblazoned above the reception area is the motto, "Journey to Citizenship."

Monarch operates according to principles of Transformation Education (TranZed), a child-centered philosophy for organizing schools (Children's Guild, 2015). "Through a process of adult and organizational transformation," the TranZed Alliance mission statement reads, "we teach children the values and life skills necessary for a successful life, one filled with caring, contribution and commitment, empowering each with the vision to see, the courage to try, and the will to succeed" (Children's Guild, 2014, p. 2).

The school's values and beliefs create a culture focused on serving the needs of children, and permeate all aspects of the school, from the curriculum and instructional aspects to the physical environment. This climate fosters a learning community that considers all participants to be partners—administrators, faculty, staff, students, families, and members of the surrounding community. Frequent events invite the public to the school for exhibitions, presentations, and performances. School leaders actively establish and sustain relationships with local agencies and organizations. Within the school, leadership is a shared responsibility. Leadership teams meet regularly to continuously improve curriculum, instruction, and assessment, while also facilitating ways to strengthen the school culture. Decision-making and implementing policy involves all members of the school, rather than being a top-down function of the administration.

The school collectively creates "norms" which govern organization throughout the school. Norms are established for many different types of interactions, such as faculty meetings, team meetings, and professional development sessions. Students are involved in the creation of norms to manage routines in different subjects, classrooms, areas of the building, and outdoor spaces. Norms can be reviewed and revised at any time during the year. EL schools also establish habits of scholarship and character ("Habits of Work") that students strive to exemplify in their efforts and interactions with others (Berger, Rugen, & Woodfin, 2014, p. 308). The Monarch Academy has seven "Habits of Excellence": responsibility, perseverance, service, compassion, collaboration, quality, and inquiry. These habits are intertwined in all subject areas and lessons, and students use them to set goals, reflect, and improve.

In Ms. T's class, a poster on the wall lists, "Our Crew's Norms," created collaboratively by the students and teacher. Each statement is written in a different color and signed by all the students in the class.

1   We will pay attention and participate in all activities.
2   We will keep a safe body.
3   We will take responsibility for ourselves and others.
4   We will get what we get and we won't get upset.
5   We will set goals and persevere to achieve them.
6   We will treat others the way we want to be treated.

On another poster, norms describe expectations for different learning activities. For example, "Sharing Norms" include listening when others speak, safely handling and passing around objects and materials, maintaining a "Sharer's" level voice, offering comments, asking questions, and responding to the sharer's comments and questions.

The Monarch Academy has adopted EL, an active learning model based on the project method. In the vignette, the students participate in an expedition about immigration. Instruction focuses on themes or issues beyond the memorization and recall of discrete or remote facts. Relating learning to the lives of the students increases their understanding of the current society and their own local community. Students consider the issues from multiple perspectives, acting in the role of "social scientist" rather than an impassive spectator to a teacher's presentation of content.

The inquiry-based approach incorporates a variety of resources, including community resources and current events. The class tours the Fells Point Visitor Center, Irish Railroad Workers' Museum, German American Museum, and the National American History Museum. The children also visit a local bakery founded by an immigrant, who relates his story during the tour. Representatives from the International Rescue Committee (IRC), an organization that helps immigrants and refugees transition to America, visit the classroom as guest speakers. Immigration is explored through the lens of a child immigrating to America from across the southern border.

Under the heading, "We are Crew," a list of the class's long-term learning targets for the overall school year states:

1   I can explain how I use targets to support my learning.
2   I can be accountable for myself and my actions.
3   I can complete work on time and explain its relevance.
4   I can explain how my whole crew depends on my thoughtful participation.

The outcomes of student learning feature a culminating public presentation of their work. For the immigration expedition, the Monarch class creates an updated resource guide for the IRC to use with the people they serve. "This was something they asked for!" Ms. T explains. The students present the resource guide to parents, community members, and the IRC at the school's Wingspan event. The students also wrote persuasive letters to the President of the United States offering their recommendations on immigration policy, and received a letter in return on official White House stationery signed by the President.

At the end of the eighth-grade year, middle school students at Monarch Academy participate in an event called Passage Portfolio Presentations of Learning. To graduate middle school, each student presents a portfolio of work completed in grades 6 through 8 to a panel of guests from the local community. As a rite of passage, the presentations focus on personal and academic growth, comparing assignments and projects that represent the students' progress. A crew leader conferences with each student to help prepare the portfolio, containing a letter to the community, a quote that represents the individual, and artifacts providing evidence of growth for each subject area. Written reflections describe struggles the students needed to overcome, relate each artifact to "Habits of Excellence," and explain how the learning experience has prepared the student for the transition to high school. The school calls Passage a "celebration" rather than an evaluation.

Monarch Academy, Bank Street, and the Park School embody the characteristics of schools designed to foster learning as a community (Table 9.1).

How Does a School Designed to Learn as a Community Define an Educated Person?

The schools we have investigated define an educated person as one who works collaboratively and cooperatively as a member of a learning community. The learner exhibits personal, social, and academic growth and assumes responsibility for setting and attaining goals. Knowledge focuses on issues important to the community and relevant to the daily experiences of the learner.

Table 9.1 Design a School (Community)

Purpose of Education	Learn as a community
Curriculum	Issues and topics from local community
Instruction	Projects ("expeditions")
Role of Teacher	Member of learning community, guide, mentor, translator
Role of Student	Collaborator ("crew"), explorer
Role of School	Learning community

Evaluate

Consistency

To be consistent, project learning would occur in all subjects and comprise a major portion of learning activities and assessment. An occasional project completed for an event such as a science or social studies fair, with the remainder of instruction focused on independent seatwork, would not represent learning as a community.

How does project-based learning differ from problem-based learning (PBL) or other student-centered activities? The steps of completing a project and a PBL lesson are essential the same. Both PBL and projects emphasize collaboration among students, with the teacher in the role of guide or facilitator. However, a problem-based activity can be completed in a single lesson. Projects are typically long-term, sustained inquiry lasting for weeks. In another difference, PBL can be applied to a single subject area or discipline, such as math. Projects are often interdisciplinary in nature, requiring gathering information from various sources.

Compatibility

This perspective views learning as social. The school creates a learning community through interaction and collaboration to socially construct knowledge and understanding. The curriculum would feature topics and issues relevant to the local community. Projects would connect the school to the community, having students participate in activities outside of the classroom and inviting members of the community into the school to mentor, offer advice, and furnish feedback.

Dewey stresses that schools need to model democratic processes and not simply impart these values as bits of information. Topics in the curriculum and methods of instruction should allow the participation of students in the reconstruction of a democratic society. Memorization of facts about the structure of democracy and the responsibilities of citizenship without simulating these conditions produces incompatible practices.

Coherence

A coherent educational program that investigates social issues using the project method evaluates success based on the development and growth of students. Attainment of external standards, measured using objective-type items on standardized instruments, may demonstrate progress toward pre-determined targets. However, such an approach does not take into account individual experiences that influence thinking, values, and beliefs. Nor do such methods assess the quality of social interactions in constructing knowledge or building relationships within a democratic community. Cumulative growth extends beyond hitting benchmarks that define achievement. The purpose of education is to learn as a community to better the social conditions for all involved. Dewey calls "absurd" the notion that adults can set up their own measures for the growth of children "irrespective of conditions" (MW 9:114). Measures of achievement need to include observations of how a child performs "from moment to moment and hour to hour" (MW 9:114).

Dewey urges continual analysis of methods and their intentions. He observes that progressive schools exhibit many common characteristics, such as respect for student differences, active learning, and less formal procedures. However, he cautions against orthodoxy. No uniform set of beliefs should be established in the name of progressive education. Dewey frequently returns to his original intentions for a pragmatic and experiential education, not a permissive or aimless one. A school that "permits improvisation to dictate its course" will result in a disjointed, incoherent program with only short-term benefits, if any (LW 3:263). For example, in attempting to individualize instruction, a teacher may provide "a succession of unrelated activities" that do not provide organized development (LW 3:264).

Dewey warns against taking an "Either-Or" position, pitting traditional and progressive education (LW 13:14). Merely reacting against traditional education does not necessarily offer a progressive education in its place, as if "all which is required is not to do what is done in traditional schools" (LW 13:14). Furthermore, taking an extreme position in opposition to a set of beliefs may be dogmatic in its own right. An education based on the experiences of the students will not invariably produce favorable results. "Traditional education offers a plethora of examples of experiences," Dewey notes. "It is a great mistake to suppose, even tacitly, that the traditional classroom was not a place in which pupils had experiences" (LW 13:12). A revolt against traditional education requires a defensible, coherent philosophy of education to effect genuine change.

Reflect

How Do Your Prior Observations and Experiences Relate to a Curriculum Designed to Learn as a Community?

You may have participated in projects in school and observed project learning. How does the purpose of learning as a community relate to your experiences? How often did the projects you may have completed or observed investigate current problems relevant to the community that resulted in a public product?

How Do Your Prior Observations and Experiences Relate to a Pedagogy Designed to Learn as a Community?

In projects you have completed or observed, did the process exhibit characteristics such as student interest and intrinsic motivation, student choice and decision-making, sustained inquiry under authentic conditions, continual feedback and revision, and reflection?

How Do Your Prior Observations and Experiences Relate to a School Designed to Learn as a Community?

In your experience, has the project method been used as the basis for learning school-wide, across grade levels and subject areas? How often do students participate in long-term group projects? Have members of the community been involved in the process or evaluation of the results? What changes would a school need to implement to permit time and resources for sustained inquiry on authentic topics?

How Do Your Own Practices and Beliefs Relate to the Purpose of Education as Learning as a Community?

In your experience, what benefits or disadvantages have you found from learning as a community? How has project-based learning contributed to your education and in what ways has this method perhaps impeded your growth? As a teacher, would you organize your instruction around projects? How would you select topics for study? What role would students play in suggesting or choosing topics and determining the process? In what ways would students critique their own performance? How could you involve families and the community in the process of learning and evaluating the results?

Learning as a community falls into the process-oriented, empirical range of the *Continuum of Educational Philosophy*. Project-based learning is social, student-centered, and often concerned with effecting change and instigating social progress. Acquiring and retaining knowledge of subject-matter cannot be regarded as distinct from the experiences of the learner. Activities conducted within the classroom setting should emulate as closely as possible circumstances and conditions that students experience outside of the classroom. Learning to achieve in school should not be detached from learning to succeed in life. "I believe finally, that education must be conceived as a continuing reconstruction of experience," Dewey expresses. "That is, that the process and the goal of education are one and the same thing" (EW 5:91).

References

Addams, J. (1935). *Forty years at Hull-House*. New York, NY: Macmillan.

Bank Street School for Children. (n.d.) Mission and credo. [Website]. http://www.bankstreet.edu/school-children/about-sfc/our-history/mission/

Berger, R., Rugen, L., & Woodfin, L. (Eds.) (2014). *Leaders of their own learning: Transforming schools through student-engaged assessment*. San Francisco, CA: Jossey-Bass.

Brown, J. S., Collins, A., & Duguid, S. (1989). Situated cognition and the culture of learning. *Educational Researcher, 18*(1), 32–42.

Children's Guild. (2014). *TranZed Alliance 2014 annual report*. [PDF file]. http://www.childrensguild.org/wp-content/uploads/2014/11/AnnualReportTZA2014.pdf

Children's Guild. (2105). Transformation education. [Website]. 09_Chapter9_community.docxhttp://www.childrensguild.org/about-us/transformation-education/

Dewey, J. (1972). My pedagogic creed. In J. Boydston (Series Ed.), *The early works of John Dewey, 1895–1898: Vol. 5* (pp. 84–95). Carbondale, IL: Southern Illinois University Press.

Dewey, J. (1976). School and society. In J. Boydston (Series Ed.), *The middle works of John Dewey, 1899–1901: Vol. 1* (pp. 1–109). Carbondale, IL: Southern Illinois University Press.

Dewey, J. (1980). Democracy and education: An introduction to the philosophy of education. *The middle works of John Dewey, 1916: Vol. 9* (pp. 192–361). Carbondale, IL: Southern Illinois University Press.

Dewey, J. (1984). Progressive education and the science of education. In J. Boydston (Series Ed.), *The later works of John Dewey, 1927–1928: Vol. 3* (pp. 257–268). Carbondale, IL: Southern Illinois University Press.

Dewey, J. (1986). How we think: A restatement of the relation of reflective thinking to the educative process. In J. A. Boydston (Series Ed.), *The later works of John Dewey, 1933: Vol.* (pp. 105–352). Carbondale, IL: Southern Illinois University Press.

Dewey, J. (1988). Experience and education. In J. Boydston (Series Ed.), *The later works of John Dewey, 1938–1939: Vol. 13* (pp. 5–62). Carbondale, IL: Southern Illinois University Press.

Expeditionary Learning Outward Bound. (2011). *Expeditionary learning: Core practices*. [PDF file]. http://elschools.org/sites/default/files/Core%20Practice%20Final_EL_120811.pdf

Expeditionary Learning. (2014). About us. [Website]. http://elschools.org/about-us

Kilpatrick, W. H. (1918). The project method. *Teachers College Record, 19*, 319–334.

Larmer, J., Mergendoller, J., & Boss, S. (2015). *Setting the standard for project based learning*. Alexandria, VA: ASCD.

Lave, J., & Wenger, E. (1991). *Situated learning: legitimate peripheral participation*. Cambridge, UK: Cambridge University Press.

Mayhew, K. C., & Edwards, A. C. (1965). *The Dewey school: The laboratory school of the University of Chicago, 1896–1903*. New York, NY: Atherton Press. (Original work published 1936.)

Mitchell, L. S. (1921). *Here and now story book: Two- to seven-year olds.* (H. W. Van Loon, Illus.). New York, NY: E. P. Dutton.

Park School. (2015). Objectives. [Website]. http://www.parkschool.net/about/philosophy/#tab-objectives

Park School. (2015). Philosophy. [Website]. http://www.parkschool.net/about/philosophy/

Park School. (2015). The principles of progressive education. [Website]. http://www.parkschool.net/about/philosophy/principles-of-progressive-education/

10 What If . . . The Purpose of Education Were to Learn to Transform Society?

Wonder

In the previous chapter, we examined schools whose purpose is to build community and serve society. Moving nearer the end of the *Continuum of Educational Philosophy* (Figure 10.1), we ask the wonder question: *"What if . . . the purpose of education were to transform society?"*

Observe

Classroom Vignette: A Tenth-Grade Lesson on Genetics

In a unit on genetics, the students in Mr. F's biology class have been discussing the Human Genome Project, which provides a complete genetic map of the genetic makeup of human beings (or *Homo sapiens*). One conclusion emerging from the project asserts that no genetic basis may be claimed for classifying humans according to race. All humans belong to a single species. Most variation exists among local populations rather than between different populations. Therefore, distinguishing people from one another by differences in physical appearance has a social or cultural foundation rather than a scientific one. This sparks a lively discussion among the students in the class.

EDUCATIONAL PRACTICES

RATIONAL   EMPIRICAL

Ideas-Focused	Experience-Focused
Content-Oriented	Process-Oriented
Fixed Curriculum	Flexible Curriculum
Teacher-Centered	Student-Centered
Teacher-Directed	Self-Directed
Pre-Determined Outcomes	Open-Ended Exploration
Whole-Class Activities	Differentiated/Individualized Activities

Objective External Reality	Internal Subjective Reality
Absolute Universal Truth	Changing Relative Truth
Pre-Existing Knowledge	Constructed Knowledge
Knowledge Independent of Experience	Knowledge Dependent on Experience
Autonomous Knowledge	Interdependent Knowledge
Absolute Universal Values	Relative Local Values
Values Independent of Experience	Values Dependent on Experience

PHILOSOPHICAL PERSPECTIVES

Figure 10.1 Continuum of Educational Philosophy (Transform Society)

"If race isn't based on genetics," Tyler asks, "then is racism based only on society and culture?"

"Of course it is!" Peter responds.

"But maybe they didn't know that back then," Sally offers. "Maybe they really believed it was genetic or whatever."

"That *what* was genetic?" Tabitha asks.

"That the races are naturally different," Sally replies, somewhat sheepishly.

"It's not just about race," Heather adds. "What does science say about sexual orientation? Is it genetic or a choice?"

Tonya interjects, "Or the sexes period. Are women supposed to be inferior? How did these decisions get made?"

"By straight white men," Alicia shouts out, inducing some awkward laughter.

"Yeah, but how?" Howard enquires. "I mean, how did men get to be in that position in the first place? Something must have given them, and everybody else, the idea they were superior. Couldn't that have come from genetics first, then the social stuff came after?"

"Or did they just make up the genetics stuff to justify the social stuff?" Sheila counters.

"But genetics is science," Howard argues. "How can you make that up?"

"People made up all kinds of things and called it science," Jermaine observes.

"Can't science be biased, Mr. F?" Maya asks. "I think it's biased against women."

"Where are the women in our science book?" Tonya asks. "Or the black people. Or black women?"

Mr. F points out both women and people of color in their science textbook, although he concedes their numbers are few.

"I thought science was supposed to be objective," Howard wonders aloud. "Maybe science can be racist and sexist too."

"Science can be biased, even so-called scientific results can be biased," Marion responds. "By money, politics, gender . . . all sorts of ways."

"Everything is biased," Justin declares. "Whoever is in power controls what we know. They decide what outcomes they want to hear and put it out there as truth and facts."

Mr. F raises his hand to call for the students' attention. As they quiet down, Alicia asks, "Isn't that an example right there? Mr. F wants us to stop and listen to him and we all do. We are all just a part of this system, right?"

"I agree," Mr. F replies. "We are all a part of this system. Therefore, all of your questions are relevant. I think we need to jot down your questions and use them in this class."

He requests that the students take a few minutes and write down all their questions pertaining to the social and ethical implications of the Human Genome Project and other science issues related to race, gender, sexual orientation, hereditary diseases, religious controversies, and other topics. They brainstorm alone, in pairs, and in small informal groups. Mr. F collects the questions and informs the class he has decided to initiate short-term inquiry projects to be conducted by small groups. Each group will select a question to research.

The next day, Mr. F begins class by displaying two quotes. One reads, "We are the ones we have been waiting for." The second states, "We must be the change we expect to see in the world."

"This first quote comes from a poem by June Jordan," Mr. F explains, "presented at the United Nations in 1978 to commemorate women and children who protested against apartheid in South Africa. The second quote is attributed to Mahatma Gandhi, who led the people of India in their fight for independence from the British Empire."

Mr. F then writes two questions on the board:

1   How can *we* be the ones we have been waiting for?
2   How can *we* be the change we expect to see in the world?

Investigate

To explore philosophies that influence this view of the purpose of education, we will investigate the following inquiry questions:

- What Do Teachers Teach? Questions About the Curriculum
- How Do Teachers Teach? Questions About Pedagogy
- How Are Schools Organized? Questions About the Role of the School

What Do Teachers Teach? Questions about the Curriculum

> "Politics is the soul of education."
>
> (Paulo Freire)

When engaged in inquiry about scientific issues, students in the classroom vignette begin to wonder how changing knowledge affects beliefs about the nature of reality. From this discussion, they begin to question the fundamental structure of the society in which they live. If assumptions about race, gender, and other indicators of one's identity may be socially constructed and culturally biased, what other possible biases exist in social, cultural, political, economic, and educational practices and decisions? What role, if any, should schools play in addressing these issues?

What Role Do Schools Play in Restructuring Society?

In a perspective known as Social Reconstructionism, all institutions, including education, are social and political constructs. Not political in the limited sense of deciding which major political party to support, but in the sense of the original Greek word *polis*, which implies self-determination. People seek autonomy and independence in governing their affairs. If the goal of Progressivism is to reform society (as described in Chapter 9), Social Reconstructionism seeks to reconstruct society. This suggests a more radical transformation. Reform may occur within the existing structures of power and control. Reconstruction dismantles, replaces, or abolishes repressive or oppressive institutions that do not better the lives of the people they are intended to serve.

In 1932, during the depths of the Great Depression, George S. Counts (American, 1889–1974) published *Dare the School Build a New Social Order?* His book attacks the passive and docile role that schools play in society. Counts begins by observing that people assume schools will provide solutions to social problems, and even help bring about the "general reconstruction of society" (p. 3). However, he protests that "instead of directing the course of change," schools are driven by the same forces that control other social institutions. Counts envisions a leadership role for schools to create "a better social order" rather than "perpetuating ideas and institutions suited to an age that is gone" (p. 5).

Counts calls on schools to "face squarely and courageously every social issue" and take an active role in shaping social practices and policies (p. 9). Schools do not operate apart from society, nor is education "some pure and mystical essence that remains unchanged from everlasting to everlasting" (p. 18). Schools live within a society affected by political, economic, and other institutional forces, and cannot retain an impartial or neutral stance toward important social issues. Indeed, the school should take an active role in influencing policy and practice. Schools should experiment and develop innovative solutions to social problems. "Perhaps one of the greatest tragedies of contemporary society," Counts charges, "lies in the fact that the child is becoming increasingly isolated from the serious activities of adults" (p. 17).

Schools must not wait for solutions to social problems to be found and enacted by others. Schools should provide leadership, initiate collaboration with other social and community institutions and agencies, and act as agents of change. If the school's role is to merely prepare the individual to adjust to social change then that leads to reacting to trends and following behind the curve of progress. "Under such a conception of life and society," Counts argues, "education can only bow down before the gods of chance and reflect the drift of the social order" (p. 26). The school should be a force for change and seek to make a positive impact on the structure of society. Not content with simply providing students with "an opportunity to study contemporary society in all its aspects," schools should "go much farther . . . [and] become centers for the building, and not merely the contemplation, of our civilization" (p. 37). This vision calls on schools to take bold action and transform society. Counts admits this "is asking teachers to assume unprecedented social responsibilities" and renounce "a role of futility" (p. 54). By continuing to remain in their present position, teachers avoid responsibility and evade their most crucial educational task.

Political, economic, and social conditions continue to revive the questions asked by Counts. Paulo Freire (Brazilian, 1921–97) speaks of the dehumanizing effects of social institutions. Restoring the humanity of people in society requires liberation from injustice, exploitation, and oppression. Freire (1985) considers education to be "a political act" (p. 188). The essence of education is political. "In metaphysical terms," Freire elaborates, "politics is the soul of education" (p. 188). The solution is to view the "the reality of oppression not as a closed world from which there is no exit, but as a limiting situation which [people] can transform" (Freire, 1970/2000, p. 49). The goal can be achieved only when the oppressor "stops regarding the oppressed as an abstract category and sees them as persons" who have been denied basic human dignity, self-determination, and justice (p. 50).

The pedagogy of the oppressed, "which is the pedagogy of people engaged in the fight for their own liberation," critically examines the role of education and the relationship of the teacher to the student. Freire (1970/2000) characterizes the traditional teacher as "a narrating Subject" who talks to "patient, listening objects (the students)" (p. 71). The teacher presents reality to the students as a fixed body of accepted knowledge that the students passively accept. Freire refers to this as "the banking concept of education," in which the teacher deposits knowledge into the students (p. 72). In this model, "knowledge is a gift bestowed by those who consider themselves knowledgeable upon those who they consider to know nothing" (p. 72). Later, the teacher will make a withdrawal from the account, usually in the form of a test or other objective assessment.

The banking concept of education perpetuates the dominant role of the teacher, who chooses the content and instructional activities. The students have no say in their own education, nor do they develop a "critical consciousness" about the world (p. 73). Students are expected to adapt themselves to society and conform to its expectations, losing any opportunity to apply their own creativity and initiative to transform the world. To overcome this structure, Freire proposes a "problem-posing" concept of education, which poses problems about authentic human issues to students (p. 79). Instead of transmitting knowledge about the world to students, teachers would engage in a dialogue with students. This creates a reciprocal relationship in which teacher and student teach each other. Neither the teacher nor the school owns the knowledge. Reality is in a constant state of being revealed. Knowledge emerges, rather than appearing fully formed with no chance for students to interact with the content, much less challenge its presumptions.

This view of education considers knowledge to be in flux, consisting of interrelated and interdependent problems, and requires commitment by students to engage with issues. Freire states, "Education as the practice of freedom – as opposed to the practice of domination – denies that man is abstract, isolated, independent, and unattached to the world" (p. 81). The content of the curriculum consists of issues that the students care about and wish to explore.

What Do Schools Teach Students about Social Issues?

Critical pedagogy (also known as critical theory) examines schools as social institutions and offers a critique of their role in perpetuating social, political, economic, and educational inequity

(Apple, 1995; Giroux, 1997; McLaren, 2003). Critical pedagogy is "fundamentally concerned with the centrality of politics and power" in how schools work (McLaren, 2003, p. 185). Schools tend to function as institutions that reproduce the dominant culture. Teachers who enact a pedagogy that challenges the status quo "interrogate the political nature of public schooling" (Giroux, 1988, p. xxix). The ethics of education and the moral obligation of educators toward students take precedence over transmitting a body of established knowledge. Critical pedagogy seeks to reconcile the tension between technical knowledge (knowledge of *what* or *that*) and practical knowledge (knowledge of *how to*) by creating a synthesis that emancipates the learner from oppressive social institutions. Instead of observing the world and explaining it in objective terms, the teacher seeks to transform society by taking action.

Critical pedagogy investigates the hidden and the null curriculum (defined in Chapter 2). The processes of school that operate below the surface of the official or formal curriculum indicate to students what conduct, attitudes, and achievements the school values. Certain knowledge receives priority and particular roles in society are positively recognized. The curriculum is viewed "as a form of cultural politics" that emphasizes the privileged positions of those in power and those who are in favor with those in power (McLaren, 2003, p. 214). School tends to reproduce that power structure and transmit it to students along with (or in many cases labeled as) approved knowledge.

According to this perspective, sources of knowledge in the curriculum should be current events, including controversial issues. Topics such as environmental concerns, economic disparity, poverty, discrimination, human rights violations, political oppression, injustice, and others should be openly examined in the classroom. The investigation into these problems should not view topics as *things* outside of the individual's experience. Subject areas are not products to be consumed, but exist in people's relationship with the world. "As a process of search, of knowledge, and thus of creation," Freire proposes, "it requires the investigators to discover the interpenetration of problems, in the lining of meaningful themes" (p. 108). The teacher cannot think for the students; students must generate and act on their own ideas. Only in a concerted effort to seek out truth can education occur. Education does not involve one who dominates and those being dominated. Education requires cooperation to bring about transformation of the world.

Incorporating multiple sources of knowledge into the curriculum suggests that no single foundation exists for all knowledge, in contrast to an epistemology based on universal truth. Issues that arise from social conditions may be perceived from different points of view, each making a claim to authenticity. Nell Noddings (American, 1929–) explains that "a certain privilege is acquired by those who experience oppression" (Noddings, 2007, p. 217). She continues, "Thus, women have access to privileged knowledge with respect to issues of gender, the poor with respect to poverty, blacks and other ethnic minorities with respect to race, and perhaps students with respect to schooling" (p. 217). Even subjects traditionally viewed as objective, such as mathematics and science, can be viewed as arising from social practice. Individual and group biases indirectly influence methods and implicitly inform conclusions.

What Do Schools Teach Students about Issues of Race and Ethnicity?

Critical pedagogy recognizes the need to transform the curriculum to be accessible and relevant to all students. Because ethnicity is an integral and salient part of the social system, students need to become "more ethnically literate" (Banks, 2006, p. 58). Multicultural education and ethnic studies have been introduced into the curriculum to familiarize students with a diverse range of backgrounds and increase tolerance and acceptance of cultural differences. This process may occur in stages, from occasionally including discrete information about different ethnic and cultural groups (such as famous leaders and important holidays) to regularly featuring topics from diverse perspectives in the standard curriculum. A more substantial approach integrates multiple points of view in all subjects as part of the overall transformation of the curriculum. At the most fully developed stage, the curriculum explicitly addresses social issues of racism, sexism, economic disparity, and injustice. Students bring their own background and experiences to serious inquiry on these topics and examine ways to take informed action (Banks & Banks, 1999; Banks, 2006).

Advocates for multicultural education believe the teacher has a great deal of influence over how students interpret the structure of social systems and perceive their role in enacting meaningful social change. Recognizing bias in the curriculum, and in the organization of school life, is a task that teachers must consciously and conscientiously undertake. Philosopher bell hooks (American, 1952–) explains, "Teachers are often among that group most reluctant to acknowledge the extent to which white-supremacist thinking informs every aspect of our culture including the way we learn, the content of what we learn, and the manner in which we are taught" (2003, p. 25). She continues, however, that experience over the course of her academic career "has shown me how easy it is for individuals to change their thoughts and actions when they become aware and when they desire to use that awareness to alter behavior" (p. 39). Moreover, teaching is not confined to the classroom, but is "always a part of our real world experience, and our real life" (p. 41). Schools tend to promote authoritarian practices that undermine efforts in the classroom. Teachers need to find ways to share knowledge "that does not reinforce existing structures of domination (those of race, gender, class, and religious hierarchies)" (p. 45). Teachers need to raise the awareness of their colleagues and students about how racist, sexist, and other biased thinking permeates the culture, including the culture of schools. Educators "must be willing to share with anyone knowledge about how to make the transition from a dominator model to a partnership model" (p. 76). Teaching is a service, and teachers must always be willing to serve the needs of all their students.

Critical race theory argues that racism is embedded in society and gradual, incremental reform efforts produce little in the way of substantial change (Ladson-Billings, 1998, 2003). The lived experience of individuals in society conveys more about the realities of racism than large-scale generalizations about the status of groups and how legal, political, and educational responses have benefitted those suffering from discrimination. As questioned by students in the classroom vignette, race is a social construct, not a biological fact. Gloria Ladson-Billings (1998) writes, "Critical race theory sees the official school curriculum as a culturally specific artifact" that follows a narrative portraying society from one dominant perspective (p. 18). In the official curriculum, voices of African Americans are "muted or erased when they challenge the dominant culture authority and power" (p. 18). Other cultures suffer the same treatment; invisible except when referred to in the context of the dominant culture. Authentic versions of history are sanitized and homogenized to present a distorted view that downplays conflict and portrays multiculturalism as one more step in assimilation.

Post-colonialism is a related perspective that focuses on the colonial aspect of the founding and expansion of Western European nations and the United States. The ethnocentric narrative presumes that civilization begins with the classical Greek era and progresses in an orderly path toward the Enlightenment and ultimately to the pinnacle of democratic and capitalistic society represented by the United States (Andreotti, 2011). Those not part of the dominant Western tradition are viewed as the Other (e.g., uncivilized, barbaric, savage, backward). Western rationality is not only judged the superior form of reasoning and discourse but is also assumed to be the universal standard.

A curriculum seeking to resist this prevailing representation of the world defies the notion that Western nations have bestowed upon other cultures the gifts of civilization for which they should be grateful. Advances in economics, education, technology, medicine and health care, and other institutional benefits conferred upon those in other parts of the world lurk beneath a pervasive subtext of conquest and oppression. For example, in the United States, the curriculum typically offers a selective account of the brutal and shameful subjugation of Native Americans (Rains, 2003).

For a nation that began as a collection of colonies, forged into an independent nation through the force of revolution, the irony of oppressing the native population is uncomfortable at best. The forced removal and relocation of people from their homelands, and the genocide that resulted from resistance, receives a carefully edited and subtly worded interpretation. When depicted, details of the persistent suffering are omitted. Otherwise, the complex story of a vast number of indigenous people becomes either stereotyped or conveniently made invisible. Their background is efficiently dealt with before being relegated to irrelevant.

A People's History of the United States (1980/1990) by Howard Zinn represents an example of restoring missing voices to the curriculum. Each chapter describes major historical events from the points of view of those involved and affected, other than from the points of view of the famous characters that figure prominently in typical textbooks. For example, the chapter on Columbus arriving in the New World opens with a description of the lives of the Arawak people of the Bahama Islands. Zinn acknowledges his history presents "a biased account, one that leans in a certain direction. I am not troubled by that, because the mountain of history books under which we all stand leans so heavily in the other direction" (p. 570). He explains that history is typically narrated as stories about heroes and saviors. This perspective not only neglects those who participated in historical events, but can have the effect of diminishing the capacity of the ordinary citizen to act. Traditional histories "suggest that at times of crisis we must look to someone to save us . . . thus surrendering our own strength, demeaning our own ability, obliterating our own selves" (p. 570). Most of history understates the role of the average citizen in favor of the roles of statesmen, generals, business tycoons, and other leaders. This teaches students that the role of citizenship is to choose others to act for us. Teachers should seek out the untold or overlooked stories to remind people of their role in shaping world events and controlling their own destinies.

The Zinn Education Project provides resources and support for planning instruction that addresses "the role of working people, women, people of color, and organized social movements in shaping history" (Zinn Education Project, 2015, About section, para 3). Students can explore history by time period or by theme to learn that "history is made not by a few heroic individuals, but instead by people's choices and actions, thereby also learning that their own choices and actions matter" (Zinn Education Project, 2015, About section, para 2). The project coordinates with two other organizations, Teaching for Change and Rethinking Schools, to offer instructional materials on topics related to reform, equity, multicultural, activism, and social justice.

What Do Schools Teach Students about Gender Issues?

In the vignette, a student raises the question if biological differences between males and females influence views on their roles in society. One might also question how schools shape and reinforce these roles. Many research studies reveal gender bias in the curriculum. One study concludes that gender bias in textbooks is near universal, remarkably uniform, quite persistent, but virtually invisible (Blumberg, 2008). The curriculum tends to represent a male-dominant perspective, highlighting the role of men in all fields. Textbooks and other instructional materials that diminish the role of women or portray women in ways that reinforce stereotypes may adversely affect the achievement of female students. Sadker and Zittleman (2007) outline seven types of bias present in curricular materials: 1) invisibility, 2) stereotyping, 3) imbalance or selectivity, 4) unreality, 5) fragmentation or isolation, 6) linguistic bias, and 7) cosmetic bias.

In the history of philosophy, the issue of women's education appears only intermittently. In the *Republic*, Socrates does not appear to distinguish between the kinds of education that males and females should receive. His concern is that each person should receive the education appropriate to his or her role in society, regardless of individual differences. In *Emile* (1762/1962), Rousseau makes a clear distinction between the education of boys and girls. In contrast to the active and strong Emile, he describes Sophie as "passive and weak" (p. 131). Her role is to please

Emile, to make a charming companion, and to be docile and dominated. Her education focuses on her appearance, household duties, and childrearing. An easygoing temperament and naturally sweet disposition are her primary strengths. "Sophie's mind is pleasing but not brilliant," Rousseau contends, "solid but not deep" (p. 149–150). Despite their differing views, for both Plato and Rousseau a woman's characteristics are natural and inherent qualities.[1]

Mary Wollstonecraft (British, 1759–97) condemns Rousseau's depiction of women. As described in *Emile*, Sophie is "formed only to please, and be subject to man" (Wollstonecraft, 1988, p. 78–79). The system of education he describes for women cultivates a subservient nature at the expense of developing reasoning and understanding. She observes that "servitude not only debases the individual, but its effects seem to be transmitted to posterity" (p. 82). The conventions imposed upon women derive not from nature, Wollstonecraft argues, but from rules dictated by a male-dominated society. Such a view of education renders women "completely insignificant," limiting the rights of human beings predominantly (if not exclusively) to males (p. 86).

Wollstonecraft pleads for her contemporaries to "arise above such narrow prejudices" and afford women the full benefits and advantages of an equal education (p. 92). She proposes for males and females to be educated "after the same model" instead of being segregated into separate kinds of schooling (p. 165). She recommends public schools be established to educate males and females in a common system, releasing women from the confines of mere domestic responsibilities. Wollstonecraft discusses the advantages an equitable education offers society, explaining, "I think the female world oppressed" (p. 178).

According to Jane Roland Martin (American, 1929–), philosophy of education has largely neglected the topic of the education of women. She argues that, throughout history, the concept of biological determinism has been used to subordinate the role of women in society. This subordination extends to the classroom. Research indicates a drop in interest by girls in subjects such as math and science after the elementary school age, leading to a decrease in enrollment by women in studying these fields. Martin (2011) suggests language denoting masculine strength and power colors views of objective, logical subjects (such as calling math and natural science "hard" subjects) while feminized language suggests a lesser status for "soft" subjects in the humanities and social sciences (p. 171).

Martin (1985) counsels that women need to assert their voices and fully participate in the "conversation" about their own education (p. 175). She blames the current state of women's educational opportunity on "the fallacy of the false dilemma – either Sophie's education or Emile's, either an education based solely on gender or one having nothing to do with gender" (p. 176). Ignorance of other alternatives, and a "failure of imagination," hinders the possibilities of claiming an education for women (p. 176). Expanding the definition of women's education needs to encompass education as a whole, not produce a separate strand or sub-category that remains either complementary or subordinate to the dominant male viewpoint. Nor should equity be viewed as offering women the same education as males, if the definition of education itself is not altered. Educational standards of excellence reinforce cultural stereotypes associated with masculinity, such as rational objectivity and productivity. However, Martin argues, "The fact that the traits incorporated in our educational ideal are genderized in favor of males does not mean that girls and women cannot or do not acquire them" (p. 194). Women increasingly participate in the productive processes of society formerly considered male-dominated arenas. "In claiming their education," Martin urges, "women . . . should not deny themselves access to all the traits our culture associates with males," such as critical thinking, abstract reasoning, and self-sufficiency (p. 194).

Similar to Martin, Noddings repudiates inserting gender-sensitive topics into the curriculum in isolated fragments or other piecemeal efforts. Instead, she recommends that the entire curriculum be redesigned around the theme of *care* (1992, 2005, 2013). Matters of interest to women, minorities, and others who feel excluded or marginalized by the content taught in schools could be integrated into the curriculum. The disciplines as currently organized tend to overwhelm or reject isolated attempts to incorporate new material. If the curriculum were organized according to themes, the study of important social issues would arise organically from the discussion of relevant topics in all subjects.

Houston (1994) argues the goal is not to try and make the curriculum gender-neutral or gender-free. The goal should be to make the curriculum free of gender bias, not absent of all issues regarding gender. Being proactive in identifying and addressing unequal access and unequal opportunities for female students will have a greater benefit for all students than avoiding the issue.

What Do Schools Teach Students about Issues of Religion?

According to critical theorists and other philosophers interested in equality and justice, schools should be places where social institutions and practices are critically examined. Noddings (2013) suggests religion should be a topic openly discussed in classrooms, as should all issues that affect the identity, growth, and well-being of members of society. The religious views present in the community should be equitably represented in a sensitive manner. This includes reading religious texts, viewing religious art, listening to religious music, and learning about the religious practices of others. Religion has affected the lives of people throughout history and continues to be a highly relevant issue. Concerns that exposure to other faiths may influence a student's choices or cause a student to question her beliefs are not grounds for excluding the study of religion from the curriculum. The dialogue is a necessary one that respects the values of others and demonstrates a caring attitude toward the experiences of students.

Critical pedagogy challenges the view of schools as neutral in regard to social issues. By declining to take a position on an issue, one perpetuates the status quo. "Washing one's hands of the conflict between the powerful and the powerless," Freire (1985) states, "means to side with the powerful, not to be neutral" (p. 122). Permitting an unfair, inequitable, or discriminatory policy or practice to remain unopposed tacitly implies consent, if not approval, of the action. "To be neutral, to be passive . . . [is] to collaborate," Zinn maintains. "And I, as a teacher do not want to be a collaborator" (Ellis & Mueller, 2004). Zinn wants teachers, and their students, to interact with what is happening in the world and to intercede when possible.

A curriculum designed to transform society would focus on local issues and global problems. As a community-oriented education, students would be active outside of the classroom in service learning projects. The curriculum would extend beyond existing content and instructional materials to locate resources in the community related to current issues. Finally, education would be future-oriented, teaching students how to plan society, rather than preparing them to fit into a planned society. The curriculum should encourage students to analyze structures of power and explore avenues for change.

How Do Teachers Teach? Questions about Pedagogy

"Problem-posing education affirms men and women as beings in the process of becoming."
(Paulo Freire)

Critical pedagogy emphasizes teachers and students taking action to transform society. The problem-posing concept of education that Freire recommends creates a dialogue between the teacher and students. This creates a reciprocal relationship in which teacher and student teach each other. Genuine problems of relevance to the students become the topics of study. Within this framework, several possible directions may develop.

An "equity pedagogy" incorporates methods and strategies that help students from diverse racial, ethnic, and cultural groups to not only function effectively within society but also to help create and sustain a more just, humane, and democratic society (Banks, 2006, p. 78–79). This pedagogy does not teach students to conform to the existing social order or perpetuate its systemic bias and discrimination. A pedagogy that is both critical and equitable urges students to question assumptions about societal structures and institutions, and become reflective and active citizens. "Equity pedagogy alters the traditional power relationship between teachers and students," Banks explains. Equity pedagogy actively involves students in knowledge construction and production, and using that knowledge to become agents of change.

According to hooks, teaching is a practice of freedom. The progressive, holistic approach she calls "engaged pedagogy" is committed to the well-being of students (1994, p. 15). Engaged pedagogy values student expression of their identities and concerns while teachers seek their own self-actualization. Teachers who encourage students to take risks must be willing to engage in risk-taking themselves.

When cultural distance or divisions exist in the classroom, a teacher may inadvertently fall into stereotyping students based on the best of intentions. Research or scholarship that generalizes how one group learns best can influence choices that create unintended consequences. Sometimes a teacher will plan or implement instruction according to assumptions that link a lack of educational achievement to race, ethnicity, cultural, socioeconomic status, or other factors (Delpit, 1995; Gay, 1999). Thinking in terms of deficiencies, teachers compare the academic success of all students to the dominant culture, which tends to reflect a white, middle-class, college-educated perspective. This deficit mindset can result in "teaching down" to students rather than teaching to their strengths (Delpit, 1995, p. 173). If the teacher does not live in the community where the school is located, misconceptions can infiltrate the learning process. Ignorance of students' lives, experiences, interests, and activities outside of the classroom presents obstacles to effective teaching. One recommendation is for teachers to learn about the local community and meet families. The professional development of a teacher needs to extend beyond identifying differences that account for deficits in learning to expand knowledge of the cultural heritage and contributions that lead to deeper knowledge and appreciation.

"Culturally relevant" pedagogy involves incorporating student culture into the curriculum and instruction (Ladson-Billings, 2009, p. 25). Teachers who practice culturally relevant teaching have high regard for others and see themselves as part of a community. They engage in the local community and encourage their students to do so. Students witness their teacher involved in their community, not standing outside of it. Teachers learn to "honor and respect" the home lives of their students (p. 151).

Like Freire, Noddings emphasizes the role of dialogue in investigating socially relevant issues. She associates this approach with the pedagogy of *care*, encouraging educators to engage in dialogue with students to interpret what caring means and how it can be expressed. Noddings (2007) asks, "If, in the name of fairness, a teacher treats all students exactly alike, do all students feel cared for? Is there a sense of fairness that is compatible with caring?" (p. 227). This kind of question can reveal how students view caring relationships. Some students might "equate coercion with caring," which would alarm a critical theorist or other educator concerned with issues of power and dominance (p. 227). Further dialogue would allow the teacher and students to "participate in a mutual construction of the frame of reference" to establish a common definition for what it means to be caring and to feel cared for. She cautions teachers, however, not to require students to engage in dialogue, but to invite them. Otherwise, the goal of helping students to perceive unequal power relationships and begin to take action to change them is undermined.

How Do Students Learn to Transform Society?

How can teachers engage early childhood and elementary-grade students in sensitive social issues? Stereotyping can begin in schools from the earliest grades, from how the curriculum depicts gender roles to other bias in textbooks and instructional materials, including omissions of different ethnic, racial, cultural, and socioeconomic groups. As discussed in Chapter 7, play is one way children socialize and portray how they view their roles and the roles of others they observe. How teachers interact with students also defines and reinforces social roles. Examples of appropriate practices include the integration of diverse images and roles in curricular materials, recognition of language differences, various cultural perspectives incorporated into learning activities and assessments, and choices offered in how students express themselves and represent their identity (King, Chipman, & Cruz-Janzen, 1994).

In 1968, Iowa teacher Jane Elliott conducted a simulation with her all-white third-grade class to give them a first-hand encounter with discrimination (Peters, 1987). On the day after the Rev. Martin Luther King, Jr. was assassinated, Jane Elliott announced she was dividing the class into two groups: brown-eyed people and blue-eyed people. Brown-eyed students were afforded a privileged status and were overtly granted privileges denied to the blue-eyed students, such as extra recess time, first in line at lunch and allowed second helpings, first in line for the buses, being permitted to use the drinking fountain, and being row leaders. Blue-eyed students were prohibited from playing with brown-eyed students on the playground unless invited, and blue-eyed students could not use the playground equipment.

The teacher, and soon afterwards the brown-eyed students, began making biting, insulting remarks to the blue-eyed students about their inferior intelligence, lack of social skills, and irresponsible habits. School became an isolating and alienating experience for blue-eyed students, and tensions eventually erupted into verbal and physical confrontations. Feelings were hurt and self-confidence eroded among the blue-eyed students. When the teacher reversed the roles, the same phenomenon occurred. Those designated superior improved in their behavior and performance while those relegated to inferior status became sullen and disheartened. The lesson in discrimination was vivid and visceral, and affected not only the students' attitudes toward each other but also their opinions about themselves as individuals.

What Is the Role of the Teacher to Transform Society?

Teachers who embrace equity pedagogy are aware of how their own cultural, ethnic, racial, and gender backgrounds and experiences affect their educational outlook and instructional practices. They are curious and respectful of the backgrounds of others, sensitive to individual and group differences, and mindful of the biased attitudes that may exist in an institutional setting. Teachers of this kind possess multicultural and pedagogical knowledge and skills that enable them to implement instruction that not only acknowledges and accepts differences based on race, ethnicity, gender, sexual orientation, language, religion, immigration status, and a host of other attributes, but also sees them as resources rather than hindrances in the classroom.

TEACHER AS CHANGE AGENT

Educational philosophers from a critical perspective speak of the role of the teacher as change agent. Teachers need to critique the educational system of which they are a part and "choose a role as either agent of change or defender of the status quo" (Ladson-Billings, 2009, p. 145).

One dimension of school reform is the devaluing of the work of the teacher as a profession. Many view teaching as a set of technical skills that, if implemented properly, should produce standardized results. This reduces the act of teaching to a simplified methodology that anyone should be able to acquire and effectively reproduce. Successful teachers carry out the methods properly; unsuccessful teachers must not be applying the procedures correctly. Teaching knowledge is broken down into discrete parts that, when reassembled, should add up to effective instruction. Standardized testing measures not only student achievement but also teacher performance, and identifies those teachers whose lower outcomes indicate a failure to execute the prescribed processes.

TEACHER AS TRANSFORMATIVE INTELLECTUAL

A reconceptualization of the role views teachers as "transformative intellectuals" (Giroux, 1988, p. 125). This defines teaching in intellectual and professional terms, not just as an application of technical skills. In addition, the role becomes a transformative one, focusing on effecting change that benefits all students in the classroom. What teachers teach and how they teach it acknowledges that schools select and exclude knowledge to transmit a particular social and cultural perspective. Teachers who are transformative intellectuals educate students to be active thinkers and risk-takers who critically examine social relations, educational discourse, and the role of schools and other institutions as sites of power and control. Teachers might also be regarded as "cultural workers" who engage in the social and political life of the community, the school, and the students, rather than attempting to maintain an objective stance as "outsiders" (Giroux, 1997, p. 224).

What Is the Role of the Student to Transform Society?

STUDENT AS CO-INVESTIGATOR

Freire proposes that the students act in the role of co-investigator with the teacher on socially relevant issues. Students need to see themselves as important and respected members of society. The issues and concerns students raise have relevance and therefore should be afforded a valued place in the classroom. Freire (1970/2000) states, "Problem-posing education affirms men and women as beings in the process of becoming" (p. 84). In the role of co-investigator, students actively contribute to the learning process. Freire explains:

> Authentic education is not carried on by "A" *for* "B" or by "A" *about* "B," but by "A" *with* "B," mediated by the world – a world which impresses and challenges both parties, giving rise to views or opinions about it.

> (p. 93)

STUDENT AS ACTIVIST

To transform society, students cannot merely receive imparted knowledge from the teacher or settle for examining social issues through classroom discussion. Students must become activists, increasing both their awareness and their involvement. Activism demands taking conscious and concerted action in the community to enact the changes students wish to see in the world.

Design

How Are Schools Organized? Questions about the Role of the School

As we have examined, concerns about social bias and inequity raise numerous educational challenges. Most schools committed to the expressed purpose of helping students transform society integrate opportunities throughout their educational programs. However, schools and programs have been designed with the mission to remedy specific social issues (Table 10.1).

Multiculturalism, diversity, and equity

The SEED Foundation was established to provide public residential schools for underserved students. SEED schools operate in Washington, D.C., Baltimore, Maryland, and Miami, Florida, with plans to expand. The boarding school environment provides a twenty-four-hour supportive environment, sets and maintains high expectations based on a college-prep curriculum, and fosters relationships within the community.

Table 10.1 Design a School (Transform Society)

Purpose of Education	Transform society
Curriculum	Relevant, real-life social issues (e.g., race, ethnicity, culture, gender, sexual orientation, poverty, etc.)
Instruction	Problem-posing, critical pedagogy (e.g., equity pedagogy, engaged pedagogy, culturally relevant pedagogy, caring pedagogy)
Role of Teacher	Change agent, transformative intellectual
Role of Student	Co-investigator, activist
Role of School	Equity, social justice

Many resources are available to assist teachers and students who wish to effect change within the existing school environment. The Critical Multicultural Pavilion, an EdChange Project, describes key characteristics of a multicultural curriculum and recommends steps for transforming the curriculum. Teaching Tolerance, a project of the Southern Poverty Law Center, offers classroom resources for addressing diversity issues in schools. One resource, Perspectives for a Diverse America, is a step-by-step tool for planning instruction from an anti-bias, social justice perspective. The National SEED Project is a peer-led group founded to develop inclusive curriculum materials in all subject areas for all grade levels on equity issues. Many other organizations and outlets publish textbooks and other materials for teachers and administrators with an interest in transforming their schools by teaching for social justice.

Gender and Sexual Orientation

Gender differences represent one area that some schools have attempted to specifically address through their organizational structure. A study by the Feminist Majority Foundation shows that single-sex classes in public schools have increased since Title IX regulations were amended in 2006, lifting the general ban on single-sex public education. Many public schools have experimented with single-sex education prior to 2006. For example, the Young Women's Leadership School of East Harlem opened in 1996 and the Young Women's Leadership Charter School opened in Chicago in 2000. Other leadership schools for girls include the Young Women's Leadership Academy (in San Antonio, Texas) and the Coretta Scott King Young Women's Leadership Academy (Atlanta). Each of these schools is designed to provide an environment focused exclusively on developing the academic skills of young women. The schools offer a college-preparatory curriculum intended to produce leaders in the community. Many of these schools emphasize mathematics, science, and technology, subject areas in which research indicates girls underperform as they progress into middle and high school. The transformative nature of the educational mission of these schools remains a priority. The founders of the Young Women's Leadership Charter School in Chicago were inspired by the vision that "every young woman would be empowered to transform her life through education" (Young Women's Leadership Charter School, 2013, Home page section, para 1).

In addition to offering classes and programs to address gender differences, how can schools address students' sexual orientation? The Pride School in Atlanta provides Lesbian, Gay, Bisexual, Transgender, Queer, Questioning, Intersex, Ally (LGBTQQIA) students, families, and educators with a safe, accepting, and understanding learning environment that honors their identities. The school climate supports the well-being of their students both inside and outside of school. At the Pride School, students create their own individualized curriculum and participate in democratic decision-making. (Chapter 11 describes other democratically structured schools based on developing individual freedom and self-identity.)

Several organizations exist to support education related to gender issues and sexual orientation. Welcoming Schools, a project of the Human Rights Campaign Foundation, offers professional development tools, lesson plans, and other resources for elementary schools on family diversity, gender stereotyping, and bullying. The Gay, Lesbian & Straight Education Network (GLSEN) offers resources to incorporate LGBT history, themes, and topics into the curriculum. The Gay-Straight Alliance (GSA) Network focuses on racial and gender justice issues, providing resources to develop a LGBTQ-inclusive curriculum and empowering teachers and students to organize and advocate for safe, welcoming school environments. Teaching Tolerance also describes best practices for creating an LGBT-inclusive school environment.

How Does a School Designed to Transform Society Define an Educated Person?

A school committed to the transformation of society would define an educated person as one who is aware of current social issues and actively participates in effecting change.

Evaluate

Consistency

Opportunities to examine issues of equity and social justice may arise in all subject areas. Works of literature in English/Language Art classes can include examples of people suffering from oppression and confronting challenges such as discrimination. The study of historical and current events in social studies classes can explore multiple perspectives and place incidents in context. In the vignette, a science lesson on genetics initiated a student discussion on social and political bias.

In an effort to appear neutral, teachers may shy away from sensitive or controversial issues or relegate these topics to the humanities and social sciences. In a school committed to transforming society, teachers in every discipline would encourage students to ask questions and express their concerns about the world they observe and experience.

Compatibility

Critical pedagogy emphasizes creating a dialogue between teachers and students. Are all types of dialogue compatible with transforming society? How does a Socratic dialogue (Chapter 3) differ from a dialogue from the perspective of critical pedagogy? Freire argues that Socratic dialogue does not "constitute a true pedagogy of knowing" because knowledge is defined in conceptual terms (1985, p. 55). The recollection of enduring truths or ruminations about permanent knowledge do not create a genuine dialectic relationship with the world. For Freire, knowledge comes from connections and actions in the world. Dialogue between teachers and students must transform the world, not merely describe and explain existing reality.

Coherence

How does critical pedagogy create a coherent system of education? Rather than simply recognizing instances of bias or inequity, each of the approaches we have investigated—equity pedagogy (Banks), engaged pedagogy (hooks), culturally relevant pedagogy (Ladson-Billings), and caring pedagogy (Noddings)—integrate these issues into the curriculum and instruction. Questions about the relationship of citizens to the political structure and the role of the individual in society occur in all schools. In a school based on critical pedagogy, these issues are not deflected or dealt with as isolated incidents. The school acknowledges injustice and invites scrutiny of power relationships.

Incoherence results when schools teach about democratic values or human rights positions then attempt to ignore, dismiss, dodge, or explain away issues students raise from their own observations or experiences. A blatant disconnect between the role of school in society and the society as lived by the participants intrudes upon the educational process and fosters suspicion and distrust.

Reflect

How Do Your Prior Observations and Experiences Relate to a Curriculum Designed to Transform Society?

In your own observations and experiences, how do schools incorporate social issues into the curriculum? From where do these issues originate—the formal curriculum (such as a textbook) or from the students and community? What topics have you noticed are not included in the curriculum? Does the subject area or the grade level of the student affect decisions on what topics to include and which to omit? If so, are these topics inserted elsewhere in the curriculum or discarded?

How Do Your Prior Observations and Experiences Relate to a Pedagogy Designed to Transform Society?

When social issues such as inequity or injustice surface in the classroom, how do teachers respond? How do you think teachers view their role in addressing such topics? How do you think teachers view the role of the student in examining these kinds of concerns? How do teachers exhibit cultural awareness and cultural literacy? How do teachers exhibit an engaged pedagogy or pedagogy of care? What relationship do teachers establish and maintain with students and how could this be altered to produce authentic dialogue on critical issues?

How Do Your Prior Observations and Experiences Relate to a School Designed to Transform Society?

How does the role of the school promote or suppress transformative education? What actions would a school need to take to communicate that all voices are welcome, respected, and of value to the entire learning community?

How Do Your Own Practices and Beliefs Relate to the Purpose of Education as Learning to Transform Society?

Critical pedagogy actively pursues solutions to social problems and issues. In your opinion, should schools take the initiative to lead change and propose solutions to social challenges? Is the role of the school to preserve society or transform it? How are these positions in conflict?

Critical pedagogy asserts that all education is political. The role of education is to improve the lives of all people, to assist in their struggles and help them overcome adversity. "I had a modest goal when I became a teacher," Howard Zinn confesses. "I wanted to change the world" (Ellis & Mueller, 2004).

Note

1 Jane Roland Martin examines the education of women as depicted by Plato and Rousseau in depth, with commentary by Wollstonecraft and a number of others, in *Reclaiming a Conversation: The Ideal of the Educated Woman* (1985).

References

Andreotti, V. (2011). *Actionable postcolonial theory in education*. New York, NY: Palgrave Macmillan.

Apple, M. (1995). *Education and power* (2nd ed.). New York, NY: Routledge.

Banks, J. A. (2006). *Race, culture, and education*. New York, NY: Routledge.

Banks, J. A., & Banks, C. A. (1999). Approaches to multicultural educational reform. In J. A. Banks & Banks C. A. (Eds.), *Multicultural education: Issues and perspectives*. (3rd ed.) (pp. 229–250). New York, NY: Wiley & Sons.

Blumberg, R. L. (2008). The invisible obstacle to educational equality: Gender bias in textbooks. *Prospects, 38*, 345–361.

Counts, G. S. (1932). *Dare the school build a new world order?* New York, NY: John Day Co.

Delpit, L. (1995). *Other people's children: Cultural conflict in the classroom*. New York, NY: The New Press.

Ellis, D. & Mueller, D. (Producers and Directors) (2004). *Howard Zinn: You can't be neutral on a moving train* [Documentary]. United States: Paramount Pictures.

Freire, P. (1985). *The politics of education: Culture, power, and liberation* (D. Macedo, Trans.). New York, NY: Bergin & Garvey.

Freire, P. (2000). *Pedagogy of the oppressed* (M. B. Ramos, Trans.). New York, NY: Bloomsbury. (Original work published 1970.)

Gay, G. (1999). Educational equality for students of color. In *Multicultural education: Issues and perspectives*. (3rd ed.). J. A. Banks & Banks C. A. (Eds.). (pp. 195–228). New York, NY: Wiley & Sons.

Giroux, H. (1988). *Teachers as intellectuals: Toward a critical pedagogy of learning*. Granby, MA: Bergin & Garvey.

Giroux, H. (1988). *Pedagogy and the politics of hope: Theory, culture, and schooling*. Boulder, CO: Westview.

hooks, b. (1994). *Teaching to transgress. Education as the practice of freedom*. New York, NY: Routledge.

hooks, b. (2003). *Teaching community. A pedagogy of hope*. New York, NY: Routledge.

Houston, B. (1994). Should public education be gender free? In L. Stone (Ed.), *The education feminist reader* (pp. 122–134). New York, NY: Routledge.

Jordan, J. (1980). Poem for South African Women. In *Passion: New poems, 1977–1980* (pp. 42–43). Boston, MA: Beacon Press.

King, E. W., Chipman, M., & Cruz-Janzen, M. (1994). *Educating young children in a diverse society*. Boston, MA: Allyn & Bacon.

Klein, S., Lee, J., McKinsey, P., & Archer, C. (2014). *Identifying U.S. K–12 public schools with deliberate sex segregation*. Arlington, VA: Feminist Majority Foundation. [PDF file]. Retrieved from http://feminist.org/education/pdfs/IdentifyingSexSegregation12-12–14.pdf

Ladson-Billings, G. (1998). Just what is critical race theory and what's it doing in a nice field like education? *Qualitative Studies in Education, 11*(1), 7–24.

Ladson-Billings, G. (2003). Lies my teacher still tells: Developing a critical race perspective toward the social studies. In G. Ladson-Billings (Ed.), *Critical race theory perspectives on the social studies* (pp. 1–11). Greenwich, CT: Information Age.

Ladson-Billings, G. (2009). *The dreamkeepers: Successful teachers of African American children* (2nd ed.). San Francisco, CA: Jossey-Bass.

Martin, J. R. (1985). *Reclaiming a conversation: The ideal of the educated woman*. New Haven, CT: Yale University Press.

Martin, J. R. (2011). *Education reconfigured: Culture, encounter and change*. New York, NY: Routledge.

McLaren, P. (2003). *Life in schools: An introduction to critical pedagogy in the foundation of education* (4th ed.). Boston, MA: Allyn & Bacon.

Noddings, N. (1992). *The challenge to care in schools: An alternative approach to education*. New York, NY: Teachers College Press.

Noddings, N. (2007). *Philosophy of education* (2nd ed.). Cambridge, MA: Westview Press.

Noddings, N. (2013). *Caring: A relational approach to ethics and moral education* (2nd ed.). Berkeley, CA: University of California Press.

Peters, W. (1987). *A class divided: Then and now*. New Haven, CT: Yale University Press.

Plato. (1997). *Complete works*. J. M. Cooper (Ed.). Indianapolis, IN: Hackett.

Rains, F. V. (2003). American Indians, white privilege and the power of residual guilt in the social studies. In G. Ladson-Billings (Ed.), *Critical race theory perspectives on the social studies: The profession, policies, and curriculum* (pp. 1–11). Greenwich, CT: Information Age.

Rousseau, J. (1962). *The Emile of Jean-Jacques Rousseau: Selections* (10th ed.). W. Boyd (Trans. & Ed.). New York, NY: Teachers College Press. (Original work published 1762.)

Sadker, D. M., & Zittleman, K. (2007). Practical strategies for detecting and correcting gender bias in your classroom. In Sadker & Silber (Eds.), *Gender in the classroom: Foundations, skills, methods, and strategies across the curriculum* (pp. 259–283). Mahwah, NJ: Lawrence Erlbaum.

Wollstonecraft, M. (1988). *A vindication of the rights of women: An authoritative text* (2nd ed.). C. H. Poston (Ed.). New York, NY: W. W. Norton.

Zinn, H. (1980/1990). *A people's history of the United States*. New York, NY: Harper Perennial. (Original work published 1980)

Zinn Education Project. (2015). About page. [Website]. Retrieved from http://zinnedproject.org/about/

11 What If . . . The Purpose of Education Were to Learn to Develop Individual Identity and Personal Freedom?

Wonder

In this final chapter of Part III, we ask the wonder question: *"What if . . . the purpose of education were to learn how to develop individual identity and personal freedom?"*

The final perspective we will investigate on the *Continuum of Educational Philosophy* (Figure 11.1) departs most fully from the paradigm that education is a search to discover external, objective, universal truths that apply to everyone. Truth in this view is a subjective, personal truth. Individuals seek the freedom to discover their own unique self-identity. With individual freedom, however, comes the responsibility to accept the consequences of one's choices.

Observe

Classroom Vignette: A Day in a Mixed-Age School

When I arrive at the Sudbury school, I am greeted by two seven-year-olds who show me to the office. After being introduced to a staff member and signing in as a guest, the two girls take me on a tour of the building, speaking breathlessly nearly in unison. A great room serves as the main

EDUCATIONAL PRACTICES

RATIONAL	EMPIRICAL
Ideas-Focused	Experience-Focused
Content-Oriented	Process-Oriented
Fixed Curriculum	Flexible Curriculum
Teacher-Centered	Student-Centered
Teacher-Directed	Self-Directed
Pre-Determined Outcomes	Open-Ended Exploration
Whole-Class Activities	Differentiated/Individualized Activities

Objective External Reality	Internal Subjective Reality
Absolute Universal Truth	Changing Relative Truth
Pre-Existing Knowledge	Constructed Knowledge
Knowledge Independent of Experience	Knowledge Dependent on Experience
Autonomous Knowledge	Interdependent Knowledge
Absolute Universal Values	Relative Local Values
Values Independent of Experience	Values Dependent on Experience

PHILOSOPHICAL PERSPECTIVES

Figure 11.1 Continuum of Educational Philosophy (Identity and Freedom)

common and meeting space. A large table sits to one side, where a staff member is conferring with two children about a topic. She welcomes me, introduces herself as the school's founder and director, and allows the two girls to continue showing me around. Two enormous sofas sit near the center of the room, with children of different ages sprawled across them. Two girls are reading, another pair are playing with dolls. On the other sofa, a teen is playing a video game on a tablet. Several comfortable chairs dot the room, and another table sits on the other side. An area is designated as the library, although bookshelves line every floor of the building, holding not only books but learning materials and games. A stage fills one end of the room, where a group of students are acting out a skit.

My tour guides show me the kitchen and eating area, where I meet a third staff member. A list of chores is displayed, with a student name beside each chore. Students check off the chore completed for that date, such as emptying trash cans, sweeping the floor, wiping off the lunch tables, and other tasks to clean and tidy the common areas. Children can eat snacks at any time during the day, once they have been "certified" to use the kitchen on their own.

On the second floor, cubbies store children's personal effects. The floor is busy with activity. In the computer lab, every station is occupied. The floor also has several cubicles where individual students can work or study. An art room filled with materials, paints, and other art supplies is open to students all day. A video room contains video cameras and editing equipment, and a student project is currently under production.

The basement holds numerous toys and games, including a pool table, ping pong table, and foosball table. A bin holds balls and other outdoor playthings. Several children are playing in the basement, but until I arrive no other adult is present. A sign-out sheet is posted at the door that leads to the backyard. The girls explain that everyone must sign out to play but they have no set times for recess. I hear the sounds of a bass guitar emanating from behind the door of a room. The girls assure me I can knock, and I meet a young man who is practicing bass guitar in a small room filled with musical equipment, an amplifier, and a computer running a recoding application. He explains that he is self-taught and spends most of each day learning new songs from the internet and recording using the computer program.

After my tour guides return me to the office, I am invited to attend a Judicial Committee (or "JC") meeting. At the school, any staff member or peer may fill out a Grievance Form on a student who has violated a rule or otherwise encroached on someone's right to "peacefully coexist." Blank Grievance Forms are available in two places at the school where they can be deposited in a box to be considered by the Judicial Committee. The JC meeting convenes at 11:30. Called to order by a student chair, defendants hear the charges filed against them by the plaintiffs. The youngest defendant is seven years old. Two older children are also charged at the meeting, as well as a teen. The JC hears the grievance, witnesses testify, a verdict is reached, and a sentence imposed. One student is less than completely satisfied with the judgment and his frustration shows, but the other students willingly confess their offenses and accept their sentences (consisting of chores).

After eating lunch with a group of students, four students inform me they are meeting with a staff member for an algebra lesson. They explain that classes are not regularly held at the school in all subjects, but a student can request a subject or topic and arrange for a class to be conducted by a staff member. All staff members are called by their first names and not referred to as teachers. The session is a combination of tutoring and peer teaching, using an algebra textbook and problems the students have located on their own. These students are high school age and have begun considering their college prospects. The staff member informs me that, although most students leave the school to enter high school, they have had several complete their secondary education at the school and been admitted to college. The school accepts children ages five through eighteen.

Later in the afternoon, the School Meeting is held. For the beginning of the meeting, all students are expected to attend. Staff members make announcements and share other news concerning all students. When the meeting proceeds to discuss matters requiring voting, the younger children are permitted to excuse themselves. Procedures and rules are raised and debated. Any new rule is entered into a Law Book. Existing laws may be revised or revoked as well. Personal responsibility is stressed, with respect for others the main method of maintaining order.

I thank the staff members and students for allowing me to visit and ask if I may arrange for some of the students from my course to visit and observe. I am told my request will be taken up at the next School Meeting, where all students may discuss how they feel about college students coming to observe. Final approval depends on their decision.

Investigate

What Do Teachers Teach? Questions about the Curriculum

The vignette describes a visit to a Sudbury school. What philosophical perspectives and concepts would support the free and spontaneous learning environment observed in the vignette?

> "Subjectivity is truth."
> (Kierkegaard)

Several major philosophers influenced what became known as Existentialism. An existentialist perspective seeks knowledge of the self and one's position as an individual in society and the universe. Meaning is derived through personal, subjective experiences rather than from external, objective sources of knowledge.

According to Søren Kierkegaard (Denmark, 1813–55), knowledge is something one can only discover for oneself "because only when *I* discover is it discovered, not before, even though the whole world knew it" (Kierkegaard, 2000, p. 120). The discovery of knowledge leads to a change in the learner, a rebirth. The individual realizes he knows nothing about the world and is no longer satisfied with recollecting knowledge (in the Socratic sense) but must go beyond suppositions to focus on the moment he becomes aware of his existence. Kierkegaard rejects discovering objective truth through a system of philosophical thinking that attempts to explain the world for him. "The crucial thing is to find a truth that is truth *for me*, to find the idea for which I am willing to live and die" (p. 8).

Kierkegaard (1834–55/1975) focuses his attention on the individual. "Every man is endowed with individuality," he remarks. "The meaning of life, then, should be to fulfill this distinctiveness" (p. 489). His philosophy seeks meaning for himself as an individual and for the life he is living, rather than relying on a logically derived model of reality that bears no deep meaning for him as an individual. "Aristotle's view that philosophy begins with wonder, not as in our day with doubt, is a positive point of departure for philosophy," he writes (p. 508). For knowledge to have meaning, Kierkegaard concludes, "then it must come alive in me" (p. 8).

Reflection leads one to an inner, subjective examination of meaning. A logical system of objective thought can be provided by outside sources, but "a system of existence cannot be given" (p. 197). If one could stand outside existence, perhaps one could see truth as something finished and complete. In actual experience, an individual is always in the process of developing his own conceptions of truth in the moment. The search for objective truth turns away from the subject toward an object. Therefore, truth becomes indifferent to or disregards the subject. Everything is always in the process of becoming, including the subject, and therefore truth is always in the process of becoming. Uncertainty is the "highest truth there is for the existing person" (p. 207).

Kierkegaard shifts the emphasis from the thought to the thinker. Objective truth concerns the *what* while subjective truth concerns the *how*. "The *how* of the truth is precisely the truth," he concludes (p. 217). Because Kierkegaard is unable to comprehend God objectively, to know God he realizes must have faith. "Subjectivity is truth," Kierkegaard concludes, which he defines as "a paraphrasing of faith" (p. 207). This paradox, that truth requires uncertainty, confirms that "the inwardness of the existing person is truth" (p. 208). A person wishes to believe and yet seeks assurance that the object of his faith exists. Faith, however, involves risk.

A person should seek self-knowledge and resist conforming to the expectations of the crowd. "There is a view of life which holds that where the crowd is, there is also the truth, that it must have the crowd on its side," Kierkegaard observes. "There is another view of life which holds that wherever the crowd is there is untruth . . . For the crowd is untruth" (p. 307–308). Public opinion and consensus are frequently wrong. Truth is neither to be found in an objective universe nor through social customs and habits. Only through introspection can one inquire into the truths of existence.

Living one's life involves committing to the act of choosing. Even poor choices are preferable to not choosing at all. "Choose despair, then, because despair itself is a choice," Kierkegaard counsels. "One can doubt without choosing it, but one cannot despair without choosing it" (p. 77). Choosing is what makes each person an individual. Kierkegaard writes:

> The richest personality is nothing before he has chosen himself; and on the other hand even what might be called the poorest personality is everything when he has chosen himself, for the greatness is not to be this or that but to be oneself, and every human being can be this if he so wills it.
>
> (p. 76)

Friedrich Nietzsche (German, 1844–1900) claims that truth comes not from rational contemplation but through direct experience. "All credibility, all good conscience, all evidence of truth," Nietzsche (2000) concludes, "come only from the senses" (p. 278). Nietzsche denies that the search for absolute truth drives philosophy. On the contrary, he believes every philosopher imparts a "personal confession" that reveals more about that individual than about universal knowledge (p. 203). General statements regarding principles and laws seek to impose one's morality and ideals on others. For Nietzsche, facts and certainties are a matter of interpretation. Hypotheses concerning the essence of things are deceptive. We infer from our own points of view and construct arguments to validate our own values. "Indeed," he asks, "what forces us at all to suppose that there is an essential opposition of 'true' and 'false'?" (p. 236). Everything exists in degrees. Nietzsche examines the motives and desires behind the need to seek inerrant explanations.

Martin Heidegger (German, 1889–1976) investigates the question of *being*, or what is meant to ask about the existence of something. By formulating an inquiry into *being*, Heidegger (1927/1962) explains that we seek something both familiar and self-evident yet at the same time elusive and difficult to precisely define. On the one hand, "everything towards which we comport ourselves in any way, is being; what we are is being, and so it is how we are" (p. 26). On the other hand, "the meaning of Being is still veiled in darkness" as a vague notion (p. 23). As human beings, we are unique in that we seek to understand being as a concept and identify it as a fact. Heidegger calls the most basic state of being for humans, "Being-in-the-world" (p. 78). This is not a property that a person sometimes has or does not have, but a constant state. Seen as a whole, being is the individual's lived experience—with the environment, with others, with the self. Being-in-the-world involves a fascination with and a concern for existence, and includes care, worry, anxiety, and projecting into the future.

For Martin Buber (Austrian, 1878–1965), the individual exists in relation to others or with objects one encounters in the environment. Such relationships do not have a fixed nature in discovering external *a priori* entities. "It is not experiences alone that bring the world to man," Buber (1923/1970) determines. "*I* experience something" (p. 55). In other words, the world is not experienced, the world "allows itself to be experienced" (p. 56). The self has the experience. All experience is subjective, rather than objective.

Existentialism in Education

"Existence precedes essence."

(Jean-Paul Sartre)

Classical philosophies, beginning with Plato and Aristotle, assume essence precedes existence. Essence comes first, born of Forms or some other first cause. From those eternal origins, things we experience have come into being. Each thing possesses characteristics bestowed on them. All things fall into categories that pre-exist whatever examples we experience.

Jean-Paul Sartre (French, 1905–80) reverses this metaphysical perspective. "Existence precedes essence," he declares (1965, p. 34). The individual exists first, and creates his own essence. As Sartre explains, "Man exists, turns up, appears on the scene, and, only afterwards, defines himself" (pp. 35–36).

For Sartre, "Subjectivity must be the starting point" (p. 34). We begin to understand the universe from our particular vantage point. "Every truth and every action implies a human setting and a human subjectivity," he observes (p. 32). Therefore, seeking an objective, external universe that operates according to fixed principles has no meaning. "There is no universe other than a human universe," he declares, "the universe of human subjectivity" (p. 61).

Like Kierkegaard, Sartre believes our individual choices construct the universe as we know it, and determine the truth and meaning of our actions. "An individual chooses and makes himself," he explains. "It is impossible for man to transcend human subjectivity" (p. 37). In the absence of an objective moral universe, ordered and structured by principles external to our existence, the individual bears all responsibility for decisions. Sartre asserts the paradoxical statement, "Man is condemned to be free . . . because once thrown into the world, he is responsible for everything he does" (p. 41)

Put another way, "Man is nothing else than his plan," Sartre asserts (p. 47). "Man is nothing else but what he makes of himself" (p. 36). This dismisses rationalizations for how we live to one's own choices and removes all excuses for our conduct. "If existence really does precede essence," he believes, "there is no explaining things away by references to a fixed and given human nature" (p. 41). Despite the emphasis on the individual, however, Sartre's philosophical viewpoint does not necessarily imply narcissism, isolation, and despair. One's behavior does not automatically justify itself, such as permitting cruelty to others. Sartre (2007) calls Existentialism a "humanism," meaning we can refer to no doctrine other than ourselves to judge our actions (p. 18). In choosing what each of us makes of ourselves, we create an image of what we believe humans to be. "Thus our responsibility is much greater than we might have supposed, because it involves all mankind" (Sartre, 1965, p. 37). Freedom bears the responsibility of accepting the consequences of one's actions of others.

Existentialism focuses on one's existence in the present moment, making choices and accepting responsibility for those choices. Tradition does not provide ethical or moral principles, only guidance. No universal human nature determines our actions. The individual makes the choice how to act, creating principles with each decision. Life has no meaning *a priori*; one develops his own values and creates his own meaning. Existentialism "defines man in terms of action," Sartre (1965) insists. "We are dealing here with an ethics of action and involvement" (p. 50).

Educator Maxine Greene (American, 1917–2014) argues that no objective meaning exists to be discovered separate from the lives of the learners. Questions should arise from one's own experiences that help bring relevance to the subject-matter. Learning should spark curiosity and imagination, not suppress such responses to engaging with new information or unfamiliar material. Greene (1995) believes the curriculum should be thought of as providing "adventures into meaning that might provoke learners to learn for the sake of repairing deficiencies in their social world as well as becoming different in their personal lives" (p. 100).

Education involves constant interpretations and search for meaning. Learning should be a transforming experience that engenders reflection and leads to action. The curriculum should permit students "to be personally present to what they see and hear and read" (p. 104). Moreover, education should encourage active participation and collaboration, and help students "develop a sense of agency" to change their lives in the immediate world of the present (p. 104).

Self-Directed Learning

Ivan Illich (Austrian, 1926–2002) criticizes schools for defining what education is for others. "School has an anti-educational effect on society," Illich (1971) paradoxically declares. "School is recognized as the institution which specializes in education" (p. 11). School monopolizes what society accepts as legitimate learning, which it alone can endorse and certify. This allows those in positions of power in society to dictate what kind of education is offered, perpetuating the status quo, keeping those in control of knowledge in power, and forcing citizens to remain dependent on institutions. "School is the advertising agency which makes you believe that you need the society as it is" (Illich, 1971, p. 163). This reduces education to a commodity that restricts access and limits choices.

As an alternative to traditional school-based education, Illich proposes individuals informally establish educational networks or webs among themselves. Groups would form based on interests or needs, with members circulating in and out of participation as they wish. This would increase access to knowledge, permitting individuals to share resources and exchange skills. Illich calls this model "self-directed learning" (p. 116). The goal is to liberate access to materials, skills, and resources from the control of schools and into the hands of individuals.

Illich's proposal predates the emergence of the Internet by two decades. Since its proliferation, his use of the terms *networks* or *webs* appears prescient. Technology permits learning to occur in virtually any location at any time of day. Groups can form according to interest or topic in innumerable variations, sharing resources and data, exchanging knowledge, and extending access to information globally. In the digital age, alternatives such as home-schooling, learning opportunities offered by community organizations, and informal associations of like-minded individuals have taken advantage of the access to resources that technology provides, freeing knowledge from local physical repositories such as schools, libraries, and other social institutions. A greater flow of information is accessible by a much wider audience.

Self-directed learning can emerge as a "mutual inquiry," grounded in shared interests, respect, trust, and care (Knowles, 1975, p. 9). The act of learning should have a liberating effect on the learner. With guidance, support, and resources, a learner can take the initiative to become more self-sufficient. Self-directed learning enables the individual to develop skills for accessing and evaluating resources and interpreting knowledge.

Self-directed learning is at the far right on the *Continuum of Educational Philosophy*. One's educational program is individualized. Students take the initiative, select the topic, set the goals, determine the method, manage the process, and assess their own progress (Gibbons, 2002). Self-directed learning, however, does not mean all learners must proceed in isolation from others or outside of school. Self-directed learning can be established in classrooms, with students working independently or in various flexible groupings. Similar to different models of inquiry, the degree of structure can vary and the process implemented in stages (Gibbons, 2002). Teachers can co-plan with students and be involved in the process until greater independence is achieved. The teacher becomes a guide, facilitator, and resource, rather than a director of learning, transmitter of knowledge, or evaluator of performance.

How Do Teachers Teach? Questions about Pedagogy

"The good teacher becomes an occasion for permitting a child to decide consciously on freedom and becoming."

(Maxine Greene)

An education to help individuals develop their own identities and experience freedom opens up possibilities for students. Autonomous, spontaneous decisions based on freedom of choice form the basis of instruction.

Greene opposes students passively accepting knowledge transmitted by the teacher. "The thinker – or the subject – does not ask *what* he can know," Greene (1967) maintains, "but *how* he can know" (p. 66). Knowledge is not given, but actively pursued by one being-in-the-world. Learning is a choice each makes consciously and individually. Learning involves attempting to make sense of the world by inquiring into it and acting upon it. Greene urges students to ask their own questions and come to know the reality of their own existence. "Each, in effect," she says, "seeks a truth peculiar to him" (p. 70). The purpose of education is to help students grasp the meaning of their own existence, providing opportunities to make choices. Content and skills should be presented as possibilities rather than as fixed accepted knowledge with no room for critical thought.

What Is the Role of the Teacher in a School Designed to Develop Individual Identity and Personal Freedom?

TEACHER AS *I-YOU.*

Buber examines the relationships people have to the world and each other. In one relationship, *I-It*, one perceives the world and those things within it (including other people) as objects. A second kind of relationship, *I-You*, implies a relationship with the things of the world (such as with nature, each other, and the spiritual). Experience of things is remote, but a direct relationship is an encounter between two things.

Life in modern society often appears to be composed of *I-It* relationships. Such participation consists of a series of cause-and-effect relationships with social institutions. Buber (1923/1970) writes, "Every *You* in the world is doomed by its nature to become a thing or at least to enter into thinghood again and again" (p. 69). This can produce a sense of isolation and alienation. An *I-You* relationship binds two people together in a unique, exclusive way. The relationship of the teacher and the students can be thought of as *I-It* or *I-You*. In an *I-You* relationship, the teacher views each student as a unique individual, rather than as a group of objects or a sum of different personalities merged into a single classroom identity. *I-It* can be detached at best and, at worst, adversarial. In *I-You*, people co-exist in a "living reciprocal relationship" (p. 94). The basis of the interaction is a dialogue between two people encountering one another.

Teachers who embrace an *I-You* relationship take the experiences and concerns of students as individuals seriously. Rather than imposing an *I-It* distance between the teacher as authority figure and the student as passive or subservient subject, the teacher realizes each student must make personal choices about the type of person they wish to become. Teachers must help students make these decisions and create meaning in a world no longer anchored to objective, dualistic thinking. Nietzsche (2000) advises, "Whoever is a teacher through and through takes all things seriously only in relation to his students – even himself" (p. 269).

TEACHER AS FACILITATOR OR MONITOR

In this perspective, one role of the teacher is to facilitate and monitor the self-directed activities of the learner. Adults at Sudbury schools do not go by the title of teacher. They are known as staff members. Students approach staff members when they need something for their learning, rather than the teacher directing the process. Sudbury calls this role "the art of doing nothing," meaning the staff does not initiate learning, the student does (Greenberg, 1995, p. 143). Similar types of schools refer to the teachers as advisors.

In contrast to the role of teacher as directing the learning of others, the role of facilitator involves transferring control to the learner (Coe, 2009). Rather than giving knowledge to passive students, the facilitator provides the opportunity and sets the stage for the learner to engage in purposeful learning. This entails fostering a dialogue between the teacher and student, enabling the student to access prior learning, set priorities, and organize and manage resources. Greene (1995) insists, "If we teachers are to develop a humane and liberating pedagogy, we must feel ourselves to be engaged in a dialectical relation" (p. 52). A facilitator is a careful and attentive listener, allowing the student to do much of the speaking to ascertain goals and assess outcomes. The learner's own experiences and reflection give meaning to the learning.

TEACHER AS RESOURCE

In self-directed learning, the educator provides access to resources to assist the learner to undertake inquiry. One suggested metaphor, teacher-as-outfitter, casts the role of educator as equipping the learner with specialized supplies to begin an adventure (Bulik, 2009, p. 54). The learner draws on the expertise and experience of the educator to offer direction and advice. The learner initiates the encounter and actively participates in the exchange to prepare for investigation and exploration.

What Is the Role of the Student in a School Designed to Develop Individual Identity and Personal Freedom?

STUDENT AS INDIVIDUAL

Students in a Sudbury school are respected as individual human beings. This view places the student at the center of learning, based on individual initiative and curiosity. "The child's agenda for its own life is as important as anyone else's agenda – parents, family, friends, or even the community" (Greenberg, 1992, p. 1). Learning is viewed at Sudbury schools as an individual process. Students can choose to play, read, practice a musical instrument, or develop a new interest. Not attending assigned classes on a fixed schedule does not equate to doing nothing (Greenberg, 1992). The learning environment at a school designed to develop freedom and self-identity should not be evaluated according to the same standards as schools that objectively measure achievement and progress. "There is no activity at [a Sudbury school] that is considered better or worse than any other activity" (Sadofsky & Greenberg, 1999, p. 299). Each individual determines the value of each thing in regards to his own personal development. This is an issue every human being grapples with for himself; it cannot be dictated by others. Schools that attempt to make that determination for students derive their authority from an objective view of reality. At schools such as those following the Sudbury model, only the individual is in a position to define what constitutes a successful life.

STUDENT AS SELF-DIRECTED LEARNER

Schools distance students from the learning process by asking them to mimic adult behaviors, memorize information selected by others, and conform to a system of education that excludes "the lived lives of children" (Greene, 1967, p. 54). Students are expected to adjust to schedules, procedures, and programs, rather than the school adjusting to accommodating the needs and developing identities of the students. The role of education is to enable students to make decisions on their own, to expand their powers of critical thinking and reasoned judgment, and to assist them in transforming their perceptions of the world. "To recognize that things, truths, and values are con-stituted by all human beings, including children," Greene (1995) proposes, "is to begin to ground what we do in the classroom" (p. 55).

The self is always in the process of becoming. "The individual child moves between limita-tions and possibility," Greene (1967) writes, "but he will only act upon his project of becoming a self if he takes seriously the responsibility of decisiveness and self-determination" (p. 101). The labels that teachers and schools place on children do not constitute their identities as students or as human beings. The school cannot prescribe the means by which any student becomes an individual, but can only offer opportunities and guidance.

Schools present students with an easy way to evade personal responsibility by defining their identity for them, dictating the rules all students must follow, setting pre-determined standards, and certifying their achievement of those standards. Schools also allow students to assume an erroneous self-concept by punishing deviation from the prescribed path and attaching failure to efforts to seek self-realization outside of established norms. Greene challenges students to avoid being submerged in a crowd and to take responsibility "for becoming, for achieving himself" (p. 20). The learner must consciously commit herself to become a responsible, free individual, "not an instance of some universal, nor yet a mere member of a group" (p. 19). The role of the student is to create his own sense of identity and define herself. "Young persons have the capacity to con-struct multiple realities," Greene (1995) reasons, once they have been introduced to the power of perceiving, conceptualizing, interpreting, and interrogating (p. 57). One approach encourages students to build relationships with one another, to encounter multiple perspectives and experi-ence vicariously as well as authentically the lived worlds of their peers.

STUDENT AS INITIATOR

As seeker of knowledge, the student will be an active participant and initiate self-directed learn-ing. "Only as he chooses can he achieve a continuity of identity and a continuity of knowing," Greene (1967) concludes (p. 163). The student who initiates learning needs to demonstrate intrin-sic motivation, willingness and persistence to learn, self-efficacy, resourcefulness, and autonomy (Ponton, 2009). This can include roles such as seeker of knowledge, problem-solver, and col-laborator. The student chooses the role, and roles can change based on topic, activity, or interest. Initiating one's own learning requires making choices and managing time, resources, and effort (Carr, 2009).

STUDENT AS PEER TEACHER

Self-directed learning can be both an independent or social activity, depending on the desires and need of the student. Sudbury schools call age mixing their "secret weapon" (Greenberg, 1992, p. 121; 1995, p. 71). Peers teach each other. Older students serve as tutors, mentors, and role mod-els to younger students. In age mixing, the variety of learning increases while serving as a much more realistic model of social interaction, working, and collaborating outside of the school setting.

STUDENT AS NEGOTIATOR

One way a student can direct her own learning in the classroom is to enter into a contract or learn-ing agreement with the teacher. The student proposes a project, for example, and with the teacher outlines the steps and timeline for completion. The teacher helps the student devise the plan and make sure it fulfills learning goals the school requires. The student may approach meeting objec-tives in a creative, inventive fashion. In addition, the student can act as self-evaluator, developing the rubric and criteria demonstrating achievement of learning outcomes.

Design

Summerhill

One well-known example of a school based on developing individual identity and personal freedom is Summerhill, founded by A. S. Neill in 1923 in Suffolk, England. Initially started as an experiment, Summerhill remains in operation, serving as a demonstration school centered on the goal "to make the school fit the child – instead of making the child fit the school" (Neill, 1960, p. 4). To create such a school, Neill recounts "we had to renounce all discipline, all direction, all suggestion, all moral training, all religious instruction" and believe children can make their own decisions and determine their own path (p. 4). Attending classes at Summerhill has always been optional. Students may attend according to age level or interest, but attendance is not mandatory. Summerhill is a school where children may spend every day playing, reading, or loafing around. No formal curriculum exists, and no distinctions are made between learning inside a classroom or outdoors, studying alone or with others, solving a problem in long division or reading for pleasure.

At Summerhill, adults and children share equal status. "We have no new methods of teaching," Neill writes, "because we do not consider that teaching in itself matters very much" (p. 5). Children who wish to learn will seek out the opportunities and resources to learn. Structured classes are offered on a timetable, but access to spaces, materials, and resources affords all students opportunities to learn on their own schedule and at their own pace. Standards for subjects are not set nor exams required. "Books are the least important apparatus in a school," Neill contends. "All that any child needs is the three Rs; the rest should be tools and clay and sports and theater and paint and freedom" (p. 25).

Summerhill is a democratic school, governed by General School Meetings where everyone has an equal vote on school rules, procedures, and operations. Adults do not run the meetings; the position of chair rotates among the students. Freedom does not mean the absence of rules. Rules are proposed, voted upon, and enforced (often by levying fines or assigning chores) to protect the safety and well-being of each member of the school community.

Sudbury Schools

The classroom vignette that opens this chapter represents observations at a Sudbury school. Sudbury Valley School, founded in 1968 in Framingham, Massachusetts, represents a model of democratic education that has its roots in schools such as Summerhill in England and the free school movement. A key component of the school organization is the School Meeting, where every staff member and every student has an equal vote in the governance of the school. "Every aspect of the school operates this way, without exception: rules, budget, administration, hiring and firing, and discipline" (Greenberg, 1995, p. 3).

Sudbury Valley School enrolls students from pre-school through high school age. The school serves as a resource for student learning. The school does not impose a mandated curriculum, require attendance in classes, or give grades. "At Sudbury Valley, a class is an arrangement between two parties" (Greenberg, 1995, p. 19). Students decide for themselves when a class begins and ends, and when they feel they have mastered the content or skill. This environment permits students to learn individually or in various mixed-age groupings. Each student makes individual decisions on what to learn, when to learn, and how to learn. Personal initiative and responsibility are emphasized. "Individual responsibility also implies a basic equality among all people" (Greenberg, 1995, p. 5). Staff members are not authority figures, but resources. Authority rests with all the members of the school community within the democratic process.

The mission of Sudbury Valley School is to help students develop "the ability to cope independently, continuously, and successfully with the demands of life" (Greenberg, 1994, p. 287). When multiple possible views of reality are considered, success has an almost unlimited variety of definitions. Each individual must construct models of reality from experience and determine how success is defined. The Sudbury model offers an environment free from restrictions on how one uses time, resources, and energy. Being permitted to devise and follow their own agendas, students learn to focus for long periods on activities of interest, persist when faced with challenges or difficulties, adapt to changing circumstances, and cope independently with life's demands. A school with the purpose of individual development instills confidence in each learner to act autonomously, with a strong sense of self and a unique identity.

Fairhaven School, which opened in Upper Marlboro, Maryland in 1998, models itself on the Sudbury Valley School. Learning at the school is "entirely self-directed" (Fairhaven, n.d., About section, para 1). Students of all ages mix freely, learning from one another and the staff. This approach fosters learning of all kinds, helping students develop a variety of skills and grow emotionally, physically, and intellectually. The Arts & Ideas Sudbury School in Baltimore, Maryland, bases its education on four principles: Personalized Study, Viral Learning, Responsibility, and Age Mixing. Free to learn at their own pace, students actively construct understanding unique to each individual. Viral learning creates a "living knowledge network" among the students and staff, where exposure to different activities and perspectives motivates students to challenge themselves (Arts & Ideas Sudbury School, 2008, Viral Learning section, para 1). The democratic governing process, characterized by school meetings and the judicial process, develops responsibility and respect for each other as individuals. Age mixing reinforces responsibility and instigates viral learning. A growing number of Sudbury schools exist in the United States and Canada, as well as countries in South America (Brazil), Europe (Belgium, Denmark, Germany, the Netherlands, and Switzerland) and around the world (such as Australia, Israel, and Japan). In each school, students create their own curriculum, direct their own learning, exercise self-government, mix with children of all ages, and take responsibility for the operation of the school.

Free and Open Schools

In addition to schools based on the Sudbury model, other schools offer self-directed learning in a democratic environment. The Albany Free School, founded in New York in 1969, is the longest running independent alternative school operating in the United States. The school has no mandated curriculum, no grading, no standardized tests, no homework, and no required classes. The Free School believes "learning happens all the time and everyone learns in different ways" (Albany Free School, n.d., About section, para 5).

Not all schools that emphasize this approach are private, independent schools. Marcy Open School in Minneapolis, Minnesota encourages student decision-making and self-directed learning. The students participate in individualized learning and practice self-assessment and self-evaluation in a flexible interdisciplinary, thematic curriculum. Jefferson County Open School in Colorado is a public option K-12 school. An advisor works with the student to plan a personalized curriculum.

Alternatives to School is an organization offering resources and support to parents and individuals who question the value of compulsory schooling and are seeking alternative public and independent options or home-schooling information and advice. The group envisions establishing learning centers in every community that provide access to technology, learning materials, supplies, and expertise to facilitate self-directed learning for all ages.

Each school or program designed to develop individual identity and personal freedom is unique. A network of schools may operate under a name that identifies the approach (such as Sudbury, free, or open) or exist as a single institution (such as Summerhill). The schools may be private or public. All share a similar perspective on education that distinguishes them from schools with a formal curriculum and methods of instruction (Table 11.1).

Table 11.1 Design a School (Identity and Freedom)

Purpose of Education	Individual identity and freedom
Curriculum	Flexible, individualized, voluntary
Instruction	Self-directed learning
Role of Teacher	I-You, facilitator or monitor (staff, advisor), resource
Role of Student	Individual, self-directed learner, initiator, peer teacher, negotiator
Role of School	Democracy, autonomy

How Does a School Designed to Develop Individual Identity and Personal Freedom Define an Educated Person?

Education from the perspective of Existentialism and self-directed learning develops skills to create one's own learning path. Individuals decide what they learn, when and where they learn, and how they learn. An educated person practices autonomy, assumes responsibility for choices, and accepts the consequences of actions.

Evaluate

Consistency

How does self-directed learning differ from other student-centered approaches? One distinction is that other models may offer choices, but within a framework produced and controlled by the school. For example, Montessori (Chapter 6) stresses the need for teachers to prepare the learning environment, supply specially designed materials, and instruct children on the appropriate uses of the materials before students are free to choose an activity. In Waldorf education (Chapter 7), all students follow a schedule and participate in common routines. In Expeditionary Learning (Chapter 9), projects are collaborative and the class and teacher develop "norms" for conducting activities.

To be consistent, in self-directed learning, every individual child is free to follow his or her own interests, arrange time in a personalized manner, move from activity to activity at any point, work with any age peer or individually, and initiate learning on any topic. The child would not need to adhere to any established routines or restrict activities to any assumed stage of development. The child would not need to follow any sequence, complete any activity, or be assessed on any task. The child sets the agenda and the adult responds to help facilitate that learning. Responsibility for choices rests with each child.

Compatibility

Because schools such as Summerhill, Sudbury, and free and open schools do not specify a required curriculum and encourage students to initiate learning, one is unable to match a set of instructional or assessment methods to prescribed educational outcomes. Allowing students to choose what to learn, when to learn, and how to learn exhibits compatibility within this design. Teachers act in the role of facilitators and resources to support self-directed learning. Students may request that certain subjects be taught and even to be administered a standardized test to document achieving learning outcomes (to enroll in another school or apply for admission to higher education).

Coherence

One might argue that a free school presents an oxymoron. A school by definition implies structure, whereas individuality exercised in its purest form connotes freedom from all restrictions.

On the *Continuum of Educational Philosophy*, these schools approach the end of the arrow without reaching the point of complete individual freedom. The education of young people operates under societal laws external to the school. For example, Sudbury schools require attendance for a certain number of hours to comply with state laws. Adult supervision is required for safety and other reasons related to the well-being of minors. Schools with the purpose of developing self-identity and individual freedom do not represent total anarchy. In fact, as we have examined, this philosophical perspective emphasizes choice, responsibility, and consequences.

In addition, schools of this nature schedule activities such as school-wide meetings at specific times. This may appear to violate creating a free and autonomous learning environment. The functioning of the school as a democratic institution, however, obligates members to demonstrate responsibility to others. In this sense, the school may overlap with schools that focus on building a community of learners. The difference lies in the roles of the teacher and student and the degree of structure. Schools such as the Monarch Academy (Chapter 9) offer a formal curriculum. Teachers plan lessons and units of study, prepare a schedule, implement activities, and assign students tasks. Collaborating on the formation of class "norms" and participating in projects creates a sense of community. Students are offered choices within a framework, but the teacher initiates instruction. Observing in a school that learns as a community and a school that fosters self-directed learning reveals significant differences in approach.

In another example, when visiting a Montessori school one might observe students choosing activities. Different students would be working on different activities, and move from one activity to another at their own pace. Again, these choices are made within a structure that differs from a school such as Summerhill or Sudbury. Selections are made from the materials and activities offered, which have been prepared by the teacher. Students may not propose new activities using different materials that do not align with the Montessori method. Students receive instruction in small groups on school-approved materials (called didactic materials). The teacher observes and records progress. A coherent school design that develops self-identify and freedom values learning initiated by the students on topics of their choice, which includes requesting activities and resources that the teacher would incorporate into the learning environment.

Reflect

How Do Your Prior Observations and Experiences Relate to a Curriculum Designed to Develop Individual Identity and Personal Freedom?

In what situations have you observed or experienced a learning environment with no set curriculum? What kind of choices were students offered? Were students selecting from a list of options or could students propose their own topics or request lessons or classes responding to their interests?

How Do Your Prior Observations and Experiences Relate to a Pedagogy Designed to Develop Individual Identity and Personal Freedom?

In what situations have you observed or experienced self-initiated, self-directed learning? How did students exercise personal freedom in that environment? How did students use time and materials? Did the teacher serve as a resource only when asked by the students?

How Do Your Prior Observations and Experiences Relate to a School Designed to Develop Individual Identity and Personal Freedom?

What kind of learning environment have you observed or experienced that openly and explicitly encouraged students to decide their own education? What would the physical layout of such a school look like? Would classrooms, furnishings and seating, supplies and materials, technology, and other resources be arranged in a way different from other types of schools?

How would decisions be made? Who would be involved in the decision-making process? How would this affect the teacher-student relationship?

How Do Your Own Practices and Beliefs Relate to the Purpose of Education as Developing Individual Identity and Personal Freedom?

Have you ever envisioned teaching in a school where students initiate and direct their own learning? Would you want to teach in a school where your role was to be available to students as a resource, tutor, or advisor based on the students' requests or expressed interests? Even in a more structured environment, how can the teacher respect the individual choices of each student and encourage autonomous decision-making?

Greene (1967) describes teachers as responsible for every act they choose. "Whether fully aware of it or not," she maintains, a teacher "is bound to be drawn to some existential mode of thinking" (p. 4). Instead of treating the act of teaching as separate from one's private life, the teacher who accepts an existentialist viewpoint acknowledges that teaching is part of the whole individual. The commitment to teaching is part of the commitment to creating one's identity. Teaching is not something *done* to others from the posture of standing outside the individual's experience. The teacher and student are both in the midst of undergoing transformation.

Teachers should not give up their freedom or personal identity and permit the educational system to define them or their role as educators. Teachers need to be constantly asking themselves probing and profound questions about the nature of learning and the act of teaching. "If the teacher does not pose such questions to himself," Greene (1973) proposes, "he cannot expect his students to pose the kinds of questions about experience which will involve them in self-aware inquiry" (p. 269).

Instead of relying upon "precedent, habit, or the dicta of authority," teachers must be aware of their own freedom to choose and be conscious of their personal existence (Greene, 1967, p. 4). An existentialist teacher does not view others, including students, as abstract categories or part of a system. Age group, grade level, reading ability, test scores, special needs classification, A. P. or honors placement, at-risk and other labels do not portray any individual student's true and complete *essence*. To consider each student as he or she actually is, the teacher acknowledges that existence comes first for the child being-in-the-world. Individuals make choices, create values, and define themselves daily as they live.

This perspective stresses the subjective nature of identity, which "no external categorization, naming, or defining" can achieve for anyone (1967, p. 8). "The good teacher," Greene (1967) concludes, "becomes an occasion for permitting a child to decide consciously on freedom and becoming" (p. 72). The emphasis is placed on the relationship between teacher and student in the struggle for meaning, the search for truth, and the act of making responsible choices. Teaching involves providing students with opportunities to deliberate, make decisions, and become individuals.

"Life gives people no choice in this matter," explains Daniel Greenberg (1994) of the Sudbury Valley School. "We are individuals, and we must act as individuals" (p. 296).

References

Albany Free School. (n.d.). About. [Website]. Retrieved from http://www.albanyfreeschool.org/about

Arts & Ideas Sudbury School. (2008). Viral learning. [Website]. Retrieved from http://aisudbury.com/viral.html

Buber, M. (1970). *I and thou*. New York, NY: Simon and Schuster. (Original work published 1923.)

Bulick, R. J. (2009). Reconsidering the metaphor for teaching in the age of self-directed learning. In M. G. Derrick & M. K. Ponton (Eds.), *Emerging directions in self-directed learning* (pp. 51–64). Chicago, IL: Discovery Association.

Carr, P. B. (2009). Resourcefulness in practice: Resourcefulness behaviors and a comment on organizational leadership. In M. G. Derrick & M. K. Ponton (Eds.), *Emerging directions in self-directed learning* (pp. 97–105). Chicago, IL: Discovery Association.

Coe, J. G. (2009). Constructing a facilitation of self-directed learning. In M. G. Derrick & M. K. Ponton (Eds.), *Emerging directions in self-directed learning* (pp. 137–152). Chicago, IL: Discovery Association.

Fairhaven School. (n.d.). About. [Website]. Retrieved from http://www.fairhavenschool.com/overview/

Gibbons, M. (2002). *The self-directed learning handbook: Challenging adolescent students to excel.* San Francisco, CA: Jossey-Bass.

Greenberg, D. (1992). *The Sudbury Valley School experience* (3rd ed.) Framingham, MA: Sudbury Valley School Press.

Greenberg, D. (1994). *Worlds in creation.* Framingham, MA: Sudbury Valley School Press.

Greenberg, D. (1995). *Free at last: The Sudbury Valley School.* Framingham, MA: Sudbury Valley School Press.

Greene, M. (1967). *Existential encounters for teachers.* New York, NY: Random House.

Greene, M. (1973). *Teacher as stranger: Educational philosophy for the modern age.* Belmont, CA: Wadsworth.

Greene, M. (1995). *Releasing the imagination: Essays of education, the arts, and social change.* San Francisco, CA: Jossey-Bass.

Heidegger, M. (1962). *Being and time* (J. Macquarrie & E. Robinson, Trans.). New York, NY: Harper & Row. (Original work published 1927.)

Illich, I. (1971). *Deschooling society.* New York, NY: Harper and Row.

Kierkegaard, S. (1975). *Søren Kierkegaard's journals and papers, Vol. 3.* H. V. Hong & E. H. Hong (Eds.). Bloomington, IN: Indiana University Press. (Original work 1834–55)

Kierkegaard, S. (2000). *The essential Kierkegaard.* H. V. Hong & E. H. Hong (Eds.). Princeton NJ: Princeton University Press. (Original work from 1834–55.)

Knowles, M. (1975). *Self-directed learning: A guide for learners and teachers.* Chicago, IL: Follett.

Neill, A. S. (1960). *Summerhill: A radical approach to child rearing.* New York, NY: Hart.

Nietzsche, F. (2000). *Basic writings of Nietzsche* (W. Kaufmann, Trans. & Ed.). New York, NY: Modern Library.

Ponton, M. K. (2009). An agentic perspective contrasting autonomous learning with self-directed learning. In M. G. Derrick & M. K. Ponton (Eds.), *Emerging directions in self-directed learning* (pp. 65–76). Chicago, IL: Discovery Association.

Sadofsky, M., & Greenberg, D. (1999). *Reflections on the Sudbury school concept.* Framingham, MA: Sudbury Valley School Press.

Sartre, J. (1965). *The philosophy of Existentialism.* W. Baskin (Ed.). New York, NY: Philosophical Library.

Sartre, J. (2007). *Existentialism is a humanism* (C. Macomber, Trans.). New Haven, CT: Yale University Press.

Part IV

How Do I Synthesize What I Have Learned into My Own Philosophy of Education?

In Parts II and III, we posed *What if* questions about the purpose of education, observed educational practices depicted in classroom vignettes, investigated philosophical perspectives and concepts, and examined school designs reflecting each point of view. Some of the vignettes and school designs may have appeared familiar. Other examples, however, may have represented a different vision of schools than what you have observed or experienced. Moreover, you may have discovered a preference for one or more approaches, combined different perspectives, or possibly conceived of an original idea. At the end of each chapter, you paused to reflect upon your own educational practices and beliefs related to each perspective.

Applying the *Wonder Model of Inquiry*, Part IV guides you through the process of imagining and designing a hypothetical school based on your own philosophical perspective.

One might question if designing a hypothetical school has practical implications, granted few (if any) of us will be given the opportunity to create a school from scratch. However, every school we have examined, and every school you have visited and observed in, has been based on a design suggested by a particular outlook on education. A set of beliefs provides the inspiration, offers the rationale, argues the justification, and defends the outcomes. We have explored the reasoning of individuals and groups of people who have shaped the way education is practiced. Policymakers, politicians, community leaders, parents, administrators, teachers, and students have all contributed to the development of systems of education. Educational policies and practices continue to evolve and change, sometimes returning to the past to revive ideas and sometimes experimenting with innovative methods. Efforts to preserve the established structure of schools represent deliberate choices as much as movements to reform schools. We need to recognize that schools are continually being designed and redesigned, not just architecturally but educationally. However, inconsistent choices, or practices and policies incompatible with one another, can be at cross-purposes. Competing or conflicting purposes of education within the same school can lead to an incoherent design.

Beyond a "big picture" view of the structure of schools, this design exercise has relevance for one's individual practice. In Chapter 1, we asked questions about setting up your own classroom, arranging the learning spaces, selecting resources, supplies, and materials, and planning your instruction. These are practical, concrete concerns of teachers that reflect a way of thinking about education. In Chapter 2, we asked fundamental questions about the purpose of education, what needs schools fulfill, how schools fulfill that purpose and meet those needs, and how schools define an educated person. Chapter 2 also recommended keeping in mind three "What if" questions to guide your overall inquiry experience:

- *What if* . . . schools taught in a different way than what I have observed or experienced?
- *What if* . . . I preferred schools taught in a different way than I have observed or experienced?
- *What if* . . . I could design my own school?

Applying the "3Cs" criteria, you can evaluate your decisions as you design your school. How will your school demonstrate consistent practices across subjects and grade levels? What instructional methods will you select that are compatible with the curriculum? Does the school reflect a coherent design, representing your purpose of education? How does your school represent your philosophical perspective?

The goal of this book has been to actively involve the reader in exploring how philosophy directly relates to the process of teaching and learning. A meaningful outcome of this inquiry is for you to assume a participatory role by designing your own school. In this way, you can begin to engage in philosophy of education *in action*.

12 What If . . . I Could Design My Own School?

"Come then, let's create a city in theory from its beginnings."

(Socrates)

To conclude our inquiry, we ask the wonder question, "*What if . . . I could design my own school?*"

In this chapter, you will have the opportunity to design a school to represent your own philosophical perspective on education. The activity is organized according to the *Wonder Model of Inquiry* (Figure 12.1).

The model borrows an idea from the Greek philosopher, Socrates. In Book II of *The Republic*, Socrates proposes creating a city from its beginnings. Starting with the premise that a city is designed based on needs, he constructs a hypothetical city-state to serve those needs. As the construction of the city progresses, Socrates critiques the purpose and value of each citizen's role. Likewise, in this chapter you will design a hypothetical school, examining the role and purpose of each element as the school develops. In making your decisions, you will be analyzing, synthesizing, and evaluating different philosophical perspectives and concepts presented in this textbook.

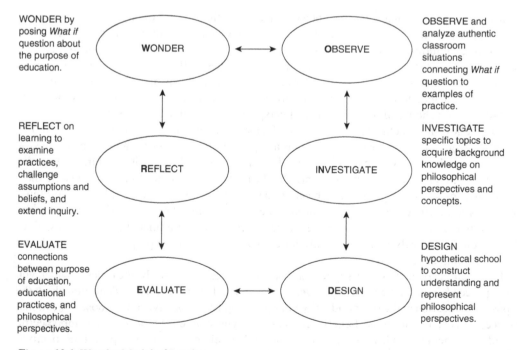

Figure 12.1 Wonder Model of Inquiry

Throughout this textbook, we have asked inquiry questions about the purpose of education, curriculum, pedagogy, and organization of schools. These questions will guide designing your own hypothetical school:

- What is the Purpose of Education?
- What Do Teachers Teach? Questions about the Curriculum
- How Do Teachers Teach? Questions about Pedagogy
- How are Schools Organized? Questions about the Role of the School

As you design your school, imagine a visitor touring it and observing in a classroom or classrooms. As in the classroom vignettes that open each chapter, offer descriptions of what an observer would see and hear. What would an observer see and hear that shows, for example, a fixed curriculum or a flexible curriculum? What would a visitor observe to show instruction that sequentially presents content or that employs experiential, hands-on methods? How would a teacher act in the role of a director or guide? How could you describe observable examples of a student in the role of inves-tigator, member of a learning community, or initiator of learning? In actual schools, one sees and hears how the curriculum is enacted, how instructional methods are implemented, teachers and students acting in certain roles, scheduling of time, organization of learning spaces, etc. In other words, a visitor observes examples of a school's philosophy of education *in action*.

This activity is an opportunity to present your personal vision of a learning environment. Design the kind of school where you would prefer to teach, to have attended as a student, or to have your own child attend. Be risk-taking in your thinking. Disregard concerns about whether your ideas are impractical or too expensive, if public officials would disagree with you or fami-lies would complain, if it varies too much from existing schools, if you doubt many students would enroll, if students might not be accepted to college or be employed due to your curriculum, or other reasons. Assume your school has been approved and fully funded. Your design should make the case as to why a student should enroll and be educated in the environment you have envisioned.

Presume no pre-existing conditions other than to fulfill the purpose of education you propose. Do not feel compelled to reproduce a "typical" school. Classes do not need to be held in a rec-tangular brick building divided into classrooms. The school does not need to group students by age or grade levels, distribute report cards with letter grades, follow set time schedules or class periods, require a core set of subjects, offer electives or specials, or mandate standardized test-ing. You may decide to include or exclude any of these elements (and others) according to the purpose of your school and the philosophical perspective your school represents.

If you believe in something, put it in; if you feel strongly against something, leave it out. For example, if you believe standardized testing is an appropriate assessment method and is consist-ent with your philosophy of education, include it. If you would eliminate all forms of grades and testing, do so. If you believe students should take physical education, art, music, dance, self-defense, or any other particular subject or class, include it in your curriculum. If you think some classes are irrelevant and do not need to be offered, omit them. If a principal and assis-tant principal are unnecessary to the governance of your school, eliminate those positions. Your school should accurately and consistently reflect your beliefs on the purpose of education and your philosophical perspective.

The *Wonder Model of Inquiry* suggests a process but does not prescribe the order in which you should proceed. You can begin at any stage. You may decide to pose a *What if* question about the purpose of education at the outset, identify your philosophy perspective, and choose educational practices consistent with those beliefs. Alternatively, you may choose to first develop specific examples of teaching and learning and later connect these elements to philosophical perspectives and arrive at the purpose of education last. Feel free to move between steps as you construct your school, revising and modifying the design as you reflect on your ideas. Under each step of the model, a series of inquiry questions will guide you to develop and describe specific details and examples of your design, and connect them to the purpose of your school. Table 12.1 provides a template for recording notes as you design your school.

Table 12.1 Design a School Template

Wonder	
Purpose of Education	*What if . . .*
School Name	
School Motto and/or Logo	
Population Served	
Purpose Statement	
Observe	

Curriculum (Examples)
   Subjects/Content
   Skills
   Sources	

Instruction (Examples)
   Method
   Assessment	

Role of Teacher (Metaphor)	
Role of Student (Metaphor)	
Investigate	
School Name	
School Motto and/or Logo	
Population Served	
Purpose Statement	
Curriculum	
Instruction/Assessment	
Role of Teacher	
Role of Student	
Design	
Instructional Time	
Decision-Making	
Role of Families	
Role of Community	
Setting and Layout	
Evaluate	
Consistency	
Compatibility	
Coherence	
Reflect	
Prior Observations and Experiences	
Own Practices and Beliefs	

Wonder

What Is the Purpose of Education?

Pose a wonder question about the purpose of education that reflects your educational beliefs: *"What if the purpose of education were . . . ?"*

You may select a wonder question from one of the chapters, modify the wording, combine two or more questions, or invent an original *What if* question to reflect your views.

What Will I Name My School?

Next, give your school an original name. The name should represent the school's purpose or your educational philosophy. Several schools we have examined include a particular philosophy in their name, such as Montessori (Chapter 6), Waldorf (Chapter 7), and Sudbury (Chapter 11). Other school names can represent the school's focus, such as Barret Paideia Academy (Chapter 3), Thomas Jefferson High School for Science and Technology (Chapter 4), and the Young Women's Leadership School (Chapter 10). The Monarch Academy (Chapter 9) is named after the Monarch butterfly and relates to Expeditionary Learning. A philosophy, philosopher, famous person or eminent educator, educational program, metaphor, or acronym can all represent a philosophy of education in the name of a school.

State a motto and/or design a logo to represent your school's purpose and philosophical perspective. The motto may be a quotation or you may write an original motto. For example, the motto of Liberty Common School (Chapter 5) is *Commvnis Scientia, Virtvtes, et Prvdentia* ("Common Knowledge, Common Virtues, Common Sense"). A motto can succinctly encapsulate the philosophy and purpose of a school.

Whom Does My School Serve?

Indicate if your school is public or independent/private. Public schools may include charter, magnet, model, or alternative schools that have a specific focus or theme.

Identify the school's student population. Indicate age groups and/or grade levels. Indicate if classes or class activities are organized by age or grade level, or are mixed-age or multi-grade.

Indicate any other relevant demographics and/or characteristics of the population of students your school will enroll and serve. You may choose to have your school focus on serving a specific population based on needs (e.g., special needs, socioeconomic status, gender, etc.) and/or interests (e.g., science and technology, visual and performing arts, etc.).

What Is the Purpose of My School?

Write a purpose statement that declares and explains your school's purpose and philosophical perspective. Use key terms from the chapters to demonstrate your understanding of important philosophical concepts. The purpose statement can also describe how your school *defines* an educated person. What would a student educated in the school know and be able to do?

The purpose statement describes your overall school to the public. Schools or school systems often publish a purpose statement, mission statement, beliefs or values statement, or philosophy statement (or an "About Us" description) on their websites and in other materials such as brochures and parent and student handbooks. For example, Bank Street School for Children (Chapter 8), the Park School (Chapter 9), and Sudbury Valley School (Chapter 11) provide statements of their educational philosophy. You may wish to view statements of one or more example schools to use as a model.

Observe

In this section, develop and describe specific examples of practice directly related to the purpose of your school for us to observe.

What Do Teachers Teach? Questions about the Curriculum

Describe your overall curriculum in one or two concise sentences. For example, possible descriptors may include:

- The curriculum is fixed; all subjects and content are required for all students.
- The curriculum is flexible, offering students choices of subjects to study.
- The curriculum is determined by the students; each individual student decides what topics to study.

The descriptor will summarize the overall philosophical perspective of your school's curriculum.

What Content or Subject Areas Does My Curriculum Emphasize?

Content is what students will know. Describe examples of content or subjects your school emphasizes. You do not need to provide a comprehensive, exhaustive list of content matter for every conceivable subject. Focus on content or subjects unique to your school. What specific aspect of the curriculum would best represent your school's purpose to a visiting observer?

Content may be structured into disciplines or subject areas (such as reading, math, science, social studies, literature, visual arts, performing arts, foreign languages, etc.). Or you may prefer to organize content using an interdisciplinary or thematic approach. Part of the curriculum may be designated as core content or core subjects, and other subjects as electives or specials. What may be electives or specials in some schools (such as the visual and performing arts, technology, physical education, etc.) could be the primary emphasis of your school's program of study. Or these subjects may be integrated into all classes in your school.

What Skills Does My Curriculum Emphasize?

Skills are what students will be able to do. Describe examples of skills your school emphasizes. You do not need to provide a comprehensive, exhaustive list of every conceivable skill. What skills are unique to your school or would best represent your school's purpose to a visiting observer?

Possible skills may include: literacy skills, scientific investigation skills, team research skills, technology skills, discussion skills, artistic or self-expression skills, leadership skills, problem-solving skills, collaboration skills, etc. Many schools, such as in mastery learning (Chapter 5), write skills in the form of objectives ("The student will be able to . . . "). Expeditionary Learning schools (Chapter 9) write skills as learning targets ("I can . . . ").

What Sources Does My Curriculum Emphasize?

Sources are where the content knowledge and skills of the curriculum come from. Describe examples of sources your school emphasizes. You do not need to provide a comprehensive, exhaustive list of every conceivable source. What sources are unique to your school or would best represent your school's purpose to a visiting observer?

Possible sources of the curriculum may include: textbooks, basal readers, *Great Books*, primary documents, research data, emerging works of world literature, current events, field-based locations or field trips, artistic representations, guest speakers or other community-based sources of information, situated learning in an authentic context, etc.

How Do Teachers Teach? Questions about Pedagogy

What Methods of Instruction Does My School Emphasize?

Describe your overall instructional method(s) in one or two concise sentences.

You do not need to provide a comprehensive, exhaustive list of every conceivable method of instruction, including the strategies and techniques. Describe the instructional methods your school emphasizes that develop a general pedagogy. What instructional method is unique to your school or would best represent your school's purpose to a visiting observer?

Possible instructional methods may include: whole-class lecture, individual seatwork, collaborative small-group work, individual tutoring, peer tutoring, inquiry-based projects, problem-solving exercises, structured and unstructured play, independent study, etc. Depending on your school's philosophy, field trips, guest speakers, community service projects, internships, etc. may also serve as examples of instruction.

What Methods of Assessment Does My School Emphasize?

Describe your overall methods of assessment. You do not need to provide a comprehensive, exhaustive list of every conceivable assessment method. What assessment methods does your school emphasize? What assessments are unique to your school or would best represent your school's purpose to a visiting observer? How are these assessments compatible with your method of instruction and how do they fit into your pedagogy?

Possible assessment methods may include: objective-type tests, worksheets, rubrics for projects and cooperative learning activities, authentic assessments such as portfolios of student-created products, oral presentations, participation in community service, interviews, etc. In addition, explain if number or letter grades are reported, or if some other kind of progress report is used. Explain if standardized state testing is required, or if some other way of reporting accountability to families and the community is used.

What Is the Role of the Teacher?

Describe the role of the teacher, and state it as a *metaphor* ("Teacher as . . . "). Explain how the teacher acts in this role.

What Is the Role of the Student?

Describe the role of the student, and state it as a *metaphor* ("Student as . . . "). Explain how the student acts in this role.

Investigate

Relate the examples (under Observe above) to philosophical perspectives and concepts we have investigated.

How Does the School Name and Motto (or Logo) Represent My School's Philosophy?

Explain how the school name and motto (or logo) relate to one or more philosophical perspectives examined in this textbook. Refer to the chapters and use the appropriate and relevant key terms in your explanation to demonstrate your understanding of important philosophical concepts that correspond to your school's name, motto, or logo.

How Does the Population the School Serves Represent My School's Philosophy?

Explain how the population the school serves relates to one or more philosophical perspectives. An independent/private school or a public school (e.g., charter, magnet, model, or alternative school) with a specific focus or theme may represent a particular philosophical perspective. Enrolling students at a certain age or grade level, mixing ages or grade levels, and/or serving a specific population based on needs (e.g., special needs, socioeconomic status, gender, etc.) and/or interests (e.g., science and technology, visual and performing arts, etc.) may also directly relate to the philosophical perspective of your school.

How Does the Purpose Statement Represent My School's Philosophy?

Explain how the purpose statement declares and explains your school's philosophical perspective. Use key terms from the chapters to demonstrate your understanding of important philosophical concepts. Explain how the purpose statement describes how your school *defines* an educated person.

How Does the Curriculum Represent My School's Philosophy?

Explain why your school emphasizes the subjects, skills, and sources of the curriculum described in your examples and how each directly relates to one or more philosophical perspectives examined in this textbook. Refer to the chapters and use the appropriate and relevant key terms in your explanation to demonstrate your understanding of important philosophical concepts that correspond to your curriculum.

How Does Instruction Represent My School's Philosophy?

Explain why your school emphasizes the instructional methods described in the examples and how the instructional methods directly relate to philosophical perspectives examined in this textbook. Refer to the chapters and use the appropriate and relevant key terms in your explanation to demonstrate your understanding of important philosophical concepts that correspond to your pedagogy.

How Does Assessment Represent My School's Philosophy?

Explain why your school emphasizes the assessment methods described in the examples and how the assessments directly relate to philosophical perspectives examined in this textbook. Refer to the chapters and use the appropriate and relevant key terms in your explanation to demonstrate your understanding of important philosophical concepts that correspond to your pedagogy.

How Does the Role of the Teacher Represent My School's Philosophy?

Explain how the role of the teacher described in the examples, and the metaphor for the role, directly relate to one or more philosophical perspectives examined in this textbook. Refer to the chapters and use the appropriate and relevant key terms in your explanation to demonstrate your understanding of important philosophical concepts that correspond to your pedagogy.

How Does the Role of the Student Represent My School's Philosophy?

Explain how the role of the student described in the examples, and the metaphor for the role, directly relate to one or more philosophical perspectives examined in this textbook. Refer to the chapters and use the appropriate and relevant key terms in your explanation to demonstrate your understanding of important philosophical concepts that correspond to your pedagogy.

Design

How are Schools Organized? Questions about the Role of the School

In designing your school, how the school is organized has a direct impact on enacting the curriculum and implementing instruction. Through its decisions, a school can support or undermine the purpose of education and reflect the philosophical perspective.

How Does My School Manage Instructional Time?

Think through the many possible considerations regarding how time is managed in relation to your purpose of education. For example, will time be divided into class periods or blocks? Will class periods or blocks be uniform across all classrooms and grade levels? Will class periods or blocks be allocated differently for different subject areas? Will the school administration create a master schedule or will grade-level teams or individual teachers manage instructional time as they determine is appropriate for their students? Will students decide how to use their time at school themselves?

These are only a few possible examples to arrange and schedule time during the school day. For thinking in a wider dimension, you can consider designing a residential school (public or private), holding classes year-round, extending the school day, offering supplementary classes after school or on weekends, or other ways to show how time is a factor in fulfilling your school's purpose and representing your school's philosophy.

How Does My School Manage Decision-Making?

Describe the decision-making process in your school. For example, will your school be managed by a principal or headmaster? Perhaps your school will have no formal hierarchy of administration. Will a committee of teachers make decisions? Will the faculty make decisions democratically? Will a council composed of faculty, students, and family members govern school business? Will democratic school meetings consisting of faculty, staff, and students make school decisions? Will each grade-level team or individual classroom teacher function independently and autonomously? Will students make decisions individually for themselves? These are only a few possible examples for designing a system of governance that reflects your school's philosophy.

Families and community members can be involved in the decision-making process. Family and community can serve in organizations such as the PTA or PTO, or participate on a board, council, or committee. "Town hall" meetings or other forums can facilitate direct input into the way the school operates. Schools can collaborate with community organizations or agencies to offer programs and services. The school building can serve as a community center for a variety of programs outside of the curriculum.

What Role Do Families and the Community Play in the Learning Process?

The relationships a school establishes and maintains with families and the surrounding community can reveal a philosophical perspective. Conversely, limits to school contact with families and the community reveal philosophical beliefs about education. Most schools host a family night (or Back to School Night) at the beginning of the year and/or semester for meeting teachers and becoming oriented to the school. In addition to this event once or twice a year, other school-based activities may involve family participation, such as family workshops or share fairs. School and classroom websites and newsletters can maintain communication with families. Teacher and other school personnel may make periodic visits to homes, neighborhoods, or community centers.

Family and/or community members may play a role in the learning process as volunteers in the classroom or guest speakers. Family or community resources can be incorporated into student assignments or projects. Families and community members may be invited to school to view student presentations, displays, and exhibits.

If I Could Design My Own School, What Would It Look Like?

The setting and physical learning environment of the school can support its purpose and reflect its philosophy. Throughout this design activity, you have been encouraged to imagine a visitor touring your school and observing in classrooms. Visualizing your school helps you develop concrete examples of your educational philosophy in action. Therefore, the final step in completing your school asks you to envision the setting.

The location and setting of a school can strongly convey a sense of what it is like and how it views the educational process. Describe the architectural features of the building (or campus composed of several buildings) and the physical setting surrounding the school. How does landscaping and the use of outdoor spaces connect to learning? Outdoor spaces may include playgrounds and athletic fields, courtyards or green spaces for recreation and studying, gardens, areas for animals, and other possibilities. The arrangement and use of public areas inside the school communicate the school's philosophy to visitors, including their color and décor.

The layout of classroom space can enable different kinds of learning to occur. Describe the arrangement and types of classroom furniture and seating, storage and accessibility of materials and supplies, access to technology, and other resources.

Evaluate

We will now evaluate your school's design based on the "3Cs" criteria: consistency, compatibility, and coherence. Your examples and explanations should be consistent, and compatible with each other and your school's purpose, to demonstrate a coherent design.

Locate each element along the *Continuum of Educational Philosophy* (Figure 12.2). The continuum displays educational practices above the arrow and corresponding philosophical beliefs below.

Mark the location (or indicate a range) on the continuum for each of the following:

- *Curriculum*: Is the curriculum more focused on the importance of ideas or more focused on the importance of students' learning experiences? Is the curriculum more fixed or more flexible?
- *Instructional Methods*: Is instruction more focused on teaching specific content or subject-matter or more focused on students' engagement in the learning process? Is instruction more focused on whole-class or whole-group activities or more on differentiated or individualized activities?
- *Role of Teacher*: Is the role of the teacher more teacher-centered or more student-centered?
- *Role of Student*: Does the role of the student focus more on achieving pre-determined outcomes or more on open-ended exploration?

EDUCATIONAL PRACTICES

RATIONAL   EMPIRICAL

Ideas-Focused	Experience-Focused
Content-Oriented	Process-Oriented
Fixed Curriculum	Flexible Curriculum
Teacher-Centered/Teacher-Directed	Student-Centered/Student-Directed
Pre-Determined Outcomes	Open-Ended Exploration
Whole-Class Activities	Differentiated/Individualized Activities

← —————————————————————————————————————— →

Objective External Reality	Internal Subjective Reality
Absolute Universal Truth	Changing Relative Truth
Pre-Existing Knowledge	Constructed Knowledge
Knowledge Independent of Experience	Knowledge Dependent on Experience
Autonomous Knowledge	Interdependent Knowledge
Absolute Universal Values	Relative Local Values
Values Independent of Experience	Values Dependent on Experience

PHILOSOPHICAL PERSPECTIVES

Figure 12.2 Continuum of Educational Philosophy

Examples do not need to be "either/or," meaning that all must be located completely on one side of the continuum or the other. The continuum indicates a wide spectrum, stretching from the extreme far left end of the arrow to the extreme far right end. Some examples may be located on one side of the arrow and some on the other side. Some may fall in the center.

Consistency

Your examples should be consistent. If the curriculum is fixed for one subject area then philosophically the curriculum for other subject areas would also be fixed. The philosophical perspectives in Part II (Chapters 3–5) emphasize enduring ideas, universal principles, and core knowledge. If, however, the curriculum is flexible for one subject area then philosophically the curriculum for other subject areas would also be flexible. The perspectives in Part III (Chapters 6–11) represent changing knowledge based on direct experiences and subjective interpretation.

Compatibility

To be compatible, practices would align with the school's purpose. For a curriculum that emphasizes receiving and mastering content, a more teacher-directed approach to instruction would be compatible. For a curriculum that values the learning process and helping students adapt to changing situations, problem solving or the project-based method would be more appropriate. If the purpose of education is to encourage individual freedom, allowing students to make their own decisions and direct their own learning would foster that educational experience.

Coherence

What if you find contradictions within your school's elements? As your school design takes shape, the elements may all land at the same location on the continuum. Even if some elements fall on one side of the continuum and some on the other, they might cluster together. In that case, you can justify your decisions. Many schools, if not most schools, demonstrate practices that at times can be located more on the left side of the arrow (e.g., more content-oriented and teacher-centered) and at other times more on the right side (e.g., more process-oriented and student-centered). One suggestion is to avoid locations far apart from one another on the continuum. You may integrate more than one perspective, but to design a school based on diametrically opposed philosophies would result in contradictions that are impossible to reconcile.

For example, you may start out locating the curriculum on the far left end of the continuum that represents a fixed body of permanent knowledge. However, you may later find you are placing elements of instruction on the opposite end of the continuum, describing individualized self-directed learning. You should pause to ask: Do you believe in a single, absolute, unchanging reality that is rational, structured, and inherently purposeful? Or do you believe in a pluralistic, changing reality that is open to interpretation based on personal subjective experience? Reflecting on these kinds of questions is where philosophy meets practice.

Consider two other examples. If you identify the role of the teacher as "guide and facilitator" but notice that your instructional examples describe the teacher transmitting facts to students, you have uncovered a contradiction. If you characterize the role of the student as "developing personal growth and a unique individual identity" yet the students in your examples receive fixed knowledge and are assessed using standardized testing, you have uncovered a contradiction. Continually ask yourself reflective questions, based on the *Continuum*, to clarify your reasoning.

Reflect

How Do Your Prior Observations and Experiences Relate to the School You Have Designed?

In what ways is the curriculum of your school similar to and/or different from the curriculum you have observed or experienced in other schools?

In what ways is the instruction of your school similar to and/or different from instruction you have observed or experienced in other schools? In what ways is the role of the teacher similar to and/or different from the role of the teacher that you have observed or experienced in other schools? In what ways is the role of the student similar to and/or different from the role of the student that you have observed or experienced in other schools?

How Do Your Own Practices and Beliefs Relate to the School You Have Designed?

Where would you place the school you have designed (or each of its elements) on the *Continuum of Educational Philosophy*? In what ways does your school represent the way you teach or would prefer to teach? What would a visitor observe in your own teaching that is consistent and compatible with the practices represented in your school design? Does your school represent practices in which you do not or would not engage?

What reasons might you have for designing a school for a purpose of education or according to a philosophical perspective that you do not implement in your own practice? How could you change your practice to be consistent and compatible with your school design to produce a coherent pedagogy?

What If . . . I Could Conduct Philosophical Inquiry in Actual Schools?

This textbook describes vignettes based on observations in actual schools and classrooms. These have served as "virtual" observations to conduct inquiry into different philosophical perspectives that underlie educational practices. At the end of each chapter, including this chapter on designing your own school, you have responded to questions that ask you to reflect on your own observations and experience in schools. Comparing the classroom vignettes and school examples to other schools you have experienced can reveal insights about different philosophical influences on education.

You may choose to apply the *Wonder Model of Inquiry* outside of the hypothetical situations offered in this textbook to conduct observations in actual schools. You can ask the same inquiry questions about curriculum, instruction, the role of the teacher and student, and the organization and design of the school and make connections to philosophical perspectives and concepts investigated in the chapters. The "3Cs" criteria can help you evaluate the consistency, compatibility, and coherence of educational practices and programs offered in authentic school environments. You may perceive inconsistencies in practice, notice incompatibility between practices, or detect incongruity between practices and the purpose of education of the school. A combination of different and perhaps contradictory philosophical perspectives may result in an incoherent school design. You may also apply the *Wonder Model of Inquiry* as a form of action research to make connections between your own practice and philosophical perspectives and concepts. By investigating and evaluating your teaching, you can continue to develop your own philosophy of education.

The theme of this textbook has been to approach the study of philosophy of education as a "wonder activity." We have investigated philosophical perspectives on education in response to questions about the purpose of education arising from observations in authentic classroom situations. The goal has been to promote critical thinking about the influence of philosophy on education, to evaluate the consistency, compatibility, and coherence of educational practices, and to reflect on one's own beliefs, exploring philosophy of education *in action*.

Index